THE PROMISED LAND?

THE PROMISED LAND?

Feminist Writing in the
German Democratic Republic

LORNA MARTENS

STATE UNIVERSITY OF NEW YORK PRESS

Published by
State University of New York Press, Albany

© 2001 State University of New York

All rights reserved

Printed in the United States of America

No part of this book may be used or reproduced in any manner whatsoever without written permission. No part of this book may be stored in a retrieval system or transmitted in any form or by any means including electronic, electrostatic, magnetic tape, mechanical, photocopying, recording, or otherwise without the prior permission in writing of the publisher.

For information, address State University of New York Press,
90 State Street, Suite 700, Albany, NY 12207

Production by Marilyn P. Semerad
Marketing by Fran Keneston

Library of Congress Cataloging-in-Publication Data

Martens, Lorna, 1946–
  The promised land? : feminist writing in the German Democratic Republic / Lorna Martens.
    p. cm.
  Includes bibliographical references and index.
  ISBN 0-7914-4859-2 (alk. paper) — ISBN 0-7914-4860-6 (pbk. : alk. paper)
  1. German literature—Germany (East)—History and criticism. 2. German literature—20th century—History and criticism. 3. German literature—Women authors—History and criticism. 4. Feminism and literature—Germany (East) 5. Women and literature—Germany (East) 6. Feminism—Germany (East) I. Title.

PT3705 .M37 2001
833'.914099287'09431—dc21
                                                            00-024106

10 9 8 7 6 5 4 3 2 1

Contents

Acknowledgments	vii
List of Abbreviations	ix
1 ■ Women, Feminism, and Writing in the German Democratic Republic	1
2 ■ "What Does a Woman Want?" Woman as the Subject of Desire	35
3 ■ Praise of the Feminine	73
4 ■ Writing Women's Images	125
5 ■ The Reality of Women's Lives	167
Concluding Remarks	205
Notes	209
Bibliography	239
Index	265

Acknowledgments

This book began as a course on Eastern European feminism, and I would first like to thank those who helped me prepare it: Nancy Kaiser for bibliographies; Nancy Lukens for the generous loan of manuscript copies of the English translations of German Democratic Republic (GDR) stories that later appeared in Nancy Lukens and Dorothy Rosenberg, trans. and ed., *Daughters of Eve: Women's Writing from the German Democratic Republic*; and the Arts and Sciences Dean's Office at the University of Virginia for awarding me a summer grant for course development.

Two grants then enabled me to get the book project underway. A Sesquicentennial Associateship from the University of Virginia gave me the necessary free time to begin research. A Fulbright grant, which provided me with the opportunity to spend ten months in the former East Berlin, allowed me to experience at first hand the ambience of what until recently had been the capital of the GDR.

I would especially like to thank the extremely helpful women I met in and through the Zentrum für interdisziplinäre Frauenforschung at the Humboldt-Universität, with which I was affiliated in Berlin. Gabriele Jähnert, the managing director, found me housing, facilitated contacts, and helped me with innumerable other practical and academic matters. Karin Aleksander, the librarian, suggested useful resources. Hannelore Scholz, Eva Kaufmann, and Brita Baume, scholars who specialize in GDR women writers, generously gave their time to meet with me, discuss my topic, and answer my questions.

Finally, thanks to Peggy Setje-Eilers for her assistance with translations, checking, and promotional matters.

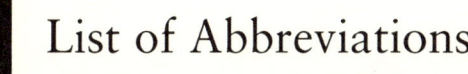
List of Abbreviations

A   Morgner, Irmtraud. *Amanda*. Darmstadt: Luchterhand, 1983.

TB   Morgner, Irmtraud. *Leben und Abenteuer der Trobadora Beatriz nach Zeugnissen ihrer Spielfrau Laura*. Berlin: Aufbau, 1974.

"Life"   Morgner, Irmtraud. "Life and Adventures of Trobadora Beatriz as Chronicled by Her Minstrel Laura—Twelfth Book." Translated by Karen R. Achberger and Friedrich Achberger. *New German Critique* 15 (1978): 121–146.

AD   Wolf, Christa. *The Author's Dimension. Selected Essays*. Introduction by Grace Paley. Edited by Alexander Stephan. Translated by Jan van Heurck. New York: Farrar, Straus and Giroux, 1993.

C   Wolf, Christa. *Cassandra. A Novel and Four Essays*. Translated by Jan van Heurck. New York: Farrar, Straus and Giroux, 1984.

DA   Wolf, Christa. *Die Dimension des Autors. Essays und Aufsätze, Reden und Gespräche 1959–1985*, 2 vols. Frankfurt am Main: Luchterhand, 1987.

FD   Wolf, Christa. *The Fourth Dimension. Interviews with Christa Wolf*. Translated by Hilary Pilkington. Introduction by Karin McPherson. London: Verso, 1988.

N   Wolf, Christa. *Nachdenken über Christa T.* Neuwied and Berlin: Luchterhand, 1970.

Q   Wolf, Christa. *The Quest for Christa T.* Translated by Christopher Middleton. New York: Farrar, Straus and Giroux, 1970.

WR   Wolf, Christa. *What Remains and Other Stories.* Translated by Heike Schwarzbauer and Rick Takvorian. New York: Farrar, Straus and Giroux, 1993.

1 Women, Feminism, and Writing in the German Democratic Republic

> We have no idea what women as women would have to say. I'm evoking for women a role that we have yet to make, in the name of a voice that, unsilenced, might say something that has never been heard.
> —Catherine A. MacKinnon,
> *Feminism Unmodified: Discourses on Life and Law*

The German Democratic Republic (GDR), a state that went out of existence in 1990 following the mass exodus of its citizens via the Hungarian border to West Germany in the summer of 1989, conjures up a negative image in the American mind, one dominated by the Berlin Wall, by a lack of civil liberties and freedom to travel, by the ubiquitous snooping of the Stasi (state security service), and by the intermittent presence of Soviet tanks, censorship, shortages, waiting in line, outmoded industrial equipment, and pollution. Even among the other Eastern bloc countries, the GDR had a negative image. "First prize: a week in the GDR," ran a Hungarian joke. "Second prize: two weeks in the GDR."

The GDR as the site of a feminist tradition is far less well known. Yet it produced the most important feminist corpus of any state socialist country. This book aims to acquaint the English-speaking women's studies audience with GDR feminist ideas. With the notable exception of Christa Wolf's works, the large body of relevant primary texts and smaller body of secondary texts has for the most part not been translated into English.* As I plan to show, GDR feminism took the form not of political action (which would have been impossible), but of revolutionizing the way in which people thought about women and how women thought about themselves by staging a radical revision—and expansion—of discourse both by and about women.

The interest in GDR feminism lies in the fact that it arose in a climate in which both the actual condition of women and the ideology concerning women and the family were distinctly different from their Western counterparts. The conjunction of the two brought with it feminist ideas which, although they have some overlap with Western feminism, nevertheless depart from different presuppositions and hence arrive at different, or at the very least differently accented, conclusions.

Social restructuring in the GDR radically changed the actual situation of women as it had existed in any previous period in German history. The GDR, like other socialist countries, successfully encouraged the full employment of women. Women constituted approximately half the labor force. The GDR provided women with an impressive and increasing array of maternity benefits and child-care facilities in order to facilitate their employment and make it compatible with motherhood. These policies in turn derive from the classic, explicitly prowoman, emancipatory socialist ideology of Frederick Engels, August Bebel, Clara Zetkin, and Lenin, policies that were tempered, in the course of the years, by political exigencies, notably a perceived need to increase the birthrate. The ideology, the policies, and the perceived exigencies were shared by all Eastern bloc countries, with the Soviet Union usually taking the lead. Yet socialist ideology was historically at odds with feminism in the Western sense—the notion of an independent women's movement, of women's self-consciousness, indeed of gender questions of any kind, in short of liberal feminism. While the emancipation of women was a socialist goal, feminism as an independent women's movement was considered contrary to socialist ideology and was therefore strictly discouraged.

---

*The titles of translated works are given in English. German titles are given in German. The reader will find the original German title of a translated work and an English translation of a German title the first time a work is mentioned.

Alongside the emancipatory public policy, a grass-roots feminism sprang up in the GDR. Its principal site was literature. The GDR produced a strong tradition of women's writing. Starting in the 1970s, much of this writing could be called feminist. Feminist by Western standards, that is; most East German women writers eschewed the label "feminist," which had negative, "bourgeois" connotations. Indeed, in GDR parlance Western "neofeminism" of the 1960s and 1970s counted as man-hating.[1] This literature was seminal for the underground political feminism that developed among GDR women intellectuals in the 1980s and surfaced immediately preceding and after the fall of the Wall on 9 November 1989.

It is important to know not only how women who live under extremely different conditions define themselves and their goals, but also what women want when, as has rarely happened, they enjoy economic independence as a social group. Women in such a position, I believe, are able to give new and different answers to the question that allegedly mystified Freud: What does a woman want? The goal of this book will be to find out what GDR feminist consciousness was—that is, feminist consciousness under the conditions established by state socialism—as it was articulated by GDR women writers.

The existence of a feminist literature in the GDR can be traced to several sources. First, feminist ideas flourish where women have already achieved a certain degree of liberation. This condition was created in the GDR. Women were more independent economically than women in most Western European countries and enjoyed a higher degree of literacy and education than in any other Eastern bloc country.[2] Lacking a political outlet, feminists turned to literature, which was deemed an important forum. As Marc Silberman puts it, "The writer worked, so to speak, under state commission, whether under accommodation or in defiance, and as a result the party and the public embued words and texts with a special power."[3] Literary production was consistently encouraged, and literature had a wide readership. In fact, the state referred to itself as a "Society of Literature" ("Literaturgesellschaft"). In 1971, following the replacement of Walter Ulbricht by Erich Honecker as first secretary, there was a general liberalization of what could be said and how. Art was for the first time—with certain exceptions—given a free license: in December 1971 Honecker called for "no taboos in art," neither in content nor in form, provided it maintained a "firm socialist position."[4] In June of the following year the minister of culture Kurt Hager, departing radically from the cultural politics of earlier times, explicitly permitted the artistic representation of "nonantagonistic" conflicts within socialist society.[5] This meant that problems faced by women could be aired in literature.

Second, East German women writers were more exposed and more receptive to the Western feminist movements of the 1970s than women writers in other socialist countries. News of Western feminist movements was accessible through radio and television.

Third, I conjecture that the emancipatory claims of socialism, in conjunction with women's new economic independence, fostered feminist self-consciousness among East German women intellectuals, in particular because these claims contrasted sharply with the strongly patriarchal German cultural tradition.

A comparison with the Soviet Union is instructive. Legislation affecting women and policies toward feminist social criticism in the GDR followed Soviet models. The Soviet Union led the way in adopting an array of legal measures that were increasingly favorable toward women; the Soviet Union was the first to declare the investigation of problems faced by women as "nonantagonistic," and hence permissible, criticism.[6] Yet in the Soviet Union, by comparison, explicitly or even mildly feminist literature is scarcely to be found. The reason often cited is Russian culture's matriarchal tendency and its construction of women as the stronger sex. Western feminism left little mark there.

Socialist Ideology on Women

In terms of ideology, the emancipation of women was central to the socialist program from the start. August Bebel, in his influential work *Woman and Socialism* (first published in 1879 and subsequently expanded), called for the full legal, social, and erotic emancipation of women. Bebel believed that the achievement of socialism was the precondition for this emancipation. Indeed, there could be no genuine emancipation of women outside of socialism; hence the "bourgeois" notion of an independent "feminism" was misguided. This was and has remained the major difference between liberal and socialist feminism. Throughout the history of socialism, women were encouraged to fight for socialism side by side with men as comrades. Class was of paramount importance. Sex was not considered class. The sexual distribution of power was seen as an offshoot of private property that would dissolve with the abolition of private property.

Beyond that, it was not explored. Frederick Engels in *The Origin of the Family, Private Property, and the State* (1884)* made a historical argument identifying primitive communism with mother right. According to Engels, in its tribal phase human society had been matrilinear and communistic. The advent of private property, which belonged to men as their labor began to produce a surplus, brought with it monogamy, patriarchy, and the institution of the state. Bebel concluded that thereafter, women were doubly enslaved: first by men, and then by capital. In both cases the sources of their enslavement were economic. The key to their emancipation was therefore also economic. Bebel, following Engels, considered productive labor, that is, paid work outside the home, to be an essential prerequisite for women's liberation from men. Women's emancipation from capital would, along with men's, come about with the socialization of the means of production.

Bebel also deemed childbearing a social service that was as valuable as men's military service and entitled women to special rights. In sharp contrast to liberal feminists, who demanded *equal* rights for men and women, Bebel and all subsequent socialist theorists advocated the position that women's work be specially protected as just compensation for their "maternal function." Hence women should have the right to adequate maternity leave and to a limitation on the hours, times, and types of work expected of them. Housework and child care, in Bebel's program, were to be performed by the community.

Socialist Ideology in Policy and Practice

The policies for women adopted in socialist countries followed these ideological precepts. In the GDR, the constitution of 1949 guaranteed equal rights for men and women, employment for all citizens, equal pay for equal work regardless of sex and age, and the right to equal education. The Socialist Unity Party (SED, for Sozialistische Einheitspartei Deutschlands) actively promoted not only the full but also the equal employment of women. It encouraged hiring women into managerial positions and technical fields. The extraordinary communiqué of 1961 "Die Frau—der Frieden und der Sozia-

---

*Dates in the text are dates of first publication.

lismus" (Woman, peace, and socialism) explicitly castigated male prejudice against women in the workplace as well as the tendency merely to exploit their labor:

> Women who are functioning in management positions are often overloaded with work, with no consideration for their obligations as mothers and housewives. More is frequently demanded of them than of a man performing the same work. Some male managerial employees are of the opinion, without expressing it explicitly, that women should "prove" themselves through special achievements. Instead of helping women and girls cope with their greater workload, they invent arguments that are supposed to prove that middle and upper management positions cannot be filled with women. In particular, these members of male management claim that the employment of a woman with a household and children is not economically "profitable"; men are more reliable and have a lower rate of "absenteeism"; yes, the "argument" is even made that women do not understand technical-organizational and economic problems as well as men. *All these and similar statements contradict the essence of our country. They inhibit the development of woman and consequently of our whole society.*[7]

From 1950 on, the state pursued a policy of accommodating working mothers. State-subsidized child-care spaces were increased, until by 1984, child care was available on demand. The GDR had the most extensive child-care facilities in the world. Single mothers were given special bonuses in order to help them combine work with motherhood. Starting in the 1970s family legislation provided increasing benefits for women on the job, benefits of which American women still only dream. Thus in 1972, mothers with three children were given a 40-hour workweek instead of the normal 43¾ hours, with no loss of pay. Paid maternity leave was lengthened from 14 to 18 weeks. In 1976 maternity leave was extended to 26 weeks. Women were allowed an unpaid baby year with no loss of job for first children and a paid baby year for further children. The workweek for women with two children was shortened to 40 hours. In 1984 mothers were given an 18-month baby leave for the third child. In 1986 the paid baby year was extended to first children. By 1986 the benefits included the following: 26 weeks of paid maternity leave; a paid baby year for each child, and 1½ years leave starting with the third child, which could be taken by the mother, her husband, or a grandmother or split among them; for single parents or parents with two children partially paid parental leave to care for sick children up to 4 weeks per year for 1 child, 6 weeks for 2 children, and so forth;[8] a payment of 1,000 marks (approximately equal to a monthly wage) upon the birth of each child, and a monthly child subsidy of 50–150 marks; a 40-hour week instead of the normal 43 ¾ hour week for all women with 2 children and for single mothers with no decrease in pay; and a paid day off monthly for housework for all mothers of children under 16 and for all women over 40.[9]

While these benefits were obviously at least in part motivated by practical rather than ideological considerations, that is, by a natalist policy designed to reverse the drop in the birthrate that had begun in the GDR in 1969, first-trimester abortion was nevertheless legalized in 1972.

The effect of this legislation on women has been documented in sociological studies and other commentaries. GDR sociology has been attacked as serving a legitimizing function, but a book by Irene Böhme, written in 1984 after the author had left for the West, and more recently post-Wall studies by both West and East German sociologists complement the GDR publications.[10] During the war women dominated family life, and after the war women moved into the jobs that had previously been men's jobs. In the new republic the law proclaimed the equality of the sexes. According to Böhme, women born between 1930 and 1940, who grew up between 1945 and 1955 under these conditions, regarded themselves as men's equals, while the men of the same generation had no sense of belonging to a privileged sex.[11] It is said that before 1961, the year the Wall was built and stopped the flow of labor to the West, any woman who wanted one could find a job with a future. Thereafter, the competition with men for jobs became more severe. Nevertheless, in 1971 the GDR still had a smaller percentage of working-age people than almost any other country in the world. At the same time, the number of women with vocational training leaped from 5% in 1950 to 83.3% in 1984, thereby closing the qualification gap between men and women in age groups up to 40. By contrast, there was still a large qualification gap in the Soviet Union. By 1985 more than 99.9% of girls who did not choose to continue their education were in a skilled worker occupation.[12] The percentage of women who worked climbed from year to year, from 76.2% in 1965 to 87% in 1977.[13] According to the post-Wall East German *Frauenreport '90*, by 1989, 91.2% of all working-age women were working, studying, or in training.[14] In 1988 women accounted for more than 50% of university and technical students and more than 80% of vocational school students. They were very highly represented in occupations requiring higher education diplomas. They accounted for more than 50% of those employed in medicine and in the educational system, although there was a gender-specific polarization into technical and nontechnical occupations, and the proportion of women decreased the higher one went in the managerial hierarchy.[15] There were also very few women professors in the GDR—only 4%.[16] At the very top, in the decision-making political organizations, there were very few women.[17] Their number peaked in the mid-'50s and then dropped off.[18] Generally, as in the West, the lower-paying job categories fell to women.

GDR family policy had the desired effect of halting the drop in the birthrate. The birthrate stopped dropping in the early 1970s, and by 1980 it had increased to 14.6 births per 1,000 persons (compared to 10.1 in the Federal Republic of Germany [FRG]). The working woman in the GDR was a working *mother*. By 1989, 91% of all women who could work did, while 91% of women gave birth to at least one child.[19] Many single women had children: 30% of first children, and 60% in Berlin, were born outside of marriage. Since in the GDR, unlike in other Eastern European countries, all contraceptives were available that were available in the West, and since abortion was legal as of 1972, the children born in the GDR were more likely to be wanted.

Women had their children early by comparison with women in the West. The average age of first-time mothers was 22; 70% of women had their first child under the age of 25, while only 9% of children were born to women over 30. By consequence, there was no "youth phase" in the GDR such as exists in the West. The early maternity of women is traceable to several causes. First, family values are said to have been very important in the GDR. Second, since employment was guaranteed and since the state actively supported the compatibility of employment and maternity, there was no reason for a woman not to have children at an early age. Finally, in a situation where all apartments were state-administered and furthermore since there was an acute shortage of apartments, it was easier to get one's own apartment if one had a child.[20]

Were GDR Women Emancipated?

Western observers have noted that GDR women presented a curious combination of self-confidence when it came to securing their independent existence and deference in the face of male dominance.[21] According to all accounts, GDR men were extremely patriarchal.[22] GDR writers interviewed in the mid-1970s noted that women's social roles lagged behind their legal and economic emancipation. Thus the writer Eberhard Panitz commented that "many women today are entirely of the opinion: 'I can lead my life alone if the man does not completely meet all my requirements!' . . . A woman knows that she can get along alone and is no longer dependent on the material support of a man." But another writer, Rolf Schneider, said:

> We have legal equality (Gleichstellung) in the GDR, which is the absolute requirement for any emancipation of women. We have neither factual equality in daily life, nor one in the general social consciousness. There are strong tendencies in our country to force the woman back into bourgeois role behavior, or to maneuver her back into it by means of compliments. Opposed to these are certain arrangements that have become statutory. Neither the people affected by these arrangements, the women, nor their partners, the men, have an exact idea of how an emancipated woman actually should be and behave.[23]

Despite women's economic independence and the party rhetoric, conservative gender roles persisted in the GDR. Dinah Dodds, interviewing East German women in September 1990, finds that little had changed: women felt that "traditional attitudes toward gender roles lay just below the surface," as the rapidity with which men had reverted to them after the collapse of the GDR showed.[24]

Sex roles and family customs did not change with the new economy. Women continued to be subjected to patronizing and misogynistic comments and attitudes. In her novel *Die Unschuldigen* (The innocents, 1975), Charlotte Worgitzky records some "minor insults": "Women are unobjective"—"Woman behind the wheel"—"You don't need to do that—you're a woman!"—"Under the roof, you broads can have things in a state of shambles if you want—the main thing's that the good Lord didn't skimp on the first floor"—"She holds her own" [literal German: she stands in for a man].)[25]

Reflecting the tension between official ideology and popular bias, the media projected an image of women that was mixed in its message. Ostensibly, the media presented a dignified image of women. Ina Merkel, writing in 1991, recalls pictures of women in "not so old magazines." These magazines did not feature young, sexy girls, but rather attractive women "in the prime of life." These women were portrayed looking self-confident, slightly ironic and distant, in their world of work, as chief doctor, head engineer, and railway supervisor.[26] No pornography was available in the GDR.[27] Yet the East German cultural theorist Irene Dölling has analyzed photos of women in the workplace in GDR periodicals and shown how their conventions subtly undermine the idea that women are equal.[28]

By the beginning of the 1970s, when 82% of women worked or were being trained, GDR women, as working mothers, were under heavy pressure.[29] Women worked a "double day"; they did the lion's share of the housework, shopping, and after-hours child care. In the next two decades the picture barely changed. The wear and tear of everyday life was by all accounts greater in the GDR than in the FRG. The working day in the GDR was longer than in the FRG (43¾ hours a week), although it was not necessarily more stressful, for it has been observed that in the GDR "working fast brought absolutely no rewards."[30] Grocery shopping, already time-consuming in West Germany by American standards on account of limited store hours, long lines, unavailability of parking, and fewer self-service items, was even more labor intensive in the East due to shortages. Buildings were in disrepair and it was difficult to get things fixed. Few people had cars; besides, roads were in poor condition. Under these circumstances, housework is estimated to have taken 40 hours per week per family in the late 1980s. Three-quarters of it was done by women—thus adding an extra 30 hours to a woman's workweek.[31] Men did not take advantage of the "baby year," and mothers, not fathers, took time off work to care for sick children. Moreover, many women were single parents. The divorce rate in the GDR was the third highest in the world, behind the Soviet Union and the United States. Women tended to be overworked and tired. One consequence of their double burden was that they failed to advance in their careers. They rarely reached the top.

Feminism in the GDR

Among GDR women generally there was little feminism in the Western sense. What was conspicuously missing was any widespread consciousness of conflict between the sexes. The consciousness of that conflict and the recognition that women constitute an independent interest group could be seen as foundational to Western feminism. Yet certain issues brought women together in the course of GDR history. These included a proposed law to draft women in 1972; GDR women mobilized against it, at about the same time that U.S. feminists were protesting at being excluded from the draft. At the start of the 1980s fear of war brought with it the formation of women's peace groups. Initiative in the public sphere was undermined by state control and the Stasi. It was said: "When three people meet, 1 1/2 of them are with the Stasi."[32] In fact, the peace and ecological women's groups were under surveillance by the Stasi.

Among the general female population there was in the 1980s a turning away from the socialist credo that productive labor is essential to women's emancipation. The younger generation of women began to move from a self-image as worker toward a more traditional self-image as wife and mother.[33] This change in self-image was undoubtedly fostered by the government's emphasis on motherhood in the previous decade and probably also reflected women's fatigue at being expected to work two jobs. The 1980s also brought a generational conflict among women: the family benefits applied to younger women and caused tension with the older generation of women, who had raised their children under much worse conditions and were also largely the ones who took up the slack at work when the younger women took baby years and sick child leave.[34]

Among groups of GDR women intellectuals the situation was different. An underground women's movement got started at the beginning of the 1980s. Women met in private circles, in large part under the umbrella of the Lutheran Church, where women's groups with all kinds of different agendas came together.[35] These discussion groups were "half-legal," that is, tolerated—unlike the peace and ecological movements. The women's groups were preceded and significantly inspired by GDR belles lettres, where the most important authors were Irmtraud Morgner, Maxie Wander, and Christa Wolf.

The influence of Western feminism was also important for the underground women's movement of the 1980s.[36] One group of cultural studies scholars, led by Irene Dölling, consistently met from 1979 to 1989 to study Western feminist texts.[37] In the GDR the breakthrough feminist idea, which was confined to intellectual circles, was that socialism had *not*, as it declared in 1971, "solved" the woman question, nor was it in fact capable of doing so, but that women constitute an independent interest group. Women came to the realization that women's interests, in important respects, run counter to men's. Immediately after the collapse of the socialist government in November 1989, in the period of "direct democracy" prior to unification, a feminist political movement sprang up in the GDR.[38] The GDR was unique in this regard; none of the other Eastern bloc countries developed a comparable feminism with the breakup of state socialism.

Did Protective Legislation Help or Hurt Women?

In the area of women's emancipation, as in every other area, what state socialism actually produced was far from being a perfect realization of nineteenth-century socialist theories. It is fashionable today to criticize the GDR as an example of "patriarchy as socialism."[39] In particular, to what extent the family policies in the GDR actually bettered the lot of women has been much discussed. Critics observe that the benefits were designed with an eye to serving the practical needs of the state rather than furthering the emancipation of women. They were intended to reverse the drop in the birthrate that had begun in the GDR in 1969 while retaining women in the work force. They were aimed at increasing the compatibility of work and *motherhood* (not fatherhood).[40] Far from rescuing the woman from the notorious "double day," they condemned her to it. For they did nothing to change the belief that child care and housework were women's work. The more time women got off work, the more they were expected to spend on child care and housework. In particular, the institution of the monthly "household day" for women reinforced the idea that it is women who do housework. Although the GDR thought of itself as trying to socialize housework, as Bebel had called for in his program, by constructing such amenities as laundromats and cantines, it certainly did not succeed in freeing women from "the petty tyranny of housework."[41] In addition, the protective legislation was a Trojan horse, for by giving women special privileges, it undermined their reputation as dependable coworkers. Women could be counted on to take time off to care for infants and sick children. The employment of a female thus became synonymous with frequent absenteeism. Special protection for women appeared, at least in the short run of approximately fifteen years, to hurt their image.

Finally, commentators note that the emancipation of women in the socialist state failed to foster a broadly based political consciousness among women. The fact that in the first free elections in the GDR in March 1990 far more East German women voted for the conservative "Alliance for Germany," which opposed abortion, day care, and affirmative action, than for any other party, caused critics, including women's studies specialists from the former GDR, to exclaim over the extraordinary lack of feminist consciousness in the GDR "woman on the street."[42] At fault, so the criticism runs, is the GDR socialist government, which encouraged a passive, "father knows best" attitude among its citizens, women included. The rights and benefits women enjoyed were handed down from on high; they were neither conceived of nor fought for by women themselves. Thus Dölling now asserts that women's rights cannot, as they were in the GDR, be legislated from above, that is, by the overwhelmingly male upper-level GDR politicians; they must be conceived of and fought for by the women themselves, that is, issue out of grass-roots movements. In Dölling's opinion the "father-state politics" of the GDR simply reproduced patriarchal structures and had the effect of making women unselfconfident and unassertive.[43] On the opposite side, the West German sociologist Gisela Anna Erler responds to these critiques by arguing that it was not the benefits that caused the image of women to suffer. In her view the image of women as unequal has its origin in much older sources; the habit of evaluating women, regardless of what they do, in terms of what they do *not* do, was not called into being by the protective legislation, but existed prior to it.[44] I myself find that the GDR government was remarkably energetic in taking measures to liberate women, even to the point of trying to combat patriarchal attitudes. Where it fell short was in not encouraging an independent feminism initiated by women.

The underlying issue in this debate is, of course, that of special protection, and whether such protection helps or hurts women. In a market economy, special protection essentially creates an ideological contradiction. It runs counter to the system of free competition and operates as an obstruction to its functioning. Consequently, a market economy tends to reinterpret protective legislation so as to make it compatible with its own competitive ends. Such reinterpretation does not necessarily work to the advantage of the protected group. Protective legislation in the United States has had a history of backfiring: women have found themselves "protected" out of well paying jobs.[45]

Title 7 of the U.S. Civil Rights Bill, by barring discrimination in employment, had the effect of securing protection for women while appearing to eschew it. The Pregnancy Discrimination Act of 1978, which modifies Title 7 to specify that pregnancy shall be treated like similar disabilities, is essentially protective legislation, but is careful not to make pregnancy appear special: women cannot be fired or not given paid leave or lose benefits on account of pregnancy (*Geduldig v. Aiello* [1974]; *General Electric Co. v. Gilbert* [1976]; and *Nashville Gas Co. v. Satty* [1977]), but they also cannot be given preferential treatment (*California Federal Savings and Loan Association et al. v. Guerra* [1985]). It is questionable, however, whether this roundabout way of "helping" women is actually effective. If one looks at the bottom line, it is hard to see how U.S. women have benefited from the antidiscrimination legislation. They are still far from being men's equals in the world of employment. At the same time women have, in the name of the same "equal treatment," summarily lost the favorable treatment they once received in the divorce courts.[46] The upshot has been the "feminization of poverty" in the United States.[47]

The problem is that the factual equality of women is not a stated objective in U.S. government policy. If it were, the reality that women are the ones who bear children would have to be taken into consideration and adequately compensated. It is women's childbearing and childrearing roles that continue significantly to retard their progress in the world of employment and make it extraordinarily difficult for them to become men's equals in that world. Childbearing cannot be shifted to men, but it could very well be conceived, as in Western European countries, as a socially valuable service that deserves to be rewarded rather than as a private affair. As for childrearing, it is difficult to shift a significant part of that burden to men as long as no incentive is offered, that is, so long as it is conceived as a job that is merely time-consuming and brings with it no material compensation. "Antidiscrimination" legislation does not adequately help a group whose time and energies are eaten up in the "private," that is, nonpaying sphere of childbearing, childrearing, and housework.

In a socialist planned economy, in contrast, where protection was much more global—for instance, where the right to work was guaranteed—explicit protection for women could not at all be regarded as an ideological contradiction in terms. Not only did the idea of special protection not have to swim upstream against a dominant laissez-faire economy, but it was fully in keeping with the socialist ethos to protect a disadvantaged group, as the GDR did initially in setting a 60 percent minimum quota of the children of workers and farmers for university admission. The *Mutterschutzgesetz* (law protecting prenatal and postnatal mothers) of 1950 (extended in 1954 and in

1958), based on women's right to work, concretized protection for women by writing maternity leave and help for single mothers into law as well as forbidding certain types of work for women.[48]

Feminist Demands after the Fall of the Wall

Interestingly, the feminist political movement that instantly sprang up during the period immediately preceding and after the fall of the Wall universally demanded yet more global protection for women. The most radical demand was for 50–50 quotas in employment. A Round Table discussion by women's studies specialists on 1 November 1989 resulted in an open letter to the Central Committee of the SED demanding, besides more political sway for women and freedom of expression for women's groups, *quotas* for men and women in civil service, in government, in the economy, and in the university. The signers also demanded that all family benefits be extended to include men.[49] A Berlin group, lila offensive (The lilac attack), worked day and night to hammer out a program within a month. In their "Standortbestimmung" (position statement), which calls for a reformed socialist society, they state that doing away with the capitalist means of production is a prerequisite but not a guarantee for the abolition of patriarchal oppression, for such oppression has a dimension that transcends class and systems. They declare that achievement must be redefined according to the abilities of individuals and not simply in terms of economic effectiveness. Their many desiderata include the sovereignty of the GDR; the universal right to work; no reorganization of the GDR along capitalist lines; quotas including a 50 percent quota in the naming of political candidates; ecological reform of industry and agriculture; reduction of work; better pay in so-called female professions; encouragement of men to go into services, child care, and health care; quotas for teaching positions; combinability of motherhood and fatherhood with work; equal responsibility of men and women for the domestic sphere; family benefits awarded not only to women; rights and responsibilities of fatherhood; abolition of all privileges bound to marriage (for instance, adoption); better pensions; better handicapped facilities; no taboo surrounding death and the dying; revision of schoolbooks and curricula to get rid of sex role stereotypes; sex education; education in shared responsibility for contraception, pregnancy, birth, and life with the newborn; enforceability of constitutionally guaranteed equal rights through lawsuits; equality for men in custody cases; change in the draft law so that women cannot be called up; more humane gynecological care; legalization of alternative medicine; strict control over, and limitation of, gene research; the possibility of sterilization if both partners want it; women's shelters; sensitization to language that is insulting to women; legalization of prostitution; a continued ban on pornography; publication of, and open access to, feminist research; development of a language adequate to women; and promotion of women's studies and the establishment of a women's studies institute.[50]

On 3 December 1989, motivated by the group lila offensive, approximately one thousand two hundred women met in the East Berlin Volksbühne to found the Unabhängiger Frauenverband (UFV, Independent Women's Association). Like the lila offensive, the UFV assumed that a reformed socialism was its goal. In its program, adopted on 17 February 1990, the UFV called for the equalization ("Gleichstellung") of men and women, which was to be achieved principally through quotas: quotas for women in areas previously dominated by men and quotas for men in feminized professions. The UFV unleashed a chain reaction in the GDR: many other women's groups sprang up throughout the country, and these largely followed suit in calling for quotas. This program of quotas was of course intended to be superimposed on a system that already guaranteed employment.

The conservative victory in the GDR Volkskammer elections in March 1990 and the signing of the unification treaty on 18 May 1990 dashed these hopes of quotas, since the GDR agreed to join the Federal Republic and to adopt its Basic Law. The UFV program became obsolete, and it became simply a question of cutting the losses.

Another, more vaguely formulated, but nonetheless conceptually radical feminist demand in the autumn of 1989 was for a new definition of achievement that is not derived from men's work but encompasses what has traditionally been thought of as women's work. Ina Merkel formulated this demand concretely as "material rewards for childrearing."[51]

On 17 December 1989, the UFV warned against unification, noting the conditions under which women live in West Germany: widespread housewife status (only 54% of women were employed vs. 91.1% in the GDR); unemployment; economic dependence; illegality of abortion; availability of drugs for children; fewer social programs;

and widespread pornography. This warning went unheeded by the majority of women voters, who did not sympathize with the demands of the UFV.

Unification then indeed drastically changed the situation of East German women. The constitutionally guaranteed right to work no longer existed, and benefits were slashed. Female unemployment soared. Tamara Jones wrote in the *Los Angeles Times* on 6 August 1991: "Ten months after the two Germanies merged, women in the eastern sector are coming to the stunning realization that, in many ways, democracy set them back 40 years." She quotes an East German woman as saying: "I don't see one single instance where unification benefited women. Not one. It's only been negative."[52] In 1993 the constitutional court finally declared first-trimester abortion illegal but not prosecutable in the united Germany if the woman had had mandatory counseling beforehand. The bill was to be footed by the woman, as insurances are not allowed to pay for abortions. This ruling met with dismay and shrieks of protest in the "New States"— as East Germany was referred to after it joined the Federal Republic.

GDR Women versus American Women

In certain important respects, GDR women had since the mid-1970s what American feminists now want: equal employment opportunities; the possibility of combining family and career instead of an either-or choice, based on the availability of child care; and legal abortion. In 1965 three-quarters of GDR women of working age worked; it took more than thirty years for the percentage of American women with a job to climb that high.[53] By 1975 in the GDR half the labor force was female; in the United States women are expected to constitute 48 percent of the labor force by the year 2008.[54] Simultaneously, the full-scale entrance of GDR women into paid employment brought with it new pressures, new contradictions, and new problems to be solved. GDR women (and Eastern European women generally) anticipated by decades the position of American women in the problem of the "double day." The thematization of this issue in the GDR is directly relevant to the direction in which the United States is now moving. The problems faced by women in the GDR are also faced by American women: women do more housework and child care than men; the divorce rate is high; many women raise their families alone; by consequence of their unequal burden of family responsibilities, women's career advancement is hindered, and they earn less than men.[55] A significant difference is that GDR women were fully employed under easier circumstances than U.S. women: employment was guaranteed, and they were supported by a social system that made it possible for them to combine employment and motherhood without heroic effort.

GDR Feminism versus Western Feminism

What forms did feminism take under state socialism, under the conditions just outlined? Although these conditions left much to be desired, in certain respects they must be seen as empowering. Bebel's precondition for women's emancipation from men was fulfilled. In the GDR women were no longer economically dependent on men. Arguably, such a state of affairs could alter women's self-conception radically. Marriage was no longer a career option. That is, a woman did not have to marry merely in order to survive; conversely, if a woman married it did not mean that she did not have to work. Women also did not have to marry in order to have, that is, support, children. Hypothetically, this could mean that women were liberated from a set of self-conceptions that had come about as a result of the necessity for pleasing men.[56] It was no longer necessary to a woman's economic survival for her to think of herself as an object of desire, or as a "helpmate" to a man's career. At the same time, women acquired the means and the independence to reformulate themselves as subjects of desire—to start making new demands.

Yet GDR feminist ideas in their specificity are not simply explainable as a function of women's better relative social and economic position in the GDR. Any comparison of GDR to Western feminism has to take into account the profound differences in the contexts in which they arose—namely, the socialist versus the liberal capitalist context. GDR feminism took a socialist context, with the guarantee of work and the extensive social net, for granted. Law basically harmonized with ideology. The major proponents of GDR feminism affirmed the system. They were committed socialists. The daring element in their feminism was to insist, in the face of an ideology that denied feminism any independent basis and in time claimed to have "solved" the woman question, that women *had* specific interests and that socialism had not addressed them. In the U.S. context, in contrast, insisting on guaranteed work and on special benefits for women would be revolutionary—not suggesting that women have specific interests.

There are certainly some similarities between feminism as it is found in GDR literature starting in the 1970s and Western feminism. Socialist ideas have undoubtedly left their impact on Western feminism, beginning with the idea that *productive labor liberates*. Western feminism has not been impervious to the legacy of Bebel and Engels. Simone de Beauvoir's *Second Sex* (1949) shows the influence of their thinking. In its turn, it was read in the GDR—the German translation was acquired by the Humboldt University library the year it appeared, 1951[57]—and surely influenced East German feminism: parallels in Irmtraud Morgner's novels are pronounced. Beauvoir's thinking is more indebted to Bebel and Engels than she admits. Even though she devotes a chapter to arguing with the prominence they give to the advent of private property in bringing about the enslavement of women, elsewhere[58] she adopts the same conclusion. Her argument on the oppression of women, according to which man reified woman in the "Other," is materialist and historical. Moreover, she believes that socialism tends to liberate women: "All forms of socialism, wresting woman away from the family, favor her liberation."[59] She asserts that nothing but gainful employment (as opposed to voting rights) can assure liberty to woman: "A woman supported by a man—wife or courtesan—is not emancipated from the male because she has a ballot in her hand. . . . It is through gainful employment that woman has traversed most of the distance that separated her from the male; and nothing else can guarantee her liberty in practice."[60]

In the United States and in West Germany, the feminist movement of the late 1960s had its roots in, and split off from, the New Left.[61] In an essay on the origins of radical feminism in New York in 1967, the radical feminist Ellen Willis observes that "despite its oppositional stance toward the existing left, radical feminism was deeply influenced by Marxism. . . . Radical feminists appropriated certain Marxist ideas and assumptions (specifically, concepts of class interest, class struggle, and materialism) and applied them to male-female relations."[62] The pathbreaking West German feminist Alice Schwarzer insisted in *Der "kleine Unterschied"* (The "little difference," 1975), similarly to Beauvoir, that employment is the sine qua non of women's emancipation.[63]

GDR feminism, in turn, was influenced by the feminist movement of the 1970s in the West.[64] Certain Western feminist literature in particular was read: Beauvoir, *The Second Sex*; Kate Millett, *Sexual Politics*; and Schwarzer, *Der kleine Unterschied*.

All this notwithstanding, the ideas that have dominated Western feminist debate played little if any role in GDR literature. To give four examples:

1. In the liberal feminist tradition, and today in the United States, equal rights, and women's equality in the workplace, are viewed as so desirable that little attention is paid to the idea of possible undesirable consequences. For if women stress undesirable consequences too much, this might be viewed as an argument against granting these rights in the first place. Feminist writers in the GDR, having had no fear that women would lose their legal equality and their right to work, focused precisely on the contradictions that full employment created in the lives of women. Believing women to be equally productive members of society, they thought they were entitled to corresponding personal fulfillment.

2. The sameness-difference debate in which U.S. feminism has been entangled since the 1960s has not been an issue in the GDR. The feminist legal theorist Catherine MacKinnon has recently argued that either answer—that women should be regarded as the same as or different from men—spells doom for women's quest for factual equality, because either way, masculinity is regarded as the norm.[65] In the GDR women had nothing to gain by presenting themselves as the same as men, and little to lose by presenting themselves as different. Most feminist writers thus represented women as *different*—often in terms of traditional domestic values—and moreover, wanted the feminine to set the standard.[66] Again, it is a question of what it is possible to say within a socialist versus a market economy. "Difference" is a losing position only when one accepts capitalism/competition as the given economic framework, as a law of life. In some ways GDR feminism sounds like a return to pre-World War I suffragist ideas with its argument for domesticity, difference, and women's values. The argument for women's difference has enjoyed a comeback in the United States under the name of "cultural feminism" in the ideas of Carol Gilligan and others. Yet in the United States one always has to fear that an argument for difference will have the effect of placing women in a losing position within the context of a free market economy.

3. In GDR literature women were not, as in the West, pervasively represented as victims.[67] Certainly, the notion that the practice of heterosexual sex victimizes women, central in Schwarzer's *Der "kleine*

Unterschied," found no resonance whatsoever in the GDR. Rather, the dominant image of women was that of strong and capable persons. This image was undoubtedly mediated by the doctrine of socialist realism, which persisted throughout the 1960s and called for positive heroes. Yet at the same time, women seem actually to have been conceived as strong; the self-image of women noted by foreigners affirms this conceptualization. In the United States the woman-as-victim image is perhaps, of the two, the more artificial construct, one that has been greatly fostered by rights law. For rights law suggests to women that their best path to advancement lies in demanding "equal rights" and encourages them to represent themselves as victims who have hitherto been deprived of these rights, or indeed excluded from the very formulation of these rights.[68] In a 1978 interview Morgner commented on the difference in tone between Western feminism and her own:

> That many women in capitalistic countries read my book [*Leben und Abenteuer der Trobadora Beatriz nach Zeugnissen ihrer Spielfrau Laura* (Life and adventures of Trobadora Beatriz as chronicled by her minstrel Laura, 1974)] zealously has reasons that surprised me. In the western countries the media are full of women's emancipation. The topic is marketed. However, there is hardly any fiction or poetry and hardly anything that is written without bitterness, without hate. But it is hard to live in negation. Many women in the Federal Republic of Germany, in Switzerland, in Austria read the book to help them cope, and as news from a country where conditions that allow women to live like human beings have already been tested, conditions that enable men to have erotic and friendly feelings for a woman simultaneously. For these women readers, the best thing about my "Trobadora" was that I write about the topic humorously, sometimes even audaciously, at any rate not grimly.[69]

4. Motherhood, an issue to which U.S. feminists' response has been sporadic, overshadowed by other concerns, and mixed in its message, is a major theme. Adrienne Rich writes in 1972, in her study of motherhood *Of Woman Born*, that in the United States "some four or five years into a new politicization of women, there was virtually nothing being written on motherhood as an issue."[70] For GDR women writers, in contrast, motherhood was among the earliest themes (it already appears with feminist overtones in Morgner's 1964 story "Notturno"), and it has consistently been regarded as an issue of the greatest importance. Untouched by

"sameness" arguments, depth psychology, and behavioral psychology, all of which have rocked the pedestal on which motherhood once stood in the United States, maternity enjoyed an untarnished image in the GDR. In a context where the value of mothers for children went unquestioned, the issue was how women could possibly be expected to juggle the conflicting demands of motherhood and work.[71]

Conditions for Writers in the GDR

The conditions under which writers wrote and published in the GDR were also very different from those in the West. The GDR was famous for its active promotion and generous funding of education and culture.[72] Literature fairly flourished in the GDR. Writers were well treated and encouraged. Material conditions were very good. Membership in the Writers' Union (*Schriftstellerverband*) committed writers to supporting and helping to build socialist society with their work. At the same time this organization helped writers find stipends and part-time jobs as editors, dramatic producers, or research assistants. All writers in the GDR, including literary writers, had a bigger and better audience than writers in the FRG. The GDR is said to have been a "nation of readers."[73] The public looked forward to new works by the top writers, and initial print runs were huge.[74] It has often been remarked that literature in the GDR compensated for deficient journalism. Christa Wolf said in 1984 in a conversation with Grace Paley: "Maybe we can't say all the things that you can say here, but, on the other hand, people listen to us much more. Not only the readers, but the politicians as well. Maybe in some cases this is not exactly an advantage because literature has to take on all kinds of tasks that maybe should not always belong to literature. Maybe these should be the tasks and themes of sociology or psychology; but now it is literature that has to do the work."[75] Other writers have observed that people read because they believed that literature contained resistance.[76] A commentator wrote retrospectively in 1996 that GDR writers had "a significance which nothing and nobody could supplant. It was something their Western counterparts could only dream of."[77]

Although writers frequently lived on very little money—say 500 marks a month—in order to be able to pursue their calling, it has been said that no one failed to write simply on account of lack of money. Writers lived largely from contracts signed with publishing houses, which usually stipulated that the writer would be paid an advance. Whereas some started writing while they held other jobs—for instance, Wolf and Morgner and Eva Strittmatter as lectors in publishing houses—there were many free-lance writers. Some made extra money on the side—for instance, Gerti Tetzner by writing children's books. Scholarships played a role. In particular, students accepted for the two-year writers' program at the Johannes R. Becher Institut für Literatur (Johannes R. Becher Institute for Literature) in Leipzig got stipends like all students. Since all the larger publishing houses were owned by the state or by organizations, all were subsidized. Thus books were accepted on artistic merit, and not with an eye to making profits through sales. In the 1970s the state declared that publishing houses should be self-supporting; intellectuals protested. But in general a lack of paper was more critical than a lack of money. Consequently, writers were under no pressure to produce highly marketable books, books with sensational or otherwise popular themes, or short books. In fact many books, such as Morgner's novels, were extremely lengthy. They were sold cheaply, typically costing between five and fifteen marks (approximately two to ten dollars).

All in all in terms of market pressure GDR writers were much freer than writers in the West. However, they had to face censorship. Every book had to be approved for publication by the printing authorization office (*Stelle für Druckgenehmigung*) in the Ministry of Culture in order to be published. The censor could reject a book completely—as in the case of three satiric stories by Christa Wolf in the mid-1980s—or insist on the deletion of certain passages. Thus sixty-four sentences were deleted from one of Wolf's *Cassandra* lectures in the GDR edition. (They appeared in the Western edition.) Publishing a book in the West *first*, as opposed to a second, licensed publication in the West arranged by the GDR publishing house, was only legal if approved by the copyright office (*Büro für Urheberrechte*). In 1979 in the case of Stefan Heym the state chose to enforce the foreign currency law and declared such publication in the West a currency violation (*Devisenvergehen*). This was a pretext. Later in the same year the criminal code was revised such that authors who attempted to disseminate antigovernment writings abroad could be jailed. The actions of the *Stelle für Druckgenehmigung* were quite unpredictable, as the committee often also included individuals who wanted to get the book through. The existence of the official censorship was experienced by writers as extremely oppressive. It created a discouraging climate and had an effect on what was written to begin with, inasmuch as it led to inner censorship on the part of the writers and "suggestions" on the part of the publishing houses.

GDR Feminist Writers and the Socialist State

David Bathrick has recently characterized GDR dissidence, in contrast to Soviet dissidence, as taking place "within the legitimizing framework of official Marxist-Leninism" and hence "a variant of the official voice."[78] This certainly holds true of GDR feminist critique. The vast majority of the women writers, as Patricia Herminghouse put it in an essay of 1985, "articulates the inadequacies of the system without shaking its foundations."[79] Only two GDR women writers could be regarded as dissidents: Sarah Kirsch, who left for the West after the 1976 expatriation of the dissident songwriter Wolf Biermann, and Gabriele Kachold, who was expelled from the Pädagogische Hochschule Erfurt (Erfurt Teacher Training College) for political activity in the 1970s and subsequently jailed for a year on account of her protest against the expulsion of Biermann from the GDR. The two most acclaimed authors in particular, Christa Wolf and Irmtraud Morgner, were committed socialists. This is not to say that either writer unconditionally applauded the politics of the SED. Rather, each engaged in intense independent reflection on current events and politics, which frequently led them to criticize not only developments in the West but also the "real existing socialism" of the GDR in the name of a more perfect, equal, humanitarian socialism.

Wolf especially came to represent a voice of integrity for many East Germans. She became an SED member at age twenty. Later, from 1963 to 1967, she was a candidate for the Central Committee of the SED. As her book *What Remains* (*Was bleibt*, 1990) testifies, her relation with the East German government did not remain smooth; for a period she was under surveillance by the Stasi.[80] She has made clear in *Parting from Phantoms* (*Auf dem Weg nach Tabou*, 1994) that she would have preferred to see an alternative society rise out of the ashes of the GDR, instead of unification.[81] She deplores the distorting, unhistorical post-Wall demonization of the GDR by the West.[82]

Wolf's feminism has been anchored in the socialist belief that women's entry into productive labor as equally privileged participants, hence their economic liberation, is the essential first step for their liberation generally. She asserted in an interview of 1983 that—and her sentence might have come directly from Engels—"patriarchy emerged with class society and private ownership of the means of production" (*FD* 124). Her 1977 introduction to Maxie Wander's bestselling and influential book of interviews with GDR women *Guten Morgen, du Schöne* (Good morning, you beautiful creature) is a hymn of praise to GDR socialism's solution to the "woman question":

> Maxie Wander's book demonstrates, without this being its intent, a significant phenomenon: Only when men and women no longer fight over the weekly paycheck, over the two hundred marks for an abortion, over whether the woman can work and if so who will care for the children; only when she is paid for her work just like the man; when a woman represents herself in court; when she, at least in the public education system, is no longer trained as a girl to be "feminine," as an unmarried mother no longer earns public opprobrium: only then does she begin to have significant experiences, which have to do not with her generally, as a human being of the female sex, but with her personally, as an individual. (*DA* 1: 203)

Wolf consistently compared the condition of GDR women favorably to that of Western women. Not only that, but—writing in the late '70s and early '80s—she compared the *state of mind* of women in the GDR favorably to that of women in "capitalist countries." We recall that West German feminist commentators were struck by East German women's timorousness in accommodating themselves to men's patriarchal gestures, while post-Wall East German feminist commentators lamented their "lack of feminist consciousness." Wolf views this state of mind—East German women's lack of a sense of conflict between the sexes—as positive and healthy. Western women, in contrast, are plagued by "inner uncertainty" and have been driven to "man hating" precisely by their lack of economic independence.[83] She predicted in 1979: "I am certain that the fashionable tendency for women to build a united front against men will not catch on in the GDR" (*FD* 88). This is not to say, however, that for Wolf the emancipation of women had been *achieved* even in the GDR.[84]

Morgner affirmed repeatedly that she was a communist. Like Wolf, in the mid-1970s she espoused a classical socialist position on women's liberation: "I am a communist who is extraordinarily moved by the special demands of women. I think it is important for women to recognize that society must first of all be changed economically in the sense that hierarchical structures must be eliminated, the exploitative structures that after all continue to breed suppression and hierarchy. . . . The first big step for women's emancipation is the socialist revolution."[85] She is unequivocal in her promotion of socialism as the system most favorable to the liberation of women. In her magnum opus *Trobadora Beatriz* she speaks, through the persona of Valeska, of Paris and Rome as "places of the past" (*TB* 431, 438), in contrast with Moscow. One of the messages of the book is that socialism is wonderful—unambiguously wonderful as an ideal, but also good as a reality. The state socialisms of Eastern Europe are held up for praise as being future-oriented, and the GDR, as the main locality of the novel, is particularly praised. In particular, Morgner praises the right to work, equal rights for men and women, and social services. Half tongue-in-cheek, but half seriously, Morgner has Beatriz refer to the GDR as "the promised land."

Yet under the umbrella of this lavish praise, Morgner does not hesitate to criticize discrepancies between the ideal and everyday GDR reality, especially regarding the treatment of women. Beatriz has been taught by the East German Uwe Parnitzke to think of the GDR as the ideal country. When Beatriz enters the "promised land," some surprises await. Not only does Beatriz have to wait for a long time at the border and have a run-in with the bureaucracy, but men and women do not seem as equal as Parnitzke suggested in his hymn of praise. Morgner blames these problems on the persistence of "custom," which is slow to change. But there is no doubt in her mind that economic change must precede any change in consciousness. The heroine Beatriz reports from Rome:

> But I can't repeat Goethe's exclamation: "Oh, how happy I was in Rome" at the top of my lungs as long as the communists have not yet taken power. For today a woman of character can only be a socialist. And she must enter politics if she wants to achieve humane conditions for herself. Above all, in Italy and similar countries she must enter politics first, anything else is just an emancipatory fad. Customs can only be revolutionized after economic conditions are revolutionized. You cannot take the second step before the first one. In the GDR the first step was taken a long time ago. Now we are occupied with the second one, and that's that. (*TB* 385)

In the mid-1970s Morgner, like Wolf, believed that "feminism," which she associates with the West and from which she emphatically distances herself, is a specific product of the "misogynistic environment" found in capitalist countries, adding: "My country is prowoman."[86]

In an interview with Alice Schwarzer a few months before her death, Morgner explains how her position changed over time. She had once thought, in keeping with the official line, that "when socialism is developed, the woman question will be a secondary problem and will somehow solve itself."[87] Similarly to Wolf, she came to realize that women had specific interests that it was beyond the power of state socialism to address.

Morgner died before unification. Her reaction to the victory of the Alliance for Germany in the 18 March 1990 election, seven weeks before her death, is not known. In her last interview, which she gave the West German women's magazine *Emma* on 28 November 1989 (updated on 21 December), she expressed her joy at the recent popular demonstrations for change and endorsed the program published by women's studies experts on 14 December in *Neues Deutschland* (New Germany).

Overview of GDR Feminist Writers

GDR feminism ran chronologically parallel to the feminist movement in the United States. The feminist wave in GDR literature started in the late 1960s, got underway and peaked in the 1970s, and became generalized, in a popularized and less radical form, in the 1980s. The liberalization of cultural politics in 1971 was the most important enabling factor. Christa Wolf, born in 1929, is the oldest of the writers. The rest of the vanguard—women who had published a significant work on women's issues by 1975—consists of women born in the 1930s: Irmtraud Morgner (b. 1933), Brigitte Reimann (b. 1933), Charlotte Worgitzky (b. 1934), Sarah Kirsch (b. 1935), and Gerti Tetzner (b. 1936). Wolf's *The Quest for Christa T. (Nachdenken über Christa T.*, 1968) is generally thought of as the first GDR novel with emancipatory tendencies, though Morgner's *Hochzeit in Konstantinopel* (Wedding in Constantinople), published in the same year, would be another candidate. In the first half of the 1970s novels about women's quest for a feminine identity are prominent. Works of fiction by Wolf, Morgner, and Worgitzky argue an explicit feminist point. A full spectrum of feminist positions is already found in these early works. In particular, writers have different views on whether women's differences from men are natural or cultural and what the feminine pursuit of happiness might concretely look like, for instance, whether women should pursue a career or reject careerism altogether.

In the second half of the 1970s and in the 1980s, in contrast to the first half of the 1970s, many women wrote expositions of women's everyday lives and narratives with a psychological orientation. The ranks of women writing about women's issues were swelled by numerous newcomers, both writers of the same '30s generation who turned to feminist questions, or indeed to belles lettres, for the first time, and younger writers born in the 1940s and 1950s. They include Brigitte Thurm (b. 1932), Rosemarie Fret (b. 1935), Christa Müller (b. 1936), Hannelore Lauerwald (b. 1936), Helga Schütz (b. 1937), Helga Königsdorf (b. 1938), Lia Pirskawetz (b. 1938), Christine Wolter (b. 1939), Brigitte Martin (b. 1939), Rosemarie Zeplin (b. 1939), Helga Schubert (b. 1940), Renate Apitz (b. 1940), Monika Maron (b. 1941), Monika Helmecke (b. 1943), Maria Seidemann (b. 1944), Renate Feyl (b. 1944), Jutta Schlott (b. 1944), Renate Koetter-Johnschker (b. 1945), Beate Morgenstern (b. 1946), Angela Stachowa (b. 1948), Angela Krauss (b. 1950), Petra Werner (b. 1951), Maya Wiens (b. 1952), and Doris Paschiller (b. 1953).

The most interesting and original feminist ideas are found in the work of Christa Wolf and Irmtraud Morgner. Both women are committed, highly consistent, and innovative feminist thinkers; both set trends and found imitators. Wolf's works were always a step ahead of what GDR cultural politics called for. Her first major novel *Divided Heaven* (*Der geteilte Himmel*, 1963) treated in an unorthodox way the subject of fleeing the GDR; *The Quest for Christa T.* implicitly criticized, in the name of "subjective authenticity,"[88] the compulsion to conform in the GDR and was, moreover, written in a complicated form that departed radically from the precepts of socialist realism. Morgner's *Trobadora Beatriz* was called the "Bible of women's emancipation" by the Western press.[89] Morgner was an innovative stylist who mixed realism and fantasy and devised a flexible, compendious novel form that helped, in her view, accommodate the interruptions that characterize women's schedules. Despite similarities between them, the thinking of the two is distinctly different. Wolf, a profoundly historical thinker, builds on the ideas of Marx, Engels, and Bebel in order to develop her own brand of what a Western perspective would call "cultural feminism"; she praises traditional feminine virtues. Morgner stands out for her iconoclastic ideas. Her main idea is that women need to jump over their shadows and liberate feminine genius—they need to dare, to be confident and self-assertive, to be monomaniacal. Though Morgner does praise traditional feminine virtues, she is not content with them. Chapters 2 and 3 will mainly concern these two writers.

Preview

In feminist literature of the GDR criticism of government policies is conspicuously absent, first, I think, because women generally approved of the direction in which the government was moving with its legislation, and second, because despite official tolerance of "nonantagonistic" feminist criticism, writing that flew in the face of government policy might well not have met with a benevolent reception. It is noteworthy, for example, that abortion became a literary topic only after abortion was legalized in 1972. Feminist writing in the GDR tended to complement rather than criticize public policies on women. In certain instances an emancipatory public policy even seems to have given the signal to women writers, who followed it with a wave of affirming fiction. For example, in the late 1960s and early 1970s the Party and the government showed concern over women's double day and urged men to take over more housework. Around the same time, in the early 1970s, women writers started writing about women's double day and the housework-shy man with a vengeance. It is generally easier to discern where women writers agreed with public policies than where they disagreed with them, because points of friction with public policies and dissatisfactions with specific conditions in the GDR tend to come packaged within a more general affirmation of socialist ideology. It is not always easy to gauge the degree of criticism intended; if it were, there would not have been such controversy over the political spirit of Christa Wolf's writings. One of the peculiarities of writing in a place where there was censorship and potential political consequences for what you wrote is that ideological criticism was discreet to the point of being self-denying. A case in point is the very existence of a feminist literature that resolutely called itself *not* feminist.

My thesis is that GDR women writers above all focused on the question of "feminizing" society by changing not laws but, rather, the conventions that shaped male and female psychology. These conventions amount to semiotic, and above all rhetorical, practices.

Wolf, Morgner, and Worgitzky all explicitly thematize the importance of women speaking out, in transgressing the norms that have traditionally governed women's speech and in refusing silence. Speech everywhere is governed by rituals and surrounded by taboos. If state socialism in the few decades of its existence curbed freedom of expression in ways that seem intolerable from the perspective of the West, the lines that centuries had drawn between the sexes in terms of who could say what and who could put whom into verbal boxes were far more entrenched. Feminist literature in the GDR focused on breaking the taboos that custom had imposed on speech by women. It called attention to the patriarchal laws and customs that communism had not managed to expunge and to the patronizing gestures and comments that men address to women[90] and suggested that current (self)-images of women, whether traditional or socialist, be replaced with more favorable ones. I distinguish four areas where GDR women writers advocate and/or perform a revision of discourse by and about women. Each forms the subject of one chapter of this book.

1. GDR women writers suggest that it is imperative to open domains of discourse now closed to women. In particular, these domains include ones that would involve reconstructing woman as the subject of desire. Whereas in the West the issue of women's desire emerged within the feminist critique of psychoanalysis, in the GDR it was voiced, earlier and differently, as a sociological and (gender-) political issue. Again and again it is suggested that women are not allowed to articulate their desires, which is as much as to say, they are not allowed to *have* desires, at least if this means writing their own independent fantasy scenarios. If they do articulate their desires, it is as good as condemning them never to be fulfilled. They fall not on receptive, but on shocked ears. The expression of desire, the rhetoric of demand, and even the rhetoric of persuasion are thus closed to women. At best women may cultivate the art of suggestion, of seduction. This is particularly true of the heartland of women's construction as passive objects, in the erotic sphere, where women have traditionally been barred from the role of active subject, but it carries over into virtually every other sphere as well.

2. The time has come to sing the praises of the feminine. In particular, there is a tendency in GDR women's writing to identify communism with the feminine. Thus Irmtraud Morgner writes in *Amanda* (1983): "A socialism that doesn't get rid of male domination can't build communism." This discourse clearly draws its authority from

classic Marxist theory, that is, from the identification of primitive communism with matriarchy. It is thus quite conservative, although GDR women writers, inspired by Western feminism, infuse femininity with a political importance far beyond anything envisaged by Bebel or Engels. The identification of communism with the feminine is particularly pronounced in the work of Christa Wolf. In her early novel *Divided Heaven* the protagonist Rita opts for the "harder, sterner life" and "the attraction of a great historical movement" in the East, with its values of community, idealism, and optimism, while her boyfriend Manfred, a scientist, cynically disbelieves in the basic goodness of man and in reason as a key to historical progress and leaves for the West, where individualism and competition rule and material rewards stimulate productivity. In this novel it seems to be pure chance that the *woman* remains in the East, and no clear connection is made between femininity and socialism (ideally conceived). But, in later works such as "The New Life and Opinions of a Tomcat" ("Neue Lebensansichten eines Katers," 1974) and "Self-experiment" ("Selbstversuch," 1973), in which Wolf explicitly thematizes men versus women, science, individualism, hierarchy, personal ambition, and competition—everything Manfred embodies—is identified with the male, along with the worst side of state socialism, the propensity to overprogram, plan, and control, while human values—caring about others, sensitivity, insight—are identified with the female. A constant theme in Wolf is that women should not envy men; it is preferable to be a vulnerable female than an emotionally bankrupt male. In *Cassandra* (*Kassandra*, 1983) Wolf elevates the woman's position to one of global political significance. Here the male/female opposition is aligned not only with capitalism/communism but with war/peace. This praise of the feminine in traditional terms of domesticity as well as in traditional Marxist terms is found in Morgner as well. Morgner, who unlike Wolf stresses that differences between the sexes are cultural rather than natural, nevertheless lauds traditional feminine virtues and asserts that society must be *feminized*. Why can't a man be more like a woman? Already in *Trobadora Beatriz*, but to a greater extent in *Amanda*, she stresses that society at large needs to adopt the feminine virtue of *nurturing* in order to save the planet from war and ecological destruction. The ideal man Benno in Morgner's *Trobadora Beatriz*, who possesses all feminine virtues, receives a title of honor: his baby stepson calls him "Mamma."

3. In the interest of creating a women's tradition and female role models, women must write themselves into history, a genre from which they have been excluded, and remake their image through lit-

erature. The entrance of women into history is Morgner's self-avowed central theme. Morgner's ideas appear to engage directly with Marxist thought and are not derivative of Western feminism's contemporaneous push for women's history and women's studies. Morgner asserts that women, like other expropriated people, have been written out of history. To compensate, they must create legends. In *Trobadora Beatriz* she herself creates such a legend in the figure of the trobadora, a woman of many adventures who sings the praises of men. In *Amanda* she rewrites myths, legends, and literary traditions in order to establish women as the real heroines of history, who once upon a time lost their beneficent power to men but whose day is finally at hand. Morgner was not the only author who occupied herself with devising new plots and forms intended to lend dignity to women's lives. Rewriting the image of women in literature and redefining the feminine role was one of the first challenges for women writers whose works can be considered feminist. In the wake of Wolf's *Quest for Christa T.* a number of women writers published works of fiction that evince a desire to seek a new feminine identity. Such writers as Gerti Tetzner, Brigitte Reimann, and Brigitte Thurm followed Wolf in adapting the genre of the novel of education (*Bildungsroman*) to the feminine subject. Some of their untraditional heroines reject male norms and try to find an alternative life-style. Others assimilate to the male model and claim their rights to career, creative self-fulfillment, and public recognition, as well as to the personal happiness that should be the reward of success. These assimilators in particular are portrayed as dynamic, enterprising, resourceful personalities who have every intention of surmounting rather than succumbing to any barriers that life may erect in their path. They "want it all, now," as Reimann has a male character say about her heroine Franziska Linkerhand.

4. The reality of women's lives must be forced into the public consciousness. Topics that are extremely important to women but that have been marginalized or elided by male discourse must be given voice. Above all, the (patriarchal) distinction between "public" and "private" life must be broken down. Especially in the second half of the 1970s and early 1980s, a great deal of literature was published on the subject of specifically feminine experience. The idea that the personal is political undoubtedly came from the Western feminist movement. The emphasis in the GDR fell on different topics, however, mainly because women's lives in the GDR were different, but also because the shadow of GDR cultural politics still fell on

the literary landscape despite the brightening dictum that there would be "no taboos in art." The point that constraints on discourse about "women's topics" must be broken down is sometimes argued discursively in this literature, but more often it is made performatively: speaking out about these topics itself breaks down the barriers against speaking about them. The boundaries of what can and should be talked about are expanded most effectively by the sheer force of repetition, by critical mass. The theme of abortion was a favorite, once abortion was legalized: fiction by Helga Königsdorf (1978), Monika Helmecke (1979), and Maya Wiens (1983), and particularly Charlotte Worgitzky's full-length novel *Meine ungeborenen Kinder* (My unborn children, 1982) describe abortions, both legal and illegal, in great detail, as well as the women's feelings about them. Worgitzky, who tells the story of one woman's seven abortions, also particularly thematizes and criticizes the *censoring* (by men, not by the state) of the topic of abortion. Should an abortion not be shown on stage? Should a woman not be able to discuss and describe her abortions publicly? Other stories collected around topics that had been not so much controversial as invisible, in particular women's exhausting double day and the problems of motherhood. Thus subjects that had hitherto been considered too trivial to be written about became, in the peak period of feminist writing, the bubbling cauldrons of GDR women's literature. My chapter on the reality of women's lives will visit the spectrum of women's issues on which feminist writers of the 1970s and 1980s opted to focus the spotlight.

2 "What Does a Woman Want?" Woman as the Subject of Desire

> All they desire is—but hist again—is that not a man's step on the stair? All they desire, we were about to say when the gentleman took the very words out of our mouths. Women have no desires, says this gentleman, coming into Nell's parlour; only affectations. Without desires (she has served him and he is gone) their conversation cannot be of the slightest interest to anyone. "It is well known," says Mr S.W., "that when they lack the stimulus of the other sex, women can find nothing to say to each other. When they are alone, they do not talk, they scratch."
> —Virginia Woolf, *Orlando*

> I always made plans right off with the first few guys I had, but never my *own* plans, always theirs. There was this potter, a neat guy, and we already saw ourselves living in a farm house in the mountains doing pottery together. And another guy, half-Portuguese, been living here for ages, wanted of all things to work at the UN in Geneva as an interpreter. So right away I had to learn Portuguese so I could go to Geneva too. We thought it was all actually going to happen. I'm only now beginning to ask myself: Where do *I* fit in all these stories? What's *mine*, anyway?
> —Maxie Wander, *Guten Morgen, du Schöne*

Even on what is termed in the United States a "level playing field," even under the conditions of legal equality and economic independence that women enjoyed in the GDR, even though women there were more empowered relative to men than they have been in most times and places, women in the GDR continued to find that they were less than men's social equals. The problem, according to Christa Wolf, Irmtraud Morgner, Sarah Kirsch, and other GDR women writers, existed both outside, in the world of social customs, and inside, in the gender-specific psychology of women. Women continued to feel as if they were living in a world that was not made for them. They failed to excel in ways that counted. What counted for them did not count for men, who held the reins. Work and achievement did not bring women the same rewards as men. Society continued to treat women like women. Women lacked power. They did not feel like autonomous subjects.

The two most prominent GDR women writers, Wolf and Morgner, inquired into this phenomenon extensively. Other writers treated limited aspects of it. Wolf's writings are reflective, insightful, ironic, nuanced, and above all moral. Perhaps one of the reasons why she has met with such resonance in the West is that she portrays women in a light familiar to Western feminism, namely, as victims. Morgner, in contrast, particularly in her acclaimed *Trobadora Beatriz*, writes energetically, radically, parodistically, and humorously: she presents an appealing recipe for change and avoids the litany of complaint.

Both Wolf and Morgner probed for the sources of women's malaise. Both writers found them in women's history of disempowerment. Both came to view the history of women as a history of oppression that stretches back for centuries until it disappears into the shadows of what is for both writers the cherished conception of primitive matriarchy. The conclusions that Wolf and Morgner draw are different, but common to both is a historical, deterministic, Marxist mode of explanation. Both presuppose that being determines consciousness.

In their quest for the material, historical sources of women's oppression they were preceded by Simone de Beauvoir, whose pathbreaking work *The Second Sex* they could have read as early as 1951, since the 1951 German translation was accessible in the GDR the same year. Wolf certainly knew Beauvoir's work by the early 1980s at latest, since she mentions her in a conversation with Grace Paley in 1984 as one of the women writers who were important to her.[1] The similarities between Beauvoir's account and Morgner's views are striking. Like Beauvoir, Morgner makes much of women's fundamental dividedness between her maternal role and her desire for self-realization. The theme already occurs in *Rumba auf einen Herbst* (Rumba to an autumn, written in 1965; published 1992).[2] One consequence, woman's historical lack of genius, obsesses her. Wolf's historical account is different and seems independent of Beauvoir's, being much more indebted to Karl Marx and Frederick Engels: she seeks the origin of women's oppression first in the rise of bourgeois, industrial society, and finally pinpoints it, following Engels and August Bebel, at the onset of patriarchy, which brought with it private property and social classes. She also has a simpler and less problematized view of what a woman "is."

Simone de Beauvoir's Theory of the "Second Sex"

Simone de Beauvoir's work appears to have been seminal for East German feminism, as it certainly was for feminism in Western Europe and in the United States. Because Beauvoir argues positions that will be echoed and elaborated on by GDR women writers, especially Morgner, it will be useful to to recapitulate her argument at some length. Beauvoir traces woman's situation to her essential, biologically determined dividedness. Unlike the male, the human female is "in the grip of the species." In this she resembles other female mammals. Maternity plays a much larger role in the lives of female mammals than in those of females of other animal classes, for gestation takes place within their bodies and the females must nurse their young after birth. Consequently, their bodies are adapted for, and subservient to, maternity. But the human female is even more beleaguered by her reproductive function than other female mammals, for she has no sterile periods and is therefore susceptible to closely spaced pregnancies. For the human female, gestation is fatiguing, childbirth difficult and dangerous; nursing tiring. An enormous portion of her life and energy is given over to reproduction. Men suffer no such biological handicap; man's body left him free to act, to invent, to create. Historically, this biological inequality led to woman's subjugation. Initially powerless to prevent constant pregnancies, which in turn rendered her dependent on man for protection and food, woman was easily enslaved by man.

Beauvoir's theoretical premise is that every existent seeks to limit and define itself, to give itself a mirror, by setting up an Other. Thus this subjugation of woman by the stronger party, man, was, existentially speaking, a matter of course. By identifying biological difference and the oppression of maternity as the original and key reason for women's subjugation, Beavoir favors an explanation that has no precedent in Engels. However, she follows Engels in arguing that the advent of private property dethroned woman from the relatively favorable position she had enjoyed in tribal, agricultural societies. Woman's reproductive function made her enslavement desirable to men, who, as the owners of the new wealth, saw fit to use her for the production of "their" children as well as for their sexual needs and the care of their households. Woman's function as Other, and her self-consciousness as a slave, in turn, imposed on her the status of *object*.

According to Beauvoir, material dependence on men, who affirmed their own status as subjects by objectifying women, had far-reaching consequences for feminine behavior and psychology, which persisted into her own time in the training of girls. Women have to learn the art of being an object. They have to learn to be desirable, to please: "The privileged place held by men in economic life, their social usefulness, the prestige of marriage, the value of masculine backing, all this makes women wish ardently to please men."[3] They must dissimulate the reality of their being: "Like all the oppressed, woman deliberately dissembles her objective actuality; the slave, the servant, the indigent, all who depend upon the caprices of a master, have learned to turn toward him a changeless smile or an enigmatic impassivity; their real sentiments, their actual behavior, are carefully hidden. And moreover woman is taught from adolescence to lie to men, to scheme, to be wily. In speaking to them she wears an artificial expression on her face; she is cautious, hypocritical, play-acting" (Beauvoir 1989, p. 259). Girls are taught passivity from the start, for "the supreme necessity for woman is to charm a masculine heart" (p. 291). "All girls . . . learn in time that to please they must abdicate. Their mothers enjoin upon them to treat the boys no longer as comrades, not to make advances, to take a passive role. If they wish to start a friendship or a flirtation, they must carefully avoid seeming to take the initiative in it" (p. 335). A man, in contrast, "occupies a privileged situation in this world" and therefore "is in a position to show his love actively" (p. 259).

Beauvoir eloquently contrasts the development of the adolescent girl with that of the adolescent boy: "The young man's journey into existence is made relatively easy by the fact that there is no contradiction between his vocation as human being and as male. . . . But for the young woman, on the contrary, there is a contradiction between her status as a real human being and her vocation as a female" (p. 336). Adolescent boys go through an "apprenticeship of violence" (p. 330): "their aggressiveness is developed, their will to power, their love for competition; and it is at just this time that the girl gives up rough games.... They are forbidden to explore, to venture, to extend the limits of the possible. In particular, the *competitive* attitude, most important to young men, is almost unknown to them" (ibid.).

Woman is denied action; instead, her life is characterized by waiting. She learns to be docile, resigned. She does not dare to be enterprising, to revolt, to invent—she has no confidence in her body, no faith in her power to change the world. The street is hostile to her, "with eyes and hands lying in wait everywhere" (p. 712); this kills spontaneity and exuberance; her preoccupation with her costume and manners "rivets her to the ground and to herself" (ibid.). Beauvoir concludes: "The constraints that surround her and the whole tradition that weighs her down prevent her from feeling responsible for the universe, and that is the deep-seated reason for her mediocrity" (p. 713).

It is through this reasoning that Beauvoir accounts for the historical paucity of women geniuses. She writes: "There are women who are mad and there are women of sound method: none has that madness in her method that we call genius. It is, above all, this reasonable modesty that has hitherto set the limits of feminine talent.... None have ever trampled upon all prudence in the attempt to *emerge* beyond the given world.... [They] have surely not enriched our vision of the world" (p. 708).

"Becoming a Subject"

According to Beauvoir, woman's historical disempowerment deprived her of subject status. The goal of "becoming a subject," of "finding oneself," is precisely the idea with which Wolf's approach to the "woman question" starts—initially in the story of the nonconformist Christa T. (1968); then in the story "Unter den Linden" (written 1969), which ends when the heroine meets *herself*; and very clearly in the sex change story "Self-experiment" (written 1972), where the heroine, after sampling life as a man, opts to change back into a woman, despite the conflicts that riddle women's lives. In

Morgner's work the question of women's self-assertion becomes central in a novel, *Hochzeit in Konstantinopel*, that appeared the same year as *The Quest for Christa T.* Morgner's heroine Bele is as much of a nonconformist as Christa T. If Christa T. hoots in public, Bele H., in a story she tells, starts up a motorbike in a motorcycle store and crashes around on it in response to unhelpful salespersons. Nevertheless, in these two novels of 1968, there are already characteristic differences between the two writers. Wolf writes seriously, philosophically, morally; Morgner writes fancifully, humorously, satirically. For Wolf, here as later, the issue is self-realization, becoming the person one "is." For Morgner, the issue is imagination and daring: having the imagination to dare, to commit transgressive acts that in turn will force other people to reconsider their conventional habits of thought.

Viewed collectively, Wolf, Morgner, and other GDR women writers suggest that woman's object status has shaped her role and deformed her psychology in four areas particularly: it has skewed her relationship to her own desire; it has placed blindfolds on her imagination; it has precluded a self-assertiveness that is the precondition of all success; and it has proscribed to her the most direct and effective modes of language and expression. These areas are interlinked: women's role in each is an aspect of the same syndrome. Woman's socialization in each area conspires to produce the phenomenon "woman." After discussing these four topics and GDR women writers' contributions to them I shall examine in detail Morgner's *Trobadora Beatriz*, the most radical feminist work the GDR produced, which unifies all the topics.

Desire

Desire is perhaps, as Morgner's work demonstrates, the most basic category of all, the wellspring of all women's other problems. Yet it is the one least theorized by Western feminisms. Beauvoir implies but does not elaborate a problematic of desire. The American Constitution identifies the "pursuit of happiness" as a right, but American feminists have made virtually nothing of it, perhaps because the issue of women's desire is the most tabooed and least objective of women's issues. (For who is to say what "women" "want"? Is the collective even appropriate here? And what counterproductive, politically incorrect notions might not come to light if women began to ask themselves what the happiness is that they wish to pursue?) Moreover, it is difficult to see how a "right to desire," which would apply first to private interactions, could be enforced.

Freud, who moved the topic of desire into the forefront of Western philosophy and was its first major theoretician, stopped short when it came to investigating feminine desire. He addressed his celebrated statement on the topic to Marie Bonaparte: "The great question that has never been answered and which I have not yet been able to answer, despite my thirty years of research into the feminine soul, is 'What does a woman want?'"[4] I would like to suggest that the cause of Freud's bafflement, and of the feminine opacity that mystified him, was the systematic social repression of women's desire. The problem can be summarized as follows: in the same sense that any subordinate is discouraged from wanting—because unruly desires are inconvenient to those in power and could upset the order of things—the expression of desire has not been tolerated in women. Whereas for men, the right to desire has been bound up with status, desire has been taboo for women across the board. For a man to express his desires may be inconvenient, but it is at least viewed as natural. If a woman, even a powerful woman, expresses strong desires, she has been viewed as unnatural, unfeminine, "domineering." More than any other aspect of the question of what it means to "be a subject," the right to desire has been the Berlin Wall that divides the sexes. One could state the matter thus: the phenomenon *woman*, the specific psychology of woman that persists even in the present day, is the product of the systematic denial of women's desire. The taboo on desire is the outstanding characteristic of feminine socialization. Women are not supposed to want.

Psychoanalysis and philosophy have taught us that the topic of desire is a complex one indeed, not at all the simple thing we imagine when we talk about desire in ordinary social contexts. All this complexity, which bears on the composition, content, and determination of desire, is not the source of GDR women writers' interest in the topic and barely figures into their treatment of it. In fact, their treatment of the subject is refreshingly free from traditional psychoanalytic and philosophical perspectives. This can be said even of Christa Wolf, the writer most interested in depth psychology. Nevertheless, since the psychoanalytic and philosophic treatment of desire sheds interesting sidelights on the social regimentation of desire, which they appear to an extent both to derive from and to reinforce and in which the GDR women writers *are* interested, it bears mention here.

The psychoanalytic appropriation of the concept of desire from Freud onward can be traced to Schopenhauer's theorizing of desire ("will") as energy, as what makes the world go round, yet at the same time as testimony to a lack: in Schopenhauer's view desire, or perpetually wanting what one does not have, is the source of human unhappiness. Freud's ontology of the self is based in desire. He posits desire as the dynamo of the psychic system. Desires, which are based in infantile fantasy scenarios, are unconscious and ineradicable, unfulfillable yet perpetually alive. Sublimated, the energy attaching to them is redirected to produce all of the accomplishments of human culture and civilization. As for the object of desire, the pleasure afforded by the mother's breast, the earliest object, and later by the attentions of the maternal caregiver, orients the subject's future desires.[5] The Oedipal mechanism, tailored to the situation of the male child, writes a scenario of desire that casts the route through identification with the father as that which leads toward an eventual substitutive fulfillment of the desire for the mother, including sublimation.

Jacques Lacan continued and expanded this line of thought. For Lacan, desire, signifying lack, is *the* constitutive psychic force from earliest infancy on. He problematizes the concept and uses it to substantiate his notion of a "rift" in the subject, or the subject's nonself-identity. He insists that the human subject not only constitutes itself through identification with desired objects, but also desires to be desired and thus internalizes the desire of the Other.

Using a historical rather than a structural argument, the literary theorist and cultural critic René Girard similarly compromised the notion of any kind of spontaneous, natural, or autonomous desire, arguing that spontaneous desire was crowded out over the centuries by a creeping ontological sickness, "mediated desire." Mediated desire operates according to a simple principle: what makes an object desirable is the fact that another, "the mediator," desires it. Behind this phenomenon is an ideal of godlike autonomy: a particular individual is chosen as the "mediator" because he is perceived to be autonomous and happy. People envy him and copy his desire. What the individual really desires is to *be* the mediator.[6] Autonomy is also signaled by indifference: "The indifferent person always seems to possess that radiant self-mastery which we all seek. He seems to live in a closed circuit, enjoying his own being, in a state of happiness which nothing can disturb" (Girard 1965, p. 107). Revealing one's desires results in loss of face: "If he reveals his desire to others, then he creates new obstacles at every step of the way. . . . The secret of success, in business as well as in love, is dissimulation" (ibid.). Again, in this reading, desire is conceptualized as a lack, as self-insufficiency, as an imperfection, and as the source of unhappiness.

In contradistinction to these theorists, all of whom conceptualize desire as lack or insufficiency, Luce Irigaray bases her feminist critique of Freud (and by implication of Lacan) on a radical rereading of desire as a privilege, as the justification for activity and self-realization in the world. This is the position that Morgner and other GDR women writers adopt as well. Irigaray attacks Freud for consigning women to passivity in his writings on femininity.[7] According to Irigaray, Freud models the concept of desire on the sperm's "race toward the ovum" (Irigaray 1974, p. 15). "Desire" thus becomes a desire for origin, that is, for the mother, whose privileged locus is the penis, capable of going back inside the mother (p. 42). All that remains to the female is penis envy. By denying woman her own independent desire—a desire that would be different from that of men—and setting her up as merely envious of the male, Freud enhances the male's narcissistic self-esteem (p. 51). The woman's function, Irigaray concludes, becomes one of "upholding the value of the penis, maintaining its stock rating" (p. 73). Applying Girard's terms to this argument, we can add to Irigaray's critique by saying that Freud not only validates male desire but also retheorizes the lack implied by desire by maneuvering one sex, the male, into the privileged position of what Girard would call the "autonomous" mediator, while consigning woman to the role of the perpetually discontented desirer and thus displacing the negative nimbus associated with desiring wholly onto the female sex!

Even in today's "democratic" societies, it is difficult for a woman to reach adulthood without noticing that the social reception of the articulation of desire is different for men and for women. The *dynamic* significance of desire is attributed to men, while the significance of imperfection, together with the loss of face noted by Girard, is attributed to women. Although a man's desires in fact appear to be largely "scripted"—circumscribed and mediated by his peer group—society nevertheless has traditionally respected these desires. A man's expression of his desire—his ideas, his beliefs—is accepted, expected, and encouraged. A man's situation is straightforward. He is to figure out what he wants, to declare this publicly, and to try to get it. For a man, a *specific* desire may not meet with public approval, but the public climate is certainly receptive to his *expression* of his desire—

indeed to the paradigmatic sequence of choice, articulation, and attempt to get what he wants. Men are even under pressure to make choices and announce them publicly. Sticking one's neck out counts as masculine. Implicitly, the world is there, waiting for men to do things to it. This paradigm is reinforced by countless literary quest plots that involve men striving to get what they want. The privilege of direct expression testifies to the prerogative of initiative, of action. In the case of women, desire does not lead in any such straightforward way to fulfillment. It is not a question of the wrong means of expression; for if women adopt men's language or men's semiotics to express their desire for conventional, even trivial things, this language does not work for them. They get odd looks.

As GDR women writers have recognized, the difference is most pronounced in situations in which men and women interact. Thus a female figure in Morgner's *Amanda* (1983) speaks of the necessity of employing the "art of suggestion" with her husband if she wants to realize her wishes: "If, for example, I wanted to take a trip with Konrad and said, 'I'd like to take a trip with you,' he'd say, 'I have no time.' In the function of wife or secretary desires must be fostered, not stated" (*A* 165). Women who want to get their way with men do best to adopt a roundabout means of persuasion, even in trivial matters. As Beauvoir claimed, women are forced to dissemble.

The difference is crassest in the erotic realm. Morgner's Laura Salmann in *Trobadora Beatriz*, a citizen of "the promised land" for women, that is, the GDR, observes: "In this country, eroticism is the last male domain; in all other areas, our laws give women equal rights" (*TB* 112). A woman who openly expresses her desire for a man loses face, according to one female character in *Rumba auf einen Herbst*.[8] Morgner remarked similarly, in an interview with Alice Schwarzer of 28 November–21 December 1989: "Simply to address a topic like eroticism or sexuality, not by beating around the bush, but directly, is a privilege that men have granted to themselves. For it requires subjecthood."[9] The division of roles within the sphere of erotic desire may be seen as the kernel and ultimate reduction of the apportionment of roles within the topic of desire generally.

The more serious the degree of involvement sought, the more fatal it is for women to be direct. To this day it is an iron law of romantic comedies that the hero gets the woman *he* wants. In the 1994 film comedy *Four Weddings and a Funeral*, for example, a work "liberated" enough so that it takes sex before marriage for granted, glorifies a homosexual relationship, and lets the heroine rather than the hero make the first erotic move, the "right" ending nevertheless consists in the hero getting the girl of *his* choice. The heroine chooses differently, but *her* choice, needless to say, proves to be a mistake. Two other women want to marry the hero, but it in no way impairs the happiness of the ending that their hopes are dashed. Literary plots conventionally turn men's desires to wishes-come-true and women's desires to tragedy. Particularly in the business of establishing permanent or quasi-permanent relationships, women have been inculcated with a stealthiness that, as the contemporary Russian author Tatyana Tolstaya brilliantly parodies in her story "Hunting the Wooly Mammoth," is the sine qua non of all feminine success. Tolstoya uses the familiar erotic metaphor of hunter and prey with a twist in her story of her heroine's quest to marry: the heroine is the hunter; the man she has set her sights on is the "wooly mammoth," for indeed, since the Stone Age there has been no progress in the customs of courtship. For the woman it is axiomatic that she must net her prey surreptitiously, by stealth, for "centuries of experience" show that if the prey gets the slightest wind of the hunt, he disappears forever: "Zoya didn't dare ask a direct question. Many centuries of experience kept her from doing that. One bad shot—and it was over, write it off; the prey runs away hard, leaving a cloud of dust and view of the soles of its feet. No, you have to lure it."[10]

An example of a GDR novel that presents this paradigm, though uncritically, is Brigitte Thurm's first novel *Verena* (1972). The eponymous heroine dreams for three and one half years of a man she once briefly worked under. She finally seeks him out. Under his unremembering gaze she feels compelled to lie: she says she came to do a newspaper report on him. When his eyes tell her that she has piqued his narcissism and he suspects her real reason, she hastily dissembles further—for nothing is more unmentionable than a woman's desire for a man—, protesting that she is only doing as her job demands: "I admit, she says softly, "that it may sound strange when a woman from far away bursts into your lunch break, unannounced, only saying she wants to write something about you that she doesn't exactly specify, and asks you curious questions about yourself and your background. Today that still seems suspicious, just because a woman is doing it."[11] In the end, she never declares herself, and her desire proves unrequited, for the man married since she last saw him.

In the same year, 1972, a film appeared in the GDR that popularized contemporary debate about the issue of who can propose to whom. The film, *Der Dritte* (Her Third), directed by Egon Günther, concerns a woman who actively seeks a new husband after two disappointing relationships with men that left her the single parent of two teenage daughters. The screenplay by Günther Rücker is based on Eberhard Panitz's novel *Unter den Bäumen regnet es zweimal* (It rains twice under the trees, 1969), but it revolutionizes Panitz's story, boldly adding the scene where the woman proposes to a man and indeed the entire theme of the heroine's quest for a new husband. The film sparked much controversy.[12] Its aim was to point out the discrepancy between women's equality with men at work and their inequality with men in private life. The heroine, Margit Fließer, finds a man who appears to her an ideal match. But, much to her own anguish and exasperation, she finds it next to impossible to approach this "wooly mammoth" except by using timeworn feminine ruses. She hovers apprehensively on the brink of declaring herself directly. Finally, she lures him "conventionally," "just like in grandma's time"—with immediate, unproblematic success. After having done so, however (and notably not before), she bursts into a tirade, ostensibly directed at her two daughters but in the presence of the man, in which she rails against the custom that dictates that a woman, even in today's age of supposed total equality, cannot propose directly to a man:

> I . . . am a mathematician. I work, think, and feel in agreement with the technical, scientific, and political standard under the socialistic conditions of the scientific and technical revolution. But when I like a man, when I need him to live, when I want him, then I will still probably make myself ridiculous if I tell him that. No! If I want to reach the goal, I have to keep my love secret, deeply conceal my desire, make it unrecognizable, because it might repulse him, right? Only he, he alone can allow himself that. Just like in grandmother's days, I have to sit there like a good girl and await merciful destiny. . . . Wait to be noticed. Wait for him to find me desirable. In matters of love I can only distinguish myself in his eyes if I maintain a quiet reserve and wait for him to make a move. If he puts his hands on me, I am still expected to hesitate, look down and at first say "No." He doesn't want anything else. It revolts him. He's had his experiences with that. This is the way he was brought up. His father and mother, too. Do you understand that I don't want to do that? That I can't? That I feel deceitful if I get into the same train purely by accident and buy a ticket just so you don't notice I'm following you. I want you to see me! I want you to really see who I am![13]

Cuts to the "mammoth's" face register his increasing sympathetic approval. The next and final episode of the film shows their wedding.

This suggestive film was the optimistic high point of the attempt to change custom. In her novel *Karen W.* (1974), Gerti Tetzner followed suit in challenging women's enforced passivity in the erotic realm. When Karen W. falls in love, she asks herself: "Why should only the man court openly?" and declares herself first—successfully.[14] Arguably, it helps matters that the man she picks is a radical communist student who believes in personal liberation. But later novelists are more skeptical. Monika Helmecke in the story "Erich" (in *Klopfzeichen* [Tapping code], 1979) lets her heroine take it upon herself to propose marriage to the man of her choice, but she fails, because she cannot engineer the right moment: after they drink wine, he falls asleep; after a concert, his thoughts are elsewhere. In Renate Apitz's *Hexenzeit* (Time of witches, 1984) the heroine declares her love to a man with whom she has had a wonderful affair, expecting that he will divorce his wife and marry her. The narrator comments: "If only you had said nothing, silly Mathilde! Perhaps things would have taken a different course." The man responds to the heroine's declaration by breaking up with her.

The sex role differences in the erotic sphere are far from being a trivial matter. Their significance is illustrated by Sarah Kirsch's "Merkwürdiges Beispiel weiblicher Entschlossenheit" (Strange example of female determination, written 1971; in *Die ungeheuren bergehohen Wellen auf See* [The gigantic mountain-high waves at sea], 1973), a hilarious story of a woman's attempt to proposition a man. This story takes as its subject a conservative example of a woman's desire: the woman wishes to have a child. It is conservative because women's wish for children is generally acknowledged, socially validated, ascribed to women by male authorities like Freud, and encouraged as politically useful. If any female desire has society's *nihil obstat*, it is this one. Yet even here, or indeed especially here, taking the initiative is off-limits for women. Children originate, the saying goes, as a "glint" in the "father's"—not the mother's—"eye." In part it is a question of erotic initiative. But the matter runs much deeper than this. It is a foundational tenet of patriarchy that children fundamentally belong to men. Women are conceived as vehicles to provide men with children, not the reverse. It is of paramount importance that the idea of the child, the desire for a child, originate with a man. The man chooses a woman (again his prerogative) and marries her in order to ensure that he will have his own biological children. (Marriage is, by convention, the closest he can come to that assurance.) Marriage, under patriarchal law, is the official deed that testifies to a man's desire for children and hence ascribes to him the responsibility for any children born in wedlock. Children unwanted by men, or expressed more precisely, children born without the stamp of male desire signified by marriage to the mother, that is, children born out of wedlock, are "illegitimate," that is, not legitimated by a man's desire for the child. The notion of illegitimacy is perhaps the most glaring example of a counterintuitive, counternatural distinction that has been institutionalized and written into law by patriarchy. Distinguishing radically between one child and another based on the marital status of the woman, which in turn testifies to the father's desire for the child, is an idea that exists only because it suits men, because men have had the power to enforce it, because our history is a history of patriarchy. The effect is to alienate woman from the activity that more than any other nature assigned to her: childbearing. It is an idea that overwrites the natural state of affairs, which writes into law and eventually into public belief the proposition that women's childbearing activity is wholly mediated by the volition of men. Adrienne Rich wrote in an essay of 1977: "The mother-child relationship can be seen as the first relationship violated by patriarchy. Mother and child, as objects of possession by the fathers, are reduced both to pieces of property and to relationships in which men can feel in control, powerful, wherever else they may feel impotent."[15] Wolf recently glossed the movement to make abortion illegal in the German "New States" in similar terms, as a renewed and only thinly disguised expression of men's desire to control women and children: "Male hypocrisy, which is complicated because the hypocrite himself is often unaware of it, conceals the ancient power play for control over woman and child behind a concern for unborn life. It makes me sick."[16]

Therefore, children originating in female desire are all wrong. A woman is, of course, permitted to want a particular man's child—this is a projection of male narcissistic fantasy. She can want a "legitimate" child—by way of supportive echo of her mate's desire. Above all, she is supposed to want a "legitimate" child when it is underway. The mother's desire for the child is politically useful; it ensures that she will care for it. Maternal feeling—however real it may be—is also a rigidly scripted scenario (differentiation and nuance could only impair its political impact), which dictates to women, in all simplicity: love your child, sacrifice yourself for your child—or yours is guilt forever! A certain amount has been written about how current divorce law perpetuates female care for, and male authority over, children in the guise of equality under the law;[17] the question of what this legislation actually does to women is then, precisely as in right-to-life arguments, conveniently buried under a justification that purports to address solely the best interests of the child. Of course, a woman is supposed to want her child's best interest. Society makes it extremely difficult for a woman to turn the discussion from the welfare of the child to the welfare of the mother without sounding like a moral monster.

Despite all this, women are not supposed to want to have children independent of, or prior to, the desire of a man. The proposition that Kirsch's heroine makes to the man she has in mind thus oversteps a firm taboo. This is evidenced first in the woman's speech, which testifies to embarrassment, desperation, lack of practice, and the nonexistence of verbal formulas for such a proposition emanating from a woman and directed toward a man. Most amusing is the contrast between Frau Schmalfuß's equality with her coworker, Friedrich, in the world of work, and her inequality with him in the world of intimate relations. In her living room Frau Schmalfuß waffles and digresses, constantly veering onto topics about which she can safely speak and then floundering ineptly back onto her main course. Her process of getting to the unmentionable point reminds one of caricatures of parents trying to tell their children about the "facts of life":

> She sighed and started to speak. At a fast pace, so as to finish everything before he can say anything. Oh Friedrich, we've known each other for so long. We both started small in the business, way back when we didn't even work for export. Now our pumps go all the way to Guinea, but I didn't want to say that at all, I was just thinking that I have also gotten round in the world, on almost as big a ship as your ice-breaker. Well, yes, I went all the way to Murmansk once, and I earn a lot. . . . She talked and talked and dragged herself slowly through the trips, the prosperity, the apartment, the social responsibility, right up to the point: . . . so, I just have to have a child, and I thought you would understand and do it, no obligations at all, I'll give you that in writing![18]

The man's reaction proves that the heroine has decidedly spoken "out of turn." The twenty-eight-year-old Frau Schmalfuß is large-footed and homely. But it is not her appearance that is her undoing, for before she begins her uneloquent speech, Friedrich thinks: "She really is a beautiful person." He himself is one-legged. Nor is it a fear of involvement—for Frau Schmalfuß promises that she won't involve him in fatherhood, and in fact believes that herself. Rather, what upsets him is the fact that *she* proposes the child, that it is her idea: "Friedrich Vogel was moved, but more as if he had been struck by lightning. . . . He felt a little over-challenged. This case here was too exceptional. He couldn't think of any examples where something similar had happened and that he could have used to guide him. He simply missed the tradition."[19] In the end, Frau Schmalfuß regrets having been honest instead of relying on vodka.

Imagination

The second aspect of the problem of the denial of women's desire is that this state of affairs works back on women's desire itself. One of Irmtraud Morgner's often reiterated convictions is that oppressed people, including women, lack the courage to desire, much less desire something unusual.[20] People desire what they are encouraged to believe they can get; thus the possibility of attaining the object of one's desire is a precondition for formulating the desire to begin with. In the dearth of such a precondition, the areas available to the imagination and to desire atrophy. The problem is psychological, but it has historical and material roots in women's entrenched lack of power. Lacking power, women have virtually been intimidated out of desire. Over the centuries their self-assertiveness and imagination have been chastened out of existence. In her novel *Die wundersamen Reisen Gustavs des Weltfahrers* (The amazing travels of Gustav the globetrotter, published in 1972, but written in 1967–1968), the heroine declares: "My parents wanted the best for me: shorthand typist. You would take a boy who dreams of being a bookkeeper to the doctors. To have strength to do something more grandiose, you need courage to want something more grandiose. I lacked this kind of courage, like all women."[21] Thus the "mediocrity" that Beauvoir diagnoses in women is born. Morgner's novel *Trobadora Beatriz* is, as we shall see, an attempt to model a way for women to break out of the vicious circle of powerlessness and passivity.

Self-assertiveness

The third part of the problem is also psychological: it has to do with women's sense of self. GDR women writers typically see a connection between men's success and their self-assertiveness. GDR women writers are astonishingly uniform in the sense of self they ascribe to men: men are seen to brim over with self-confidence. Thus Beate Morgenstern's story "Im Spreekahn" (In the Spree boat, in *Jenseits der Allee* [Beyond the avenue, 1979]) describes how a young woman goes out for a drink with a young man, a student, who does nothing but praise himself and make belittling comments about her. The narrator reflects: "He used her as his object to find himself. . . . His strong self-confidence fascinated the young woman. . . . Belief in oneself was not at all a guarantee for success. But maybe an important precondition? A precondition that she did not have because self-doubt had been implanted in her early on."[22] Although such self-confidence is often irritatingly unjustified, the greater problem, according to Morgner, is that women do not have it, because it limits their ambition and hence their potential for significant and original achievement. This is the theme of her story "Gospel of Valeska" ("Die gute Botschaft der Valeska"), which forms the coda of *Trobadora Beatriz* and which will be discussed in the next section. Christa Wolf's Other in "Self-experiment," after her two sex change operations in a uniquely privileged position to compare the sexes, tells us that "man and woman live on different planets" (*WR* 211). In her account a man feels good, like someone who has succeeded in finding a gap in the fence (*WR* 203). He looks on the world as a place of opportunities, as a place for realizing his ambitions. Men are thing- and fact-oriented, not person-oriented, and are indifferent to what others think of them. In fact, they are free of affect generally: indifferent (*WR* 223). A woman, in contrast, feels guilty (*WR* 205). She is filled with a sense of conflict between career and personal life. For her the world is a place of (largely romantic) hopes (*WR* 213). Women are dependent on others' glances and are always watching others for signs; they think men are bad-mouthing them (*WR* 210).

Language

A fourth aspect of the problem bears on women's language. In contrast to the question of women's desire, Western feminists have devoted a great deal of space to discussing women's language. Linguistic studies have elaborately demonstrated that women's speech and speech habits are different from men's. Robin Lakoff's pioneering study *Language and Woman's Place* (1975) posits that there is such a thing as women's language, and that it, along with language about women, both reflects and reinforces women's lack of power in society.[23] One of Lakoff's most interesting observations implicitly relates constraints on women's language to the denial of women's desire. The source of a desire, we tend to believe, is a strong feeling. Lakoff observes that women's speech shows that women are not allowed to feel strongly about things: "women's speech is devised to prevent the expression of strong statements."[24] Thus women are not allowed to show temper, to bellow in rage, or to use strong language like "shit," "damn," or "hell." The ban on the expression of strong emotions as "unladylike" testifies to women's nonsubject status: "If someone is allowed to show emotions, and consequently does, others may well be able to view him as a real individual in his own right, as they could not if he never showed emotion. Here again, then, the behavior a woman learns as "correct" prevents her from being taken seriously as an individual, and furthermore is considered "correct" and necessary for a woman precisely because society does *not* consider her seriously as an individual."[25]

Subsequent feminist linguists concur with Lakoff that women's speech—or worse, their silence—is traceable to their lack of power. The German feminist linguist Senta Trömel-Plötz, largely citing the research of others, notes that men dominate conversations, interrupt women more than women interrupt them, speak much more than women, introduce topics that are talked about, and determine how long conversations last. Women, in contrast, tend to support men's topics; ask more questions; speak more tentatively, less forcefully, and less directly; and, in mixed company, have a great deal of trouble getting their own topics discussed. She concludes: "Language is on the side of the powerful."[26] She as well as most other feminists consider speech a form—indeed a very important form—of action, so that constraints on women's speech both reflect and constitute restraints on their action generally. Trömel-Plötz asserts: "Speaking is acting."[27] Another German feminist linguist, Luise Pusch, concurs: "Language, speaking, speech acts are probably the central domain of what is called "reality" today."[28]

The American legal theorist Catherine A. MacKinnon has similarly argued, in the context of a critique of First Amendment rights and elsewhere, that women's powerlessness has deformed and muffled their speech. She writes in *Feminism Unmodified*: "When you are powerless, you don't just speak differently. A lot, you don't speak. Your speech is not just differently articulated, it is silenced. Eliminated, gone. You aren't just deprived of a language in which to articulate your distinctiveness, although you are; you are deprived of a life out of which articulation might come." She pointedly disagrees with Carol Gilligan's thesis that woman's speech is inherently different from men's: "I do not think that the way women reason morally is morality 'in a different voice.' I think it is morality in a higher register, in the feminine voice. Women value care because men have valued us according to the care we give them, and we could probably use some. Women think in relational terms because our existence is defined in relation to men." Her recommendation: "I say, give women equal power in social life. Let what we say matter, then we will discourse on questions of morality. Take your foot off our necks, then we will hear in what tongue women speak."[29]

Feminist linguists assert that when women speak, they are less likely to be listened to than men. And if women are listened to, they are less likely to be believed. Lakoff believes that there is a connection between the restrictions on strong language for women and the reception of women's speech. She writes: "Allowing men stronger means of expression than are open to women further reinforces men's position of strength in the real world: for surely we listen with more attention the more strongly and forcefully someone expresses opinions, and a speaker unable—for whatever reason—to be forceful in stating his views is much less likely to be believed."[30] Lakoff's view needs qualification: the fact that a *woman* speaks rather than the way she speaks or what she says is decisive. As we have seen, men are credited with having beliefs, convictions, desires, and passions. These beliefs, convictions, desires, and passions are, we tend to believe, directly and immediately legible in their actions and in their speech. The signs that men utter are therefore motivated. But women are believed not to desire, not to have strong feelings, not to have convictions. Consequently they are opaque, mysterious. Freud famously viewed feminine psychology as a "dark continent."[31] A woman's externality stands in no readily apparent relation to her depth. In the case of her speech—what is it exactly? What lies behind it? It is not perceived as directly expressive of anything. A tangle of mysteries lies between woman's speech/behavior and what is behind it. In *Three Essays on the Theory of Sexuality* Freud professed to be able to speak only about men's sexuality, complaining that women's was shrouded in obscurity: "The significance of the factor of sexual overevaluation can be best studied in men, for their erotic life alone has become accessible to research. That of women—partly owing to the stunting effect of civilized conditions and partly owing to their conventional secretiveness and insincerity—is still veiled in an impenetrable obscurity."[32] As Freud's statement testifies, women are more easily believed to utter falsehoods than men. For this reason too, their testimony is less likely to be believed than men's; an outstanding recent example has been the testimony of Anita Hill versus that of Clarence Thomas. The bias of police and juries against the word of the female victim in rape cases has been frequently remarked.[33]

Similar views were articulated by GDR women writers early on: implicitly in stories like Kirsch's, explicitly in an essay by Annemarie Auer of 1976 on *Trobadora Beatriz*. Auer argues that society receives women's words differently even though they are identical to men's. She writes:

> When a man makes a statement, people accept it. A man's word always carries weight. It has to be a mere trifle before it forfeits that response; and even then it still takes a while until he is found out.... It is more awkward when a woman has something serious to say. She has to expect that people will dismiss it. It is ignored. And the technique of disregard, which her word runs up against, is developed to perfection. She has to first become unpleasant, or better prominent, or at least old, before she has the chance of being heard.[34]

The work of the GDR writer Rosemarie Zeplin in particular is rich in instances where a man's words dominate, cut off, and silence a woman's perspective (*Schattenriß eines Liebhabers* [Silhouette of a lover, 1980]).[35] Morgner's views correspond to those of MacKinnon. Particularly *Amanda* (1993), the sequel to *Trobadora Beatriz*, a novel that contains a brilliant collection of parodies of forms of discourse and nondiscourse, makes plain Morgner's assumption that powerlessness deforms speech. For women in patriarchally structured social contexts beginning with the family and ending with the state, this essentially means silence. As a child Laura was trained that "a smile or a curtsy in response to a question is better suited to girls than an answer" (*A* 47). Vilma Tenner boasts of her invention of "body-speak," which consists of swallowing her words (*A* 185–86).

Beatriz, reincarnated as a siren for the purpose of urging the seemingly uncontroversial message of peace on earth, has her tongue cut out. Helga Königsdorf in "Bolero" (in *Meine ungehörigen Träume* [My improper dreams], 1978) highlights to what extent her passive and superficially uncomplaining heroine has lost her initiative and her voice by having her express her long-term dissatisfaction with her lover in an act of unpremeditated violence: she pushes him off her balcony. Even men noticed that women were supposed to speak with feminine vagueness and charm. Günter De Bruyn has the hero of his "Geschlechtertausch" (Sex change, 1975), another sex-change story, decide to reverse his sex-change operation because no one listens or takes him seriously when he, as a woman, speaks.[36]

Christa Wolf's work of the late 1970s and particularly of the early 1980s is of importance in this connection. Wolf's ideas sound, in certain respects, both like those of Carol Gilligan and like those of Catherine MacKinnon. Initially, she expresses the Gilligan-like idea that women have their own voice. More and more this idea came to be overlaid with the conviction that, as MacKinnon says, women's lack of power silences them. Like Gilligan, Wolf, from the beginning a believer in difference and an ardent proponent of the superior ethos of woman, assumes that woman has her own voice and that it is a "different voice": Wolf believes not only that women say things differently, but that they have different things to say. The first time she raises the question of women's voice, in "Self-experiment," she identifies it as the voice of truth—as opposed to the masculine voice of fact. The character Other, having opted to change back into a woman, first dutifully writes the required factual "report" on her sex-change operation, and then the inofficial, unsolicited "notes"—a feminine form of discourse—that constitute the story and that tell the "truth," as opposed to the facts. In the late 1970s Wolf then embarked on a series of historical studies of women, by her own testimony in order to find the sources of women's—and society's—present-day malaise.[37] She first sought the causes in the onset of the bourgeois era after the French Revolution; this led her to study the women Romantics. In her 1979 essay on Karoline von Günderrode, "The Shadow of a Dream" (*AD*; "Der Schatten eines Traumes"), Wolf formulates an idea that anticipates the work of MacKinnon: men determine what reality is. Her thesis in this and other contemporary essays is that the division of labor, utilitarian values, and instrumental reasoning that intensified in the wake of the French Revolution were hostile to women and to their demand for "wholeness."[38] The upshot is that whereas men became (psychologically maimed) subjects, women were squeezed to the peripheries of the new culture and did not become subjects at all. In the Günderrode essay, Wolf continued to espouse the position that women spoke with a better and truer voice than men—in her explanation, precisely because they were not bound to the new society by wage slavery. But one year later, in the essay "Speaking of Büchner" ("Von Büchner sprechen," 1980), Wolf concludes that the new bourgeois society robs women of everything: history, soul, emotions, work, art—and also speech. "Rosetta . . . lets herself be forbidden to speak" (*AD* 181). Bourgeois society turns women into *objects*.

The Frankfurt Poetics Lectures that Wolf wrote in the early 1980s show that she changed her opinion: not about the historical objectification and silencing of women, but about the precise historical moment when it began. Her new view is that the advent of patriarchy itself, which in her orthodox Marxist interpretation is coeval with the advent of private property, is responsible for women's fate. Not the late eighteenth and early nineteenth centuries are the crucial period, but the overthrow of the Minoan by the Mycenean culture three thousand years ago. Central to Wolf's investigation is the idea that women have *lost their voice*. "Studying early civilization, I was shocked to discover that in our culture women have had no voice for three thousand years" (*FD* 109). In *Cassandra* Wolf goes back to an era when she believes, with J. J. Bachofen and August Bebel, that women were empowered—the era of primitive matriarchy, with its presumptive peaceful and communistic conditions, in order to reconstruct what she feels must have been woman's true voice at the moment when patriarchy prevailed over matriarchy and began definitively to silence woman's voice. Cassandra is a representative of the "last" woman's voice. Already, her prophecies were not believed: "Now I have taken up the first voice to be handed down to us, and have tried to scrape the overlay of male mythology from it: the myth that she was a seer who was not believed because the god Apollo had divested her of all credibility. . . . That was my work of demythologization: to analyze the syndrome of alienation which patriarchy has inflicted upon every female voice in this culture" (*FD* 109). In the novella itself Wolf greatly problematizes the simple, seemingly unexamined connection between women, true seeing, and true speaking that she proposed in "Self-experiment." She investigates how both seeing and speaking depend on power rather than attributing them to sex. Thus in the crucial period of military escalation and war in

Troy, her Cassandra figure operates in the space between the *seeing* that is the privilege of the powerless and the *nonspeaking* of the protegée who has something to lose.

Irmtraud Morgner's *Trobadora Beatriz*

Irmtraud Morgner's *Trobadora Beatriz* is an explicit attempt to overcome—in the guise of literary work—the barriers that custom has imposed on women's actions and their speech, and at the same time it is a summation of the themes of women's desire, women's imagination, women's action, and woman's speech. Morgner was not only a novelist with a runaway imagination, but an original thinker with a developed set of feminist ideas, and a political thinker who wanted her ideas to leave a mark upon the world. She recognizes the fetters that Beauvoir asserted bind women, but instead of resigning herself, she energetically and inventively sets about finding ways to burst them. For Morgner, art—writing, speech—is valuable inasmuch as it becomes action. In an interview she gave while working on *Trobadora Beatriz* she replied in answer to the question of what she would like to write in the future:

> Well, what I would like to write: the gospel of a prophetess. . . . I don't mean that in a religious sense. I mean that women, if they want to take on the task of becoming human, could use a genius, less art, a genius! . . . I would like to write the gospel of an inspired woman who leads women into history. Literature is good and useful, but more important for this purpose would be deeds. Action, that would be more important. . . . I am not talking about art. I would like to describe it: not as art. Naturally with the greatest possible impact of words that I have. My motivation would not be to make art, my motivation would be to make world.[39]

In *Trobadora Beatriz* her "gospel" comes sugar-coated as the story of a fantastical woman's picaresque adventures, starting in France in 1968 and ending in the GDR in 1973. In what her fictional avatar Laura calls an "operative montage novel" (p. 170), Morgner, who was educated as a Germanist, adeptly plays hocus-pocus with literary history and generic conventions.[40] *Trobadora Beatriz*, which parades, in mock eighteenth-century style, as a fictitious document, is a portmanteau novel: the main plot alternates with parts of Morgner's unpublished novel *Rumba auf einen Herbst*, and is also interrupted in Jean-Paul style by numerous independent stories. For her heroine Morgner picks the twelfth-century Provençal poet Beatriz de Dia, and brings her to life in the present day. This heroine, whom Morgner presents to her readers as a model, is also stylized as a feminine Faust.

Primarily Western critics of the novel have commented astutely on Morgner's techniques of montage and polyphony, on her use of fantasy, parody, quotation and self-quotation, and her juxtaposition of different genres and forms of discourse.[41] These techniques have lent themselves to interpretation in terms of Bakhtin's theories of the novel[42] and have even been labeled "postmodern."[43] The earlier GDR critics, in contrast, accustomed to socialist realist fare, found Morgner's style hard to digest; they tended to ignore its complexity and overlook its irony, opting for univocal readings that domesticized the work to GDR ideology on women.[44] It has rightly been pointed out that Morgner's techniques of montage tend to destabilize meaning. Yet they do not counteract and undermine closure as completely as some Western critics, who in their turn are troubled by the seeming collapse of an initial, promising, radical feminism into an affirmation of pro-GDR ideology, would wish to have it.[45] The book's feminism certainly does not reduce into its pro-Marxist, pro-GDR line without a remainder, as Ingeborg Nordmann has pointed out.[46] Yet there are undeniably what Monika Meier calls "monologic tendencies" in the novel.[47] Morgner gave a good many interviews, and in these interviews she states her opinions directly, unambiguously, and repeatedly, often with very little variation from interview to interview. Morgner's collected interviews leave little room for argument about her opinions on politics, women's issues, and literature. The "monologic strands" that one can read out of her novels—because they are spoken by positive figures at crucial junctures, repeated, or based in fictional "fact,"[48]—are, for the most part, heavily underwritten by her interview statements. Thus, in interviews Morgner gave around the publication date of *Trobadora Beatriz*, she affirms socialism as the precondition for women's emancipation;[49] at the same time she deplores, and wishes to change, the persistence of patriarchal "custom" under socialism;[50] she believes that women need to acquire self-confidence,[51] courage,[52] even "megalomania";[53] the task of the writer is to help them acquire this confidence by giving them a history,[54] legendary if necessary.

In the GDR currently, according to Morgner in interviews of the '70s, women are more empowered than they ever have been before.[55]

In the real world, all that remains to be transcended is the tenacity of custom ("Sitte"). "Customs are worse than people," says Laura in *Trobadora Beatriz*, "and longer-lived" (*TB* 142). It should be stressed that this insight, which Morgner reiterates in numerous interviews, is not at all original to her, but is a common and accepted argument in the GDR in the early 1970s. Precisely the same argument is made apropos of sex roles and psychological gender characteristics by GDR psychologists writing in the early 1970s, such as Adolf Kossakowski and Karlheinz Otto, eds., *Psychologische Untersuchungen zur Entwicklung sozialistischer Persönlichkeiten* (Psychological investigations into the development of socialist personalities, 1971) and Heinz Dannhauer, *Geschlecht und Persönlichkeit* (Gender and personality, 1973). Both blame "customs" and "thousand-year old traditions" for the persistence of inequality between the sexes despite the "socialist image (Leitbild) of man and woman," which mandates their complete equality, not just in employment but also in matters of housework and child care.[56] Morgner's recipe is that of an activist: Women can accelerate the demise of these repressive customs if they jump over their own shadows, emancipate their imagination, and change their own outlook on life. According to Morgner, women have to start to trust themselves.

Morgner stated in an interview in 1984 that her earliest and strongest identification was with Faust.[57] The earliest of her mature novels, *Hochzeit in Konstantinopel* (1968), already features a female daredevil as its heroine. In *Trobadora Beatriz* Faustian female genius, or what Morgner calls "megalomania" ("Größenwahn") blossoms into a major theme. The message is that women must learn to desire, to dare—to throw off submissiveness, deference, and passivity and to be, as she says, megalomaniacs—after the model of men. Like Goethe, Morgner chose a historical figure around whom to construct a legend. The heroine of *Trobadora Beatriz*, Beatriz de Dia, is conceived as a female Faust. "Beatriz is a transgressor of boundaries, a heretic on the order of magnitude of a Faust," Morgner said in an interview in 1984. She adds later in the same interview: "Faust was my youthful identification figure. The fascination for the heretic Beatriz de Dia is grounded in the fascination that the Faust figure radiated then and still radiates now."[58]

Faust is not a psychological character but—particularly in Goethe's realization—is supposed to represent a, even the, quintessential human (male) type, the type of the overreacher who is not content to lead his life within the lines that God's universe has laid down for him, harmoniously with the rest of creation, but strives for the knowledge and power of the godhead. Numerous allusions in *Trobadora Beatriz* to the Faust legend, especially to Goethe's *Faust*, remind us that Beatriz is a woman with the soul of Faust. She has Faust's genius, enterprise, daring, and resilience. In a famous scene Goethe's Faust ponders the best translation for "logos," which according to St. John was at the beginning of all things, and, after rejecting the possible translations "word," "sense," and "power," arrives at the formulation: "In the beginning was the deed." Morgner's epigraph for the novel is a quotation ascribed to Beatriz de Dia: "In the beginning was the other deed."

Many of the fantastical elements in Morgner's novel can be read as direct or indirect allusions to *Faust*. Like Faust, Beatriz uses magic. If Faust relies on the supernatural powers of Mephistopheles, Beatriz relies on those of the sphinx Melusine—a creature who, like Mephistopheles, can change herself into many different shapes. Like Goethe's *Faust*, the novel is peopled by legendary and fantastical creatures. Morgner launches the plot by having Beatriz, a twelfth-century noblewoman and poet, make a Faust-like deal with oppositional supernatural forces, albeit with the friendly, if comical, feminist goddesses Demeter and Persephone, who oppose the patriarchal rule of "the Lord God" (*TB* 20) and are willing to expend some of their magic on Beatriz in exchange for work hours. At this point, a parodistic "Sleeping Beauty" story is interposed: Beatriz arranges to have herself put to sleep until time (as she hopes) will have changed conditions for women.[59] She awakens in her castle in Provence in May 1968, 808 years later but still inwardly and outwardly "in the zenith of life" (*TB* 15), just as the student and worker revolt is taking place in Paris.

Although Faust has several misadventures as well as many adventures, it would be impossible to think of him as a victim. That characterization is reserved in Goethe's play for Gretchen—who, incidentally, is criticized in *Trobadora Beatriz* as a product of culture rather than nature: "For Gretchen is by no means a little wild 'flower' in the sense of being a part of nature, but a cultivated plant" (*TB* 275). The same goes for Beatriz as for Faust. In marked contrast to the stereotypical image of woman propagated by Western feminism, Beatriz, despite her many misadventures, is not a victim. Initially her adventures resemble those of a runaway hippie. She wanders through the French countryside, takes drugs, spends time in jail, sells ice cream, writes poetry, sells lavender, rescues a child from drowning, works as a servant, takes up with various men, works as a prostitute, marries a customer, takes a communist lover, and reads Marx. But as a woman of the '60s, she demonstrates her Faustian character. She starts to earn her living through her creative talent, as a street singer. She takes many lovers. She becomes a terrorist. In book 8, she travels around the world like Faust.

In *The Second Sex* Simone de Beauvoir expounds in great detail woman's essential conflict, which results from her trying to be a subject and an object at the same time. The two identities of woman are at odds with each other. Every successful sally that a woman makes into the male world diminishes her value as a woman, while the more she cultivates her femininity, the more firmly she closes herself out of the male world. Morgner's novel thematizes the dividedness of women by juxtaposing the exotic, brilliant, impractical heroine Beatriz to the down-to-earth, more typically feminine Laura Salmann. Laura, a single working mother in Berlin, is unable to continue work as an S-Bahn (suburban train) driver on account of her infant son's frequent illnesses, and therefore caves in to Beatriz's offer to work as her "minstrel." The two are not explicitly one person, as Laura and Amanda are in *Amanda*, where Morgner expands the device of splitting and endows it with greater nuance. Yet numerous hints invite the reader to conclude that Beatriz is Laura Salmann's fantasized alter ego. The novel begins with an outrageously phony (and funny) authentic-document fiction: supposedly, the story of the 843-year-old Beatriz[60] is a manuscript that Laura sells to Irmtraud Morgner, who then functions merely as editor. This opening already suggests, according to the eighteenth-century convention, that Morgner, Laura, and Beatriz are one person. Explaining why she is working for Beatriz, Laura says to the Aufbau-Verlag: "I revere Beatriz. I'm lining my own pockets, so to speak. Do you want to warn me of myself?" (*TB* 169). It is strongly hinted that Laura is the author of a montage novel that is identical to *Trobadora Beatriz*.[61] The physical appearance of the three women indicates the nature of their identity. Morgner's encounter with Laura in the opening pages of the novel is a meeting with her mirror image: both women are dragging a small child, and the dark-haired Laura bears some resemblance to the actual Morgner. Beatriz, in keeping with her role as the suppressed side of Laura's personality, is her physical opposite, tall and thin while Laura is short and fat.

Morgner gives the issue of female dividedness a new twist. Whereas Beauvoir saw it essentially as a misfortune—nowhere in her book does she suggest that it might have advantageous aspects—Morgner, in *Trobadora Beatriz* and also in *Amanda*, gives it a literary spin that takes away its tragic edge. To be divided is the fate not merely of woman, but of Faust: "Two souls, alas! reside within my breast,"[62] complains Faust—and goes on to identify one as the spirit that ties him to the earth, the other as the one that attracts him to the godhead. Faust's dividedness is responsible for making his story a tragedy, but it also makes Faust the restless, never-contented genius that he is; it is the specific cause of his characteristic striving. Thus dividedness has positive, dynamic, Faustian implications, not just crippling ones. In Morgner's novel, the Beatriz-Laura duo, which unites imagination and practicality, presents a formidable female match for the social constraints that inhibit feminine self-realization.

Whether Morgner wanted to make her readers reflect or whether she shied away from straightforward manifesto-like feminist statements on account of fear of censorship (the work "stinks of internal censorship," she writes in *Amanda*[63]), certain aspects of the work present themselves as puzzles that lend themselves to more than one interpretation. One such puzzle is the opposition between the two friends Beatriz and Laura Salmann. Beatriz and Laura agree on ends, but disagree on means. They are both in stature and in character like Don Quixote and Sancho Panza: Beatriz quixotic, Laura practical. If Beatriz is a radical, Laura urges *Realpolitik*. In the terms of *Faust II*, Beatriz is a vulcanist who favors quick, revolutionary solutions, while Laura is a neptunist who believes that change must take place gradually. Thus Beatriz finds it necessary for women to seize power in order to make the world a better place for them (and everybody else). As a start, she contemplates hijacking an airplane in order to force the government to get rid of the anti-abortion law. Laura is equally firm in insisting that change requires patience. Laura diagnoses Beatriz for "emancipatory fanaticism" (*TB* 171). In order to channel this fanaticism in a benevolent direction, she sends Beatriz on a harmless adventure: chasing a unicorn. The unicorn's brain, she tells Beatriz, would yield a medication that, ingested, would change the mentality of millions in a positive, peaceful, communistic direction and free the world from capitalism, wars, hunger, and patriarchy.

Which position does Morgner underwrite, Beatriz's or Laura's? Early critics read the novel, whether regretfully or in relief, as a sustained flirtation with Beatriz's radicalism that ultimately validates Laura's pragmatism.[64] This reading gives too much weight to the novel's ending, the segment from the eleventh book onward, where Morgner begins to wind in her main plot, and not enough emphasis to its—admittedly divergent—beginning. Particularly the final chapter, which suggests that Beatriz's story was "just a story" told by Laura's new husband, the "perfect man" Benno, to Laura, gives the impression of having been written out of a compulsion to produce a "happy ending," to pull in the reins that had been so liberally extended before, to safely domesticate Beatriz.[65] But the fascinating, transgressive Beatriz character was drawn. She, not Laura, was set up to capture the reader's imagination from the outset; neither her portrait nor the reader's early identification can be negated, at least not by an ending pulled out of the box of standard writers' devices. Melusine, the revolutionary socialist sphinx, the most positive and benevolent supernatural character, a female Robin Hood of the skies who is working for a "third" social order that is neither matriarchal nor patriarchal but "human," suggests, in a scene where she appears to speak for the author (*TB* 182), that Beatriz is a theoretical model, similar to Marx's model of a communist society, whose function is to show what is possible. Beatriz models a variety of women's desires and fantasies. She is meant as a imaginative stimulus. We can assume that Morgner was not really in favor of hijacking airplanes. Yet Beatriz is the heroine of her novel. While the figure is undercut by the irony of being a fictional creation of Laura's, she is not psychologized away, or reduced to a storybook figure. Morgner wants to show that Beatriz's radical type is necessary.

Thus at the beginning of the eighth book Beatriz informs Laura that "women [need] neither Persephonic opposition, nor art, in order to emancipate themselves, but rather a genius" (*TB* 163). Later Beatriz furiously refuses to sign a book contract for a montage novel with the publishing house Aufbau-Verlag that Laura has procured for her precisely on the grounds on which Laura hoped to persuade her to sign it: that the proposed novel will be easy. Beatriz responds to Laura's proposition with a tirade:

> She declared Laura's plans for getting the book written disgraceful. You couldn't write either a good book or a bad book that way, but rather no book at all. As long as Laura was incapable of convincing herself that she would be creating the greatest minstrel poetry in the world, she should not even consider that kind of project. Raimbaut d'Aurenga used to write even the most inane occasional verse with the conviction of a revelation; nothing would produce nothing. The worst mistake a woman can make is to lack megalo-

mania. To be able to do something more grandiose, you first need the courage to want something more grandiose. Laura lacked this like most women. (*TB* 179)

Morgner herself used almost identical words in a 1972 interview: "I think that men do not normally lack in megalomania. But women lack it almost completely."[66] Laura—whose realism is reinforced by the presence of her infant son Wesselin—responds to Beatriz's letter by forging Beatriz's signature on the contract. This act gets her an advance from the press. Inundated by the cares of everyday life, she reacts angrily to Beatriz's principled letter. She throws a book at the wall and cries: "Impatience and megalomania will be your downfall!" (*TB* 180). But for this she is punished by a supernatural power: the sphinx Melusine. Crashing into Laura's apartment through her heating stove, Melusine chastises Laura: "You committed a serious wrongdoing. Recant! Stop this sinful interference! For impatience is the unique talent of Beatriz de Dia, megalomania her exceptional virtue" (*TB* 181).

Programmatic statements made by members of the novel's huge cast of characters must always be read with a degree of suspicion, depending on their provenance and on their corroboration or disconfirmation by the events in the plot. The theme of megalomania receives an extensive airing toward the beginning of the eighth book in an interview that Melusine conducts with the Soviet chess master Dr. Solowjow. Solowjow pronounces negatively on women's ability to become single-minded—only to be immediately contradicted by the plot. The issue is why there has never been a world-class woman chess champion. Solowjow purports to know the reason: "Because a woman cannot become a complete fanatic" (*TB* 164). There are no female Bobby Fishers, in his opinion, because *children* prevent them from becoming chess fanatics—or fanatics of any kind: "The presence of children puts intellectual projects in relation to reality, relativizes them, sometimes also ironicizes them dramatically"(ibid.). Hence, he opines, women are realistic, not fanatics. Additionally, chess in his view is a warlike game—Bobby Fisher aimed to destroy his opponents' ego—and this aggressiveness is perhaps something that does not appeal to women. Even though Solowjow himself appears as a self-satisfied egotist, complacently observing that if his wife didn't absorb the practical problems of life for him he never would have risen to the top as a chess champion, we are tempted to take his analysis as Morgner's. With an important restriction:

Morgner implicitly regards women's inability to become fanatic as a contingent disability, not an essential one. For in the very next section of the eighth book it becomes clear that Beatriz is contemplating yet another phase as a terrorist.

Later, in book 11, when the GDR finally legalizes abortion—the triumphant high point of the novel—Laura cites another reason for women's historical lack of originality: the fear with which they must live, in particular, fear of pregnancy. Laura says (sounding like Simone de Beauvoir): "In general, personalities that live in fear grow, if at all, in a completely different way than others. They think differently, feel differently, produce differently with hands and heads. Plainly, physical bondage cripples a person hardly any less than political bondage. And no original achievements are to be expected from cripples" (*TB* 336).

It comes as a disappointment to many readers that Beatriz dies in the penultimate book of the novel. Finding a justification for her accidental death, and also for the peculiar personality change that precedes it, is another of the novel's puzzles—perhaps even retrospectively for Morgner, who resurrected Beatriz in her next novel, *Amanda*. The very suddenness and improbability of her death suggests that it is a cipher, and critics have not hesitated to interpret it as a "political death," much like Christa's T.'s death in Wolf's *Quest for Christa T.* As in the case of *The Quest for Christa T.*, they have imposed diametrically opposed readings on it. Thus it has been argued that Morgner's intent is to show that Beatriz's megalomania and eccentricity are unviable and to validate Laura's pragmatism[67]; or to show precisely the opposite, that Beatriz is punished for her loss of genius, for her "overadjustment" to GDR society.[68] Alternatively, it has been maintained that Beatriz's characteristics of megalomania have become unnecessary because of the improved political climate,[69] as well as the opposite, that the GDR has successfully stifled these characteristics.[70] Of these readings, the last interprets the novel very much against its own grain. The first, the one that asserts that Beatriz is punished for her megalomania, is also implausible, given that in the stretch of plot before her death, Beatriz undergoes a drastic personality remake into a docile GDR citizen, writer, and housewife. This radical alteration reveals the scaffolding beneath the already less-than-lifelike, allegorical figure of Beatriz; it substantially weakens Beatriz's already tenuous claim on our credibility to being an independent character and urges the interpretation that she is Laura's fantasy. Thus when Beatriz "shrinks"—also physically, into a Laura-like figure (*TB* 397)—we can interpret that it is the Beatriz-in-Laura that is scaled down to size; indeed Laura, who is on her way to completing her montage novel and takes an imaginative "trip" to Paris, seems to have assimilated aspects of the itinerant trobadora Beatriz. The third reading, that Beatriz is no longer "necessary" for Laura as a separate character and radically different alter ego, best accommodates the interpretation that Beatriz is Laura's invention.

Beatriz's death can probably be read as a further allusion to Goethe's *Faust*. Faust's death is ambiguous. Mephisto's cohorts swoop down because they believe that Faust has uttered the fatal words, testifying that he has been seduced by a beautiful moment and is tired of striving. Yet they misunderstand; Faust is in the midst of reclaiming land from the sea, where he envisions, in the future, a "free people" living on "free land"; and Faust's soul is carried off by angelic hosts to heaven because, "For him whose striving never ceases we can provide redemption."[71] Faust's final visionary speech does, however, imply that there might be *utopian limits* to his striving—that is, if Faust ever came to see his ideal community, he might indeed rest. Beatriz's death is likewise preceded by an apparent curious diminution in her striving. She gives up travel, becomes modest, and becomes a homebody. Beatriz evaporates, so to speak, into Laura. On the day of the Vietnam cease-fire Laura notices that Beatriz even resembles her outwardly: "Why are you domesticating yourself so?" she asked, shocked. "Do you want to become my double? Do you want to make yourself superfluous?" (*TB* 397) Beatriz takes a turn for the housewifely and indeed plunges to her death while washing windows. From a narrow, Mephistophelian point of view, then, her death can be seen as a punishment for her loss of megalomania. While polishing windows Beatriz waves at Melusine, a figure from her old days of genius and in fact the character who pronounced her a genius, who declared that "Megalomania . . . is her exceptional virtue" (*TB* 264). She cannot balance her genius character with her new domestic role, and thus "must . . . have lost her balance" (*TB* 404). This phrase, "to lose one's balance" ("die Balance verlieren"), still rings in the reader's ear as the cause of the physicist-single mother Vera Hill's plunge from her metaphorical tightrope (*TB* 394). Yet Beatriz's turn toward the normal, which ends with her death, parallels important political victories for women and for the Left both at home and abroad. Just before Beatriz returns from her travels, the GDR legalizes abortion. The South Vietnamese partisans win significant victories during April 1972. Whereas Faust settles down after his travels in order to occupy himself with a concrete social project, Beatriz increasingly becomes a committed socialist, interested in following, as a writer, the "Bitterfeld Way" (Bitterfelder Weg) of writing about the lives of workers. Finally, to the great rejoicing of Laura, Benno, and Beatriz, the Left wins in the French elections (in 1973). It is immediately in the wake of this victory—in fact, under the influence of a postcelebration hangover—that Beatriz plunges to her death. Perhaps with an upswing in the political fortunes of the Left and of women, hence with concrete utopia dawning, Morgner thought that Beatriz, as the personification of feminine megalomania, could afford to relax and therefore be killed off.

The fact that the heroine is a female *troubadour* is significant. The role of a singer of love, who selects a lady as an object of desire and announces or advertises his desire through his song, was reserved for men: "A female singer of medieval courtly love poems is paradoxical" (*TB* 28). And more explicitly: "A passive troubadour, an object that sings the praises of a subject is logically unthinkable. Paradoxical" (*TB* 112). In Beatriz Morgner creates the model of an erotically aggressive woman, who breaks the taboo of erotic passivity for women in speech as well as action. Not only does Beatriz have many love affairs, but in the course of such affairs, she writes sexually explicit love poems. One of Beatriz's first acts upon crossing the border to the GDR is to praise the border policeman's physical beauty: "[She] praised the sparkle of his white, evenly-formed teeth, which advantageously accentuated his bronze complexion" (*TB* 91). This compliment falls flat: "The smile disappeared, throat clearing. Embarrassed coughing. Passport returned through the slot with best wishes for a good recovery" (*TB* 91). In short, the policeman quickly decides to naturalize the incident by classifying Beatriz as crazy. Morgner's prognosis for this aspect of "customs" in the GDR, as spoken by Laura, is hopeful. According to Laura, if Beatriz should give up her career as a troubadour in the "promised land," it is not because women couldn't get the erotic initiative there—which is not inevitably man's, but in a land of emancipation simply the last male prerogative to go—but because a woman troubadour as yet has no objects worthy of her song (*TB* 163).

Morgner conjecturally gives Beatriz's proclivity for taking the erotic initiative the stamp of male approval. In Beatriz's strongly idealized version of Raimbaut d'Aurenga, the medieval troubadour whose praises she sang, Raimbaut recognizes that women's expression of their erotic desire has simply been squashed out of existence:

> Our lives will not be boring when women finally do what they want to do, and not what they should do. . . . What will happen when they express what they feel, and not what we expect them to feel? Recently the wife of a poet said that there were no love poems written by women. This wife was right, only few women would be willing to sacrifice their reputations to the odor of abnormality. Women without suppressed love lives are viewed as sick (nymphomaniacs). Men of this kind are considered healthy (sound as a bell). (*TB* 39)

This whole speech is then later quoted with minor variations by the "ideal man," Benno (*TB* 274).

The theme of megalomania, which becomes explicit in the eighth book and glimmers up elsewhere, returns as the principal theme of the Valeska story at the end of the novel. The "Gospel of Valeska" is one of the famous GDR sex-change stories that were commissioned for Edith Anderson's anthology *Blitz aus heiterem Himmel* (Lightning out of a blue sky, 1975). The publisher Hinstorff found the sexual explicitness of Morgner's story offensive and rejected it.[72] Instead, it appeared at the end of *Trobadora Beatriz*, as a "gospel" that Laura reads as a "revelation" on Beatriz's burial day. It functions as the novel's coda, summarizing many of its themes. Beatriz's words are echoed apropos of Valeska: "Women need a genius." Valeska, a certified biologist, previously appeared in book 9 of the novel. She can be taken as an avatar of Beatriz, since Beatriz "sends" Valeska's papers to Laura "from Hades" (where Valeska was delivered clinically but not actually dead), having translated them "from the Hadian." These papers reveal an a original and energetic feminist personality who gets divorced from her first husband, Uwe, as soon as she gets pregnant, because her husband's function has been fulfilled in inseminating her, and who fantasizes about a commune consisting of women with their children.

Valeska's gospel, which is couched in mock-religious terms and composed in short, Bible-like verses as the message of a prophet who experienced revelation, walked on water ("Life" 127), acquired disciples, and rose from the dead ("Life" 125), and whose goal is the salvation of humanity, tells the story of Valeska's sex change into a man. The story "Gospel of Valeska" finds Valeska unwillingly contemplating moving into the same apartment with her second husband, the scientist Rudolf, a living arrangement which, Valeska suspects, will destine her to a life of housework and destroy her relationship. Rudolf cherishes the conviction that he is the greatest scientist in his field. Valeska herself has no such inflated sense of self. Then, however, she has a vision of herself, which reveals to her: she *is* a special scientist after all. Her mission will be to invent synthetic food, which will make human beings' predatory characteristics superfluous and thus promote the more general goal of peace. When, thereafter, she muses: "One would have to be a man . . ." for the third time, this wish is granted: she becomes outwardly a man. Unlike Wolf's character Other, Valeska sees the advantages in being male and decides to remain a man, at least in the daytime. For a man, life and work are much easier; moreover, Valeska can live in the same apartment with Rudolf without having to fear that he will expect her (i.e., him) to do all the housework. At night she changes back into a woman for Rudolf's sake. Also unlike Other, she undergoes only physical, not psychological changes. Her brain remains her own. Morgner believed that the differences between the sexes were cultural, not natural: "The physical differences between men and women were insignificant in comparison to the cultural ones" ("Life" 132).

Valeska's sex change, physical in the story, can be taken as a metaphor for a mental sex-change operation. Valeska's message is straightforward: women should start to believe in themselves; and they should, like her, learn to think in the self-confident male mode. In addition, Valeska's transformation becomes a metaphor for women learning an outward behavior—a behavior mimicking that of men—that will help to break down the barriers that custom traditionally places in the path of women simply because they are women. Valeska's sex change figures as a quick, miraculous solution to a problem that in fact takes "generations" ("Life" 127) to solve. It is essential, but at the same time not enough, to acquire a new mindset, to believe in oneself. One must also act in a way that will demolish the old prejudices that hinder the realization of the most convinced self-belief. The Valeska story thus posits seriously that women have to take on the characteristics of men to get anywhere. For example, women should simply throw off the unilateral obligation of housework: "Why don't you simply set your daughter on your companion's desk for once—here, what you don't know you'll have to learn—and head for the airport yourself" ("Life" 142), Valeska counsels a young mother. For in this "treadmill" (ibid.) women have no hope of realizing their potential. As Laura said earlier to justify her giving up her profession as a Germanist, "the imposition of back-and-forth trips, repeated daily, between the stooped, down-to-earth activity of housekeeping and those heights where thoughts, after all, dwell" appeared to her "too exhausting" (*TB* 174). Valeska's story emphatically restates Beatriz's message that "women need a genius"; but the actual method she proposes inverts the one Beatriz herself follows and thus infuses the project with new hope. Beatriz, inwardly a genius, takes on the outward characteristics of a traditional woman and—plunges to her death. Valeska's point is precisely that a woman of genius needs to take on the outward comportment of a man.

In *Amanda*, Morgner's sequel to *Trobadora Beatriz*, the idea that women must assume the characteristics of men will be seriously modified. In the later novel Morgner concludes that if women co-opt men's means, that is, grab power and use violence, the end result will be no better than it was under male domination (*A* 80). Gone are the days when Morgner saw fit to ascribe terrorist acts to her heroine.

Morgner always makes explicit that she is not for matriarchy, but for equality. Yet her constant tactic is to overshoot her goal, to show what might be possible (though not necessarily desirable) for women, to rattle and dislodge the encrusted patriarchal presuppositions that to this day inhibit the functioning of women's brains. One of Morgner's favorite devices is to lampoon patriarchy, where women are held in subservience, by flipping the man-woman relationship in an area where the patriarchal prerogative is part of our mental software. Thus in the parodistic utopia of the Amazons in *Die wundersamen Reisen Gustavs des Weltfahrers*, which is intended, as a note indicates, to give an exaggerated counterexample to extreme patriarchy, the women are in power. Men are on a reservation, clothed, and ashamed of their genitals; they do the washing, sewing, and child care. The race is perpetuated by sperm banks, to which 11 percent of the men are selected to donate. Women rule and occupy themselves with intellectual pursuits, in particular, writing postdoctoral theses (*Habilitationsschriften*) for export. *Trobadora Beatriz* contains a similar scene, recounted by Laura, in which Laura, in the company of her women's brigade, aggressively tries to pick up a man in a bar. She whistles and stares at her prey, buys him a drink, sits at his table and presses her knee to his, and finally leaves the bar with him, sliding her hand over his buttocks. Beatriz herself, as a personality who never adopted the typical feminine passive erotic role, pays for a man's drinks, to his "consternation" (*TB* 99). She exhibits surprise that a woman's magazine doesn't feature photos of naked men, since men's magazines feature photos of naked women (*TB* 113). Beatriz also writes a congratulatory address for the poet Guntram

Pomerenke on his admission to PEN on the model of the congratulatory address given for her, praising exclusively his physical attributes. Benno, the man Melusine conjures forth for Laura initially as an apparition in a float moving through the air, is Laura's "Helena"—with the same initial supernatural, merely physical appearance. Like a piece of merchandise or a pet in a pet show, he has a tag attached to him giving information about him. This is "the man on the pedestal": woman's ideal man, who will prove to be completely egalitarian, share child care, and tell Laura Scheherazade-style tales at night. In *Amanda* Morgner has him die after wasting away with jealousy over Laura's professional success; he expresses superficial joy initially, only to drown his frustration later in drinking bouts.

It would be a mistake to think that Morgner uses this device of reversal in order to suggest that what women want, or should want, is to secure male prerogatives for themselves and/or objectify men the way they themselves have been objectified. The reversal scenes are parodistic, not programmatic. Morgner avoids defining feminine desire mimetically. In *Trobadora Beatriz*, in fact, there is little attempt to define the proper or actual objects of feminine desire at all, although it is taken for granted that the main female figures share utopian political goals: all hope that the world will turn into a perfect communist society with no more hunger or war. Morgner's focus is enablement—liberating women psychologically and actually so that they dare to imagine, formulate, and pursue goals—and not the definition or prescription of specific goals. In the sequel, *Amanda*, as we shall see in the next chapter, the picture changes: Morgner suggests that women's and men's desires have been different from time immemorial. Men have desired, and still desire, to "lay the world at their feet," while women have wanted and still want to be undivided, indivisible, and "have an island at their feet." Thus in the later novel, Morgner does ascribe a goal, an object of desire, to women.

3 Praise of the Feminine

One might be able to interpret the fact of being deprived of a womb as the most intolerable deprivation of man, since his contribution to gestation—his function with regard to the origin of reproduction—is hence asserted as less than evident, as open to doubt. An indecision to be attenuated both by man's "active" role in intercourse and by the fact that he will mark the product of copulation with *his own name*. Thereby woman, whose intervention in the work of engendering the child can hardly be questioned, becomes the anonymous worker, the machine in the service of a master-proprietor who will put his trademark upon the finished product. It does not seem exaggerated, incidentally, to understand quite a few products, and notably cultural products, as a counterpart or a search for equivalents to woman's function in maternity.

—Luce Irigaray,
Speculum of the Other Woman, trans. Gillian C. Gill

The mother-child relationship can be seen as the first relationship violated by patriarchy. Mother and child, as objects of possession by the fathers, are reduced both to pieces of property and to relationships in which men can feel in control, powerful, wherever else they may feel impotent. Legally, economically, and through unwritten sanctions . . . the mother and her child live under male control although males assume a minimal direct responsibility for children.

—Adrienne Rich,
"Husband-Right and Father-Right"

> You should develop, modify and direct . . . the traditions and the education of the private house which have been in existence these 2,000 years. . . . And let the daughters of uneducated women dance round the new house, the poor house, the house that stands in a narrow street where omnibuses pass and the street hawkers cry their wares, and let them sing, "We have done with war! We have done with tyranny!" And their mothers will laugh from their graves, "It was for this that we suffered obloquy and contempt! Light up the windows of the new house, daughters! Let them blaze!"
> —Virginia Woolf, *Three Guineas*

One of the most striking characteristics of the writings of both Christa Wolf and Irmtraud Morgner is the earliness, definiteness, consistency, and confidence with which they praise femininity. If their respective oeuvres leave one overwhelming impression, it is that of an affirmation of the feminine—one culminating in the prose fiction that each writer published in 1983, Wolf's *Cassandra* and Morgner's *Amanda*. These works tell us not that women are merely as good as, as capable as men; they leave us with the impression that women are better than men, and that femininity is better than masculinity. The key to both writers' positive imaging of the feminine is their equation of feminine characteristics with a utopian social form: an ideally conceived communism. Implicit at first, this equation becomes more and more definite and finally explicit in the works they published in the same year, 1983. Wolf's slim novella *Cassandra* and Morgner's immense novel *Amanda*, written in the shadow of a nuclear threat to Europe and out of each writer's urgent desire to promote peace, bear, no doubt coincidentally, the same message: male culture has led the world to the brink of disaster; women have, since prehistoric times, cherished different ideals and cultivated different qualities; if the world is to have a future, feminine virtues must prevail.

Feminism may have been taboo in state socialist countries, but it is difficult to imagine that any such decided claim for the superiority of femininity could have been made without the underpinning of classic Marxist theory from which state socialism derived its ideological justification. One of the purposes of this chapter will be to trace the genesis of the association of femininity with communism, which both writers make initially almost instinctively, later highly consciously.

While both writers appear indebted to classic Marxist theory for their positive imaging of the feminine, their affinity for this idealizing construction of women is fueled by their strong antipathy toward what they see as the values of a dominant masculine culture. In the work of both, a detailed negative image of masculinity emerges first, vis-à-vis an implicitly positive but undetailed image of femininity. In their works focusing on female figures, the female figure is the "I," the developing and learning subjectivity, the normative viewpoint and point of identification for the reader; her male vis-à-vis is a more predictable, preformed if not static type. The negative male is the same for both writers: he is rational, competitive, hierarchical, and frequently a scientist.

This chapter will begin by introducing the communist theory of the family and the nineteenth-century sources for that theory, which served as a background for Wolf's and Morgner's ideas. Puzzlingly, this genealogy has hitherto been entirely overlooked not only in discussions of GDR feminism, which usually attempt to disengage it from the socialist legacy, but also in criticism that focuses on the construction of woman as mother in GDR women writers.[1] Thus in her recent book *Post-Fascist Fantasies*, Julia Hell inscribes even the work of Christa Wolf in a *paternally* oriented discourse centering on the image of the antifascist hero-father, which she regards as the dominant discourse in the GDR literary tradition of reactivity to fascism.[2]

A look at the nineteenth-century theoreticians of matriarchy or "mother right"—Lewis Henry Morgan and J. J. Bachofen—and their reception by communist theoreticians of women and the family—Frederick Engels and August Bebel—will help to lay bare some of the strands that form the ideological fabric of GDR feminism. In particular, it will elucidate the equation of communism with *femininity* that informs the work of Wolf and Morgner. I shall then present an account of the development of Wolf's and Morgner's feminist ideas.

Is Communism Feminine? The Nineteenth-Century Sources

The association of communism with femininity has a long history that begins in the middle of the nineteenth century, enters the Marxist canon with Engels's *Origin of the Family, Private Property and the State* (1884), and culminates in the picture of primitive communistic matriarchy drawn by Bebel in the 1891 and later editions of his influential *Woman and Socialism*, the classic Marxist work on the woman question. It is worthwhile to trace in the works of Morgan and Bachofen the genesis of this idea, which has played a determining role in forming the positive image of women, along with the construction of woman as mother, which was currency in the state socialisms.

The story begins with Lewis Henry Morgan's discovery of matrilineal descent among the Iroquois, which he published in *League of the Iroquois* (1851). In his major work *Ancient Society* (1877) Morgan greatly expanded his study of kinship and tied it to the rise of property, to the growth of the idea of the family, and to the development of the state. He studied tribal society worldwide—all the known North and South American Indian tribes, the Greek and Latin and other European tribes, and also the Asian, African, Polynesian, and Australian tribes—and concluded that humanity everywhere progressed through certain distinct stages: the Lower, Middle, and Upper Status of savagery, the Lower, Middle, and Upper Status of barbarism, and civilization. Each period is characterized by its own economy, form of government, type of family, and system of descent. The most dramatic turning point in the history of humanity came at the beginning of the Upper Status of barbarism with the manufacture of iron. According to Morgan, the production of iron was the "event of events in human experience, without a parallel, and without an equal."[3] This was the event that made civilization possible. The production of iron tools, the first tools "able to hold an edge and a point," brought an "accelerated progress of human intelligence,"[4] after which inventions crowd on one another. It also led to the accumulation of property, and, by consequence, to a hitherto unknown passion for property.

Morgan believes that private property brought with it three significant changes: descent was changed from the female to the male line; the monogamian family replaced the syndyasmian or pairing family; and the government, which had formerly been based in the gens (clan) and the tribe, became in the period of civilization the state.

Before this watershed, the form of government was gentile. The archaic gens, which existed from the Middle Status of savagery through the Lower Status of barbarism, was, Morgan hypothesizes, invariably matrilinear. The reason for this is that only the maternity, not the paternity, of children was certainly ascertainable.[5] The gentes were organized into phratries (brotherhoods), tribes, and at their point of greatest development, a confederacy of tribes. There was no state and little personal property. Morgan paints a sympathetic picture of the ancient gentes, repeatedly stressing that they rested on the principles of liberty, equality, and fraternity.[6]

While the gens were matrilinear, they were not therefore matriarchal. According to Morgan Iroquois women as well as men voted for sachems (chiefs),[7] but the sachems were men. Women were, however, in a better position in matrilinear society than they were when the descent was changed to the male line and monogamian marriage became the rule, because they lived in a household where members of their own gens predominated and were not isolated in the household of their husband.[8]

The transition from matrilinear gentile society to the patriarchal state took place, in Morgan's view, as follows. Already in the Middle Status of barbarism, the rise of "property in masses"—flocks and herds—brought about a change from descent in the female to descent in the male line within the gentes. Where paternity was becoming more assured, men wished to bequeath their property to their own children instead of to their gentile kindred.[9] According to Morgan this changeover would have been effected in a fairly simple and peaceful manner, even by consensus.[10]

In the Upper Status of barbarism property of all kinds then greatly increased. By the end of it even land was owned by individuals instead of by the tribe. Descent was firmly established in the male line, and the monogamian marriage, which allowed the women (though not the men) only one partner and was desired by the men because it assured the paternity of their children, replaced the syndyasmian or pairing marriage.[11]

At length the dispersion of persons out of the gentes and their territories, the increase in the numbers of persons belonging to no gens (in Rome, the plebeians), and the rise of townships and cities (notably Athens and Rome), combined with the rise of property including slaves, caused a complex state of affairs that gentile government was incapable of dealing with. The state, founded on property and on territory rather than on persons, was born. Thus in Rome, Servius Tullius (576 B.C.) instituted social classes and reorganized the assembly of the people—originally a gentile institution—so as to put control of the government in the hands of the propertied classes.

The ideas of Bachofen in *Das Mutterrecht* (Mother right, 1861), were only partially compatible with those of Morgan. Morgan became aware of Bachofen's work in 1872.[12] Bachofen's study, which pertains to Lycia, Crete, Athens, Lemnos, Egypt, India and Central Asia, Orchomenus and the Minyae, Elis, the Eizephyrean Locrians, Lesbos, and Mantinea, is entirely different from Morgan's in its method. It is not founded on anthropological studies, like Morgan's, but is based chiefly on a study of myths, from which Bachofen extrapolates his conclusions about ancient cultures. Like Morgan, he finds pervasive descent in the female line among pre-Hellenic peoples. Like Morgan, he traces this "mother right" to the fact that maternity is certain, while paternity always has "a certain fictive character."[13] Unlike Morgan, he also posits an era of actual matriarchy ("Gynaikokratie")—of female domination in the family and female rule in the state.[14] Morgan mentions Bachofen's "gyneocracy," or political supremacy of women, in *Ancient Society*, published sixteen years after Bachofen's study, with interest and notes that universal descent in the female line would be its prerequisite.[15] He does not, however, build Bachofen's findings into his own conclusions.

Bachofen posits three cultural stages. The first, Aphroditean natural law, involves unregulated hetaerism, for which wild plant and animal life served as the model, and descent was in the female line. The second is characterized by matrilinear descent, matriarchy, and monogamous marriage. It came into being because women rebelled against the debasing state of hetaerism, of being the sexual prey of any man at any time.[16] Initiated by the Amazons, who fought for it,[17] it was founded on a cult of Demeter, the primordial tellurian mother, was bound up with an agricultural way of life, and took agriculture as the prototype for motherhood.[18] The third stage is father right and patriarchy, which marked the triumph of the spiritual over the material principle; it supervened in Athens with the transition from the Demetrian (chthonian) to the Apollonian (solar) religion, and is found in its perfected form in the Roman state.

Bachofen differs from Morgan, first of all, in his description of the second stage or matriarchal period. Morgan does not document female rule in any period of any society. For Morgan exclusive marriage is bound up with patriarchy, desired by men so as to guarantee the paternity of children. For Bachofen it is an invention of matriarchy, desired and fought for by women so as to limit their sexual accessibility to men. Different too is Bachofen's hypothesis that the transitions between the three phases could only have been violent and bloody: "Every change in the relation between the sexes is attended by bloody events; peaceful and gradual change is far less frequent than violent upheaval."[19] The Amazons enacted "bloody vengeance against the male sex."[20] Finally, unlike Morgan, Bachofen gives no economic or structural explanation for why patriarchy may have come to supplant matriarchy.

Bachofen holds the matriarchal states up for high praise. He stresses not only their "universal freedom" and "equality"[21]—characteristics that Morgan too ascribes to the ancient gentes—but particularly their harmonious, even nonviolent character. They were internally peaceful (although matriarchy encouraged warlike courage among the men, who were chiefly occupied with warfare far from home[22]): "Matriarchal states were particularly famed for their freedom from intestine strife and conflict. . . . The matriarchal peoples . . . assigned special culpability to the physical injury of one's fellow men or even of animals. . . . An air of tender humanity . . . permeates the culture of the matriarchal world."[23] Moreover, "the matriarchal peoples feel the unity of all life, the harmony of the universe."[24]

Frederick Engels then, in *The Origin of the Family, Private Property, and the State* (1884), synthesizes Morgan, whose analysis of ancient society had greatly intrigued Marx;[25] Bachofen; and his and Marx's own ideas in order to formulate a communist theory of the family. Although he prominently and repeatedly acknowledges Bachofen, he in fact prefers Morgan's conclusions on every major point of difference. Indeed, he adopts Morgan's findings wholesale: his stages of prehistoric culture, his genealogy of family types, his description of gentile society, and his ascription of a key role to property in the change to descent in the male line, monogamian marriage, and the foundation of the state. He mentions Bachofen's "gyneocracy"[26] but himself stresses, like Morgan, that in the gentes "all are equal and free—the women included."[27]

Engels paints a much more specific picture than Morgan of the way in which private property led to patrilinear descent, specifying that the property was owned *by the men*. Since it was the man's job to find food for the family, Engels reasons that the man owned the instruments of labor necessary for the purpose, and later the cattle and the new instruments of labor, the slaves. He concurs with Morgan that the transition was simple and peaceful:

> According to the custom of the same society, his children could not inherit from him. . . . Thus on the one hand, in proportion as wealth increased it made the man's position in the family more

important than the woman's, and on the other hand created an impulse to exploit this strengthened position in order to overthrow, in favor of his children, the traditional order of inheritance. . . . Mother right, therefore, had to be overthrown. . . . This was by no means so difficult as it looks to us today. . . . A simple decree sufficed.[28]

Engels dramatizes conclusions drawn by Morgan about the resulting decline in the position of women. In his famous words:

The overthrow of mother right was the *world historical defeat of the female sex*. The man took command in the home also; the woman was degraded and reduced to servitude; she became the slave of his lust and a mere instrument for the production of children. This degraded position of the woman, especially conspicuous among the Greeks of the heroic and still more of the classical age, has gradually been palliated and glossed over, and sometimes clothed in a milder form; in no sense has it been abolished.[29]

Engels emphasizes that the increase in productivity and wealth also brought with it class society, slavery, and institutionalized warfare. Already in the Middle Stage of barbarism additional labor was needed. War provided it by bringing in slaves. In the Upper Stage of barbarism war became an institution, waged simply for plunder.[30]

Marx and Engels had already excoriated bourgeois marriage in the *Communist Manifesto*. Thus it comes as no surprise that Engels in *The Origin of the Family* parts ways with Morgan in denouncing the institution of marriage. Morgan, an admirer of monogamous marriage, believed that in its highest, modern form it implied a perfect equality between the sexes, and found that as it progressed toward that form the condition of women vastly improved.[31] Engels is likewise an admirer of monogamy, but he emphasizes the suspect origin of monogamous marriage, and is a bitter foe of the institution as it exists in his day. He inveighs against marriage as an institution that, based on male supremacy, exists expressly to produce "children of undisputed paternity" for the man.[32] Thus it allows the man every freedom while fettering the wife. Engels even identifies the antagonism between man and wife in monogamous marriage as "the first class opposition that appears in history"[33]: "Monogamous marriage comes on the scene as the subjugation of the one sex by the other."[34] Contemporary bourgeois marriage, by definition a marriage of convenience, has nothing to do with love. Engels discerns love between the sexes only among the proletariat, where there is no property. Marriage reduces women to servitude; they perform housework as a private service: "The modern individual family is founded on the open or concealed domestic slavery of the wife. . . . Within the family [the husband] is the bourgeois, and the wife represents the proletariat."[35]

This train of thought brings Engels to his recipe for the liberation of women: "The first condition for the liberation of the wife is to bring the whole female sex back into public industry."[36] According to Engels women have no hope of becoming men's equals until they enter production on a large scale and reduce the amount of time they spend on private domestic labor to nearly nothing.[37]

Engels also differs from Morgan in his evaluation of private property and the institution of the state. Morgan deplored the passion for property that had arisen in human society. At the conclusion of *Ancient Society* he urged that "a mere property career is not the final destiny of mankind."[38] Engels, a communist, goes much further in his denunciation of private property and calls for its abolition. With property collectively owned, the single family will also cease to be the economic unit of society: "Private housekeeping is transformed into a social industry. The care and education of children becomes a public affair."[39] Whereas Morgan, an American, admired democracy, believing it the highest form of government,[40] Engels dislikes the state as an institution and calls for its overthrow. He notes that the state is the invention of the most powerful, economically dominant class; it gives it the means of holding down and exploiting the oppressed class.[41]

Whereas Morgan esteems the ancient gentes for their liberty, equality, and fraternity, Engels esteems them for their lack of private property. He picks this characteristic out of Morgan's description, as well as out of Morgan's few references to "communism" in living in the household and to the "communal household" of the American aborigines, and makes much of them.[42] He indeed writes of the "communistic traditions of the gentile order" and ascribes "collective production" to early societies.[43] He posits that "at all earlier stages of society, production was essentially collective."[44] Thus an equation between ancient gentile society and communism is born.

August Bebel's *Woman and Socialism*, first published in 1879, was a best-seller in its day. The most read Marxist work before World War I,[45] it went into fifty editions by 1909.[46] Written in a lively, popular language, it brought many people, especially women, into the ranks of the Social Democrats. More than any other work it formed socialist thinking on the woman question. Bebel's most important ideas were that economic independence, and not just civil equality, is essential to woman's liberation; that women's work must be legally protected; that accomplished socialism is a precondition for women's emancipation; that women's childbearing function substantiates their claim to equal rights; and that housework and child care should be performed by the community.

The book's publication record shows the high regard in which it was held in the GDR. It was one of the first books to be republished in the Soviet Occupation Zone, and from 1946 through 1979 it was reissued eleven times in the Eastern part of Germany.[47] The Central Committee of the SED believed that its public policy on women executed Bebel's testament.[48] Like the other state socialisms the GDR followed Bebel's precepts in declaring women's equality, actively promoting women's employment, and socializing child care. Although Bebel's idealistic goal, the emancipation of women, was increasingly overshadowed by the practical necessity of retaining women in the labor force while keeping the birthrate high, the state explicitly aimed to make motherhood and paid labor compatible by helping women with their maternal responsibilities. At the international conference that the Central Committee of the SED sponsored in honor of the one-hundredth anniversary of the book in 1979, the speaker, Inge Lange, declared that the GDR had "accomplished the equality of man and woman with the building of socialism."[49] In the same year the Central Committee of the SED published a special edition of the book with photographs and a new foreword, which emphasizes that Bebel's ideas have become a reality in the Soviet Union and in other state socialisms, not least in the GDR.[50]

Bebel repeatedly added to and modified *Woman and Socialism*. Banned by the German government a month after it first appeared in 1879, the work was issued in a second, enlarged edition under a different title in 1883. Bebel made further major changes in the ninth edition of 1891, for in the interim he had read Engels's *Origin of the Family*. In particular, he expanded and changed the first section, called "Women in the Past." In the second edition Bebel had stated that woman was the first human being to be oppressed. He traced her oppression to her reproductive function: pregnancy, childbirth, and motherhood made her dependent on man's protection.[51] In the ninth edition Bebel continued to assert that woman was the first human being to be oppressed, but dropped the rest of his argument, substituting for it Engel's contention that the oppression of women dated from the advent of private property.

In the post-Engels version of the book Bebel writes, in a lucid, simple, and dramatic style, about women in ancient societies, synthesizing Engels, Bachofen, and Morgan. Yet his account is not only more readable and accessible, but also different in its emphasis and drift from theirs. Whereas Engels tends to adopt Morgan's conclusions rather than Bachofen's, Bebel is strongly attracted by Bachofen. He adds to Engels's conclusions major theses of Bachofen's and supplements Engels's picture of ancient society with a plethora of details drawn from Bachofen.

First, Bebel goes beyond Engels in playing up the idea of matriarchy, that is, of women's actual power as opposed to their mere equality in gentile society. Thus he asserts that the mother was the head of the family, indeed the leader of the communistic gentile kinship organization.[52]

Second, Bebel like Bachofen idealizes the era of mother right as peaceful: "Generally, relative peace prevailed under mother right" (Bebel 1979, p. 21). Quite in contrast to Morgan, according to whom Indian tribes were theoretically always at war with each other,[53] Bebel asserts that "the individual tribes . . . mutually respected each other's territory."

Third, whereas Engels adopts Morgan's views in saying that the transition from mother to father right was peaceful, Bebel pointedly juxtaposes to this view Bachofen's observation that such changes are never peaceful: "Fr. Engels believes that this great transition took place entirely peacefully and that once all the preconditions for the new right were present, only a simple vote in the gentes was necessary to replace mother right with father right. Bachofen in contrast, basing his view on classical sources, is of the opinion that women were fiercely opposed to this social transformation" (p. 27).

Finally, Bebel dramatizes Engels's identification of the gentile organization and mother right with communism: "Like the previous forms of the family, the gens was based on common property, in other words, on a communistic economy. The woman is the head and leader of this family cooperative" (p. 20). And later: "*The authority of mother right meant communism, equality for all; the appearance of father right meant supremacy of private property, and at the same time it meant the oppression and subjugation of woman*" (p. 26; also beginning of chap. 7; italics Bebel's).

Bebel's affection for mother right and matriarchy may well stem from his extreme respect for woman as mother, as the person who gives birth. Already in the first edition of 1879, in the context of arguing for women's right to vote and to hold public office, he castigated men who find pregnant women "unaesthetic" and called for the social recognition of the childbearing woman in outspoken language that he would only slightly vary subsequently: "*A woman who bears children performs at least the same service to the community as a man who risks his life defending country and hearth against an enemy thirsting for conquest*" (p. 242; italics Bebel's). He observes that the risk women run in giving birth is greater than the risk men run on the battlefield: "*The number of women who die or languish as a result of childbirth is far greater than the number of men who fall or are wounded on the battlefield*" (ibid.; italics Bebel's).

Rewards for Motherhood?

In subsequent decades the argument that maternity is a social service and therefore deserves to be rewarded became extremely widespread. It blossomed into one of the principal contentions of a spectrum of pre–World War I feminist movements. According to Werner Thönnessen, the Erfurt Program of the German Social Democratic Party of 1891, which called for universal suffrage, did not contain special provisions for the protection of women, but Eduard Bernstein in *Die Neue Zeit* (The new time) called for it: a woman needs special protection "in her role as the agent of the coming generation, the one who gives birth. . . . The woman fulfils a special sexual function, and with regard to this she has a claim to special protection by society." Two years later, in 1893, Clara Zetkin argued the same point in an article in *Die Gleichheit* (Equality).[54] In 1901 the socialist feminist Lily Braun declared that motherhood was a social function.[55] In 1911 Social Democratic women, following Bebel, argued that women's productive labor, along with "the service that women provide to society through maternity" should earn them the vote.[56] Gisela Bock shows that in France, where the rewards-for-motherhood movement was strongest, the socialist feminist Léonie Rouzade, followed by Hubertine Auclert and Nelly Roussel, called for state payment of mothers in return for their essential social service; the Conseil National des Femmes Françaises (founded in 1901) and the Union Française pour le Suffrage des Femmes (founded 1909) demanded recognition of motherhood as a social service. Women in England, Norway, Sweden, Italy, and the United States voiced the same demand.[57]

After the war the heyday of the idea was over. To be sure, Virginia Woolf on the brink of the Second World War called for a legal wage to be paid by the state to mothers.[58] But many feminists shied away from identifying woman as mother, preferring to insist on her sameness with men.[59] Yet child and family subsidies paid by the modern European welfare states can be traced to the pre-World War I maternalistic feminist demands, although they fall far short of them, as well as to concern over the birthrate, which has dropped dramatically in the twentieth century.[60] Even the United States had the Sheppard-Towner Maternity and Infancy Act from 1921 to 1928, guaranteeing government funds for mothers' and children's health care. But it was repealed, and thereafter in the United States motherhood was regarded as a purely individual matter.[61]

The idea that women should enjoy *social rights* (or benefits) on account of the *social service* they perform through maternity is an emancipatory idea. It is not at all to be confused with declaring women essentially *mothers* as an excuse for excluding them from productive labor; nor is it the same thing as controlling and exploiting women's maternal function by offering honors to mothers according to how many children they bear, as was done in Hitler's Germany in 1939[62] and in Stalin's Russia in 1944.[63] The fact is that childbearing is time-consuming and work-intensive. The burden of pregnancy, the disabling period of childbirth and postpartum recovery, and the nursing and care of the infant that fall to the mother in fact do represent, alone and quite aside from any subsequent childrearing, a commitment of time and energy which, in the case of a single child, could plausibly be compared to two-year military service.

Some Western feminists have recognized, as Shulamith Firestone says, that "the heart of woman's oppression is her childbearing and childrearing roles."[64] The real reason why women have been excluded from careers and relegated to the lowest-paid, lowest-status productive labor, is not, first and foremost, any social construction of femininity, but rather the fact that their childbearing function and childrearing activity make them uncompetitive on the labor market. The United States has given women "equal" opportunity in the labor market. But the government has never and still does not recognize that women make a specialized, unique, and essential contribution to society in the form of childbearing. By not recognizing this contribution and compensating women for it, current legislation guarantees that women will remain unequal. The Pregnancy Discrimination Act of 1978 protects women from being fired or losing benefits on account of pregnancy; it defines pregnancy as a disability. It would be more honest to define pregnancy—not on the labor market to be sure, but within the larger social framework—as an asset. In an era of birth control and legal abortion, when women can choose whether or not to bear children, it is hypocritical to dismiss childbearing as a "natural" function that "happens." In the nineteenth century, the birthrate was high. Today, in the Western industrial nations, it is at an all-time low. Children have become valuable—both to governments, whose planning for the future depends on stability in the birthrate, and to would-be parents. Today, U.S. couples wishing to adopt children greatly outnumber the domestic children available for adoption. Child-hungry individuals are willing to pay substantial sums to surrogate mothers.[65] Yet paradoxically, women who bear children enjoy no advantages; at best they are not discriminated against; de facto they are generally *disadvantaged*. Legislation is ostensibly attempting to move some of the responsibility for childrearing onto fathers, largely by giving divorced and single fathers rights at their own option,[66] but the subtext of this legislation is an ethos that gives absolute priority to genetic property, namely, the old foundation of patriarchy. The interests of women are neither an explicit consideration in this legislation, nor indeed visibly served by current trends in divorce law.[67] Moreover, divorced women are, with the demise of alimony, pushed onto a labor market that their prior childbearing and childrearing and, in most cases, factually continuing primary responsibility for their children, has tilted sharply against them.

The Maternal Construction of Women in the GDR

There is no question that the GDR conceptualized woman not only as *worker* but also as *mother*. From the inception of the state the SED routinely addressed women in political speeches as "Frauen und Mütter" ("Women and mothers"). Here one sees the ideological legacy of Bebel and Zetkin directly put into practice. Dölling asserts in her study of photographs of women in GDR magazines that a "stereotype of motherliness" is present in nearly all of the photos of women in private life.[68] It is true that the persistent GDR construction of woman as mother, as well as its effort to make work and maternity combinable, may well have increasingly acquired a secondary agenda of maintaining the nation's birthrate. Since the fall of the Wall East German women intellectuals have attacked GDR "Mommy politics" for painting women into a maternal corner.[69] However, it is worth pointing out that this obviously deeply entrenched maternal construction of woman brought women not only disadvantages but also some very considerable advantages.

First, women's advancement in employment had absolutely no negative effect on their status in the area of family law. The GDR did not, as did the United States, open the doors of employment to women in the name of equal rights only to close down the presumption that they would make the better custodial parent, also in the name of equal rights. It also did not use a woman's employment as grounds to deny her custody of her children "in the best interest of the child," as has happened in the West. In the GDR the criterion for granting custody was the "welfare of the child," and the mother received custody in 93 percent of divorce cases (compared to 85 percent in the FRG), while fathers paid child support and had visitation rights. Single mothers had sole custodial rights. Unmarried fathers were required to pay child support, although they did not have visitation rights.[70]

Second, GDR politics actually did make it possible for a woman to combine motherhood and work successfully, which from the Western perspective is no small accomplishment. *Pace* the East German women intellectuals, the general run of GDR women, as exemplified by those Maxie Wander interviewed in *Guten Morgen, du Schöne*, appeared by and large content with their lot as working mothers. In general the "feminism" of the women Wander interviewed amounts to a desire for "equal rights" ("Gleichberechtigung"); some say they want men to participate in child care and housework; two fantasize about living in a commune ("Großfamilie")—an idea that is echoed in fiction.[71] But these are not overriding obsessions, and the women are not bitter. One of the principal arguments cited by GDR women for believing themselves better off than their sisters in the West is their ability to combine work and motherhood. Thus in a 1972 interview with an argumentative West German man Morgner successfully defends her characterization of the GDR as a better place for women by pointing out that unlike in the FRG, "as a single woman you can very well live with children—with one or more children—and be socially accepted." She emphatically affirms that "having a child is simply not a private affair, raising a child is a significant job that someone performs and that a humane society must recognize, also through support."[72]

Matriarchy Theory, Wolf, and Morgner

The classic Marxist ideas on women not only found their way into the work of Christa Wolf and Irmtraud Morgner, but found their most radical expression there as these writers disengaged them from their doctrinaire framework and reattached them to modern feminist ideas. Both Wolf and Morgner make the leap, as Virginia Woolf had in *Three Guineas* (1938), from the peaceful image of maternal femininity conjured up by Bachofen and Bebel to regarding war as the direct consequence of patriarchy.[73]

Engels and Bebel certainly cannot be considered Wolf's or Morgner's unique sources of information on primitive matriarchy. In the Frankfurt Lectures on Poetics Wolf lists her reading for *Cassandra*, which includes more recent works, including *Mütter und Amazonen* (by Berta Eckstein-Diener; published in 1932 under the pseudonym "Sir Galahad"; translated into English as Helen Diner, *Mothers and Amazons*); George Thomson's *Studies in Ancient Greek Society: The Prehistoric Aegean* (1949); and Robert von Ranke-Graves's *Griechische Mythologie* (well known in English as Robert Graves, *Greek Mythology*).[74] Several critics have documented that Ranke-Graves's mythology handbook served as the principal source for Wolf's account of the Trojan War—probably, as Rose Nicolai and Christine Maisch point out, because Graves is a proponent of matriarchy theory.[75] Matriarchy theory was "in the air" in the GDR long before Wolf wrote *Cassandra* and Morgner *Amanda*: for example, in the noted 1975 anthology *Blitz aus heiterem Himmel*, containing short stories on the theme of sex change, one story (Karl-Heinz Jakobs's) is about matriarchy, another (Gotthold Gloger's) mentions it, and the concluding essay by Annemarie Auer gives an account of primitive matriarchy that follows and elaborates on Engels and Bebel. Moreover, matriarchy had been rediscovered by Western feminism starting with Elizabeth Gould Davis's *First Sex* (1971), a work that Wolf also lists (it was published in German in 1979 under the title *Am Anfang war die Frau*). Davis uses Bachofen's assertion that matriarchal states were peaceful to buttress her argument for the moral superiority of women.[76] Two years later in *Beyond God the Father* the radical feminist theologian Mary Daly followed suit, summarizing matriarchy theory as portraying matriarchal societies as "egalitarian" and "not bent on the conquest of nature or of other human beings" like men's "technical controlling knowledge."[77]

Yet the GDR writers' enthusiasm for matriarchy emerges with so little rupture from their previous thinking about women, and with such emphasis on the link with communism (absent in the American treatments), that it seems plausible to conclude that the explosion of Western feminism in the 1970s mainly gave them the courage to stage their own feminist coup on Marxist historical materialism, and not their ideas. Engels and Bebel are the works that cement the connection between matriarchy, communism, and peace that form the core of both writers' treatment of the subject. The major revision that both Wolf and Morgner perform on classic Marxist doctrine is to downplay the role of private property, which for Engels is the crucial factor leading to patriarchy, monogamous marriage, and the state. Instead, patriarchy itself appears as the villain.

The Work of Christa Wolf

In response to the question, "Why do you write?" put by the Paris newspaper *Libération* to European authors in 1985, Christa Wolf stated:

> The intellectual adventure of writing consists for me in recovering and possibly unleashing forces in myself, forces that, during the course of my life under our historical conditions, were suspected of being useless, superfluous, harmful, unneeded, inappropriate, trivial, disadvantageous, unauthorized, detrimental, anarchical, amoral, unscrupulous, punishable, illegal, unsuitable, unfit, inadvisable, disgraceful, unlawful, incompetent, ridiculous, pathological, foolish, worthless, arbitrary, despicable, inane, insane, immoral, irresponsible, misguided, improper, unseemly, indecent, destructive, egoistic, inadmissible, ungrateful, radical, rebellious, unreasonable—in short, subjectivistic, those forces upon which a verdict was imposed, that were repressed, narcoticized, fettered, and paralyzed. The shock over the fact that in industrial societies the selection of the "useful" forces and ambitions of a person functions at the cost of his "useless" needs and desires, and the grief over the consequences of this split and amputation, certainly flow into my writing.[78]

Writing, then, is self-exploration, self-expression, and protest for Wolf. It is a liberation of the emotions and ideas that, Wolf believes, have been repressed by the rationalization of modern industrial society. Consistently, the strongest element in Wolf's writing has been social critique. Her ideal has consistently been utopian communism.[79] Friendliness and a sense of community appeal to her, as well as a life-style that does not "divide" people or privilege rationality over feeling, forcing people to repress aspects of themselves, but, rather, favors self-realization and personal fulfillment. A constant motif in her work is an ideal inclusive recognition of the "whole." She shows a strong antipathy not only toward such cornerstones of the capitalist mentality as competition, individualism, and materialism, but toward what she calls, following Critical Theory, "instrumental reason." In the course of what the GDR termed its "scientific and technological revolution," the New Economic System of 1963 adopted a program devoted to systematicity, technologization, and achievement. Wolf was one of several GDR writers who, following the stimulus of Western European Marxists, criticized this trend, which led away from Marxism's original goal of the full development and self-realization of the individual.[80]

There is nothing at all novel about Wolf's social critique, which orients itself on the Marxist humanitarian model of nonalienated existence. What is new about Wolf's formulation of the problem is her ascription, in the early 1970s, of her preferences and of the "good" characteristics specifically to women.[81] Implicitly and instinctively at first, but increasingly definitely and openly, she identifies the positive concepts with the feminine, and the negative ones with the masculine. In rejecting masculine ideals, Wolf goes far beyond the Marxist classics.

In an initial phase, in the early 1970s, Wolf does little to avert the conclusion that these feminine and masculine characteristics are biological. In the story "Self-experiment" (1973), the fact that a sex-change operation suffices to turn a woman mentally into a man suggests that in this period Wolf believed that gender differences are sex-specific.[82] If Wolf did indeed entertain such a view, it would have been at odds with GDR psychology, which believed, following the Marxist-Leninist conception of the human being as fundamentally transformable and thus reeducate, that psychic differences between the sexes are largely socially determined and thus modifiable through education.[83] As seen in the last chapter, Morgner's ideas on this subject were in complete conformity with the official view. In an interview of 1983 Wolf finally explicitly distanced herself from biological determinism, asserting that the differences between the sexes have historical causes.[84] Most commentators on Wolf's feminism quote this statement with relief.[85] Wolf's historical studies and her engagement with Western feminism in the intervening period may well have caused her to change her mind. In any case, she was and remains a difference feminist, regardless of how she has accounted for men's and women's differences.

Wolf's work in the second half of the 1970s sought the historical causes of the present-day malaise, of the origin of "men's values" and the reasons why women escaped from them. Her approach is Marxist in its method and in its conclusions. To this period belongs her work on the Romantics.

Around 1980 came a major shift in her thinking, which climaxed in the publication of her Lectures on Poetics and *Cassandra*. At this stage—in the immediate wake of the East-West nuclear arms escalation of 1977–1979, which, with Soviet nuclear-armed missiles aimed at Western Europe and Nato nuclear-armed missiles aimed at Eastern Europe, threatened Europe and especially Germany with a nuclear catastrophe—Wolf was intensely preoccupied with the danger and the evil of war. She realigned the masculine-feminine polarity prominent in her earlier work with the polarity war-peace. The contemporaneous women's peace movement that arose spontaneously in both West and East Germany in response to the arms escalation seemed to bear her out. Sibyll-Anka Klotz observes in a 1989 study that women's support of peace has a venerable history, and is in fact the single most important common denominator among the women's movements of the day.[86]

Male culture, Wolf asserts, has driven us to the brink of destruction. What is radical about this equation, for a GDR writer like Wolf, is that she takes a giant step away from socialist doctrine on the woman question and toward a feminism, in the Western sense, that asserts that the antagonism between the sexes is a primary one, not, as Bebel had argued, a secondary one that will disappear with accomplished socialism. Wolf puts traditional Marxist explanations on the shelf and pinpoints the origins of the malaise at the beginning of patriarchy—that is, at the beginning of history. She occupied herself extensively with historical studies pertaining to mother right and matriarchy, as well as with Western feminist writing. Up to the present Wolf has retained her belief that patriarchy brought about a revolution of all values. Her 1996 novel *Medea*, which like *Cassandra* is set at the historical moment when patriarchy suppressed matriarchy, dramatizes the nefarious consequences.

While Wolf's thinking on women develops, it does so logically and consistently. The novel that established her fame as a writer,

Divided Heaven (1963), a work that is still indebted to the techniques of socialist realism, features a woman protagonist, Rita. Set in the period immediately prior to and encompassing the building of the Berlin Wall in August 1961, it tells the story of this young woman's experiences working in a factory—she is sent to work temporarily in a train car factory in preparation for her profession as a teacher—and as a student; of her love affair with the ten-year-older chemist Manfred; and of her decision not to follow Manfred to the West, but to remain to help build up a communist society in the East. The pros of socialism, argumentatively contrasted with the cons, are the main theme of the novel, which is, first and foremost, the story of Rita's political coming of age. It seems fortuitous that, in this extremely pro-Socialist and even pro-Wall novel, it is the *woman* who stays in the East and opts for the values of community and socialism while the *man* leaves for the West, preferring individualism, competition, and materialism. Manfred and Rita are divided not only by sex but by a generation gap that might be held accountable for the former's cynicism and the latter's optimism and idealism. Like Wolf herself, Manfred, whom Hell dubs "the fascist body of the past,"[87] grew up under Hitler; his father was an SA (Nazi storm troopers) member who opportunistically joined the Communist Party after the war and rose to the position of factory director; his mother is a nonworking wife who aggressively pushes her husband's career, hates the GDR, and wishes herself in the West. Rita, the daughter of an artisan who was killed in the war, saw the war only as a child and grew up in a village with her widowed mother. The positive characters in the novel, all committed communists, are, besides the heroine Rita, men. Nevertheless, because Rita is the heroine, because the novel is about her education, and because her lover Manfred leaves for the West, a connection is created in the reader's mind between women and socialism, and between men and capitalism. This connection is supported by the novel's pronounced antiscientist theme: Manfred's scientist colleagues, arrogant, materialistic, hierarchical GDR chemists who are disdainful of the GDR, are all men.

Women's issues receive explicit treatment in the novel in the form of a critique of sexism in the workplace. When Rita enters the train car factory the male workers are nonplussed: what can this woman possibly be good for? Rita then quickly learns to handle screws and drills and proves herself to be a competent coworker. Manfred's mother, Frau Herrfurth, a dependent, nonworking housewife who disapproves of employment for women and who nags Rita to vacuum rugs, represents the negative female type. The feminism of this early novel thus in every point supports, and does not go beyond, the current official policies of the GDR on women, which encouraged women to enter the labor force.

The next work in which Wolf stages a confrontation between the sexes is the "The New Life and Opinions of a Tomcat," written in 1970 and published in 1974 in *Unter den Linden*. Whereas *Divided Heaven* followed the style of socialist realism, with its typical characters, positive heroine, and clear, accessible style, this story, which borrows its idea from E. T. A. Hoffmann's *Lebensansichten des Katers Murr (The Life and Opinions of the Tomcat Murr)*, is a parodistic satire, quirkily written by a cat narrator in a pompous, congested facsimile of "scientific" prose. Wolf's objective here is to attack the wrong kind of socialism, or misplaced scientific rationalism. At the same time she targets male chauvinism, which she identifies with the scientific and rationalistic spirit, by joining them in the personages of the cat and psychology professor who is his owner. The conceited, vain, pompous, uninsightful male chauvinist tomcat fancies himself a scientist like his master. Convinced that animals are the highest form of being, he sets about "psyching out" his human subjects. His master, who has an ulcer and is impotent, insomniac, and constipated, is engaged in research that attempts to rationalize all the humanity out of people. The satire on socialism is obvious. The psychology professor wants to set up a single system—SYMAHE—that will be good for all and lead to ultimate, complete human happiness. Specifically, he undertakes to merge two files: the catalog of all human qualities and capabilities and the system of maximal bodily and mental health. SYMAHE "would represent the triumph of an all-cognisant, all-explaining, all regulating ratio."[88] Humanity turns out to be incompatible with SYMAHE: one would have to delete creative thought, courage, unselfishness, pity, loyalty to convictions, imagination, a sense of beauty, reason, and sex—leaving only the reflex system!

Women in this story are the subversive element in the male rage for systematicity. The professor's wife compensates for her sexual frustration by having an affair with one of his colleagues. The professor's daughter sabotages her father's experiment with the effects of hunger on cats by feeding the tomcat secretly—an action the tomcat finds methodologically deplorable but gastronomically welcome—and throws a wild party in her parents' absence. The professor lusts after the neighbor's sixteen-year-old daughter, while the cat is equally prone to sexual temptation. He castigates the neighbor's female cat, the mother of his offspring, for being impudent, arrogant, greedy, and uninhibited—"in short, a female" (*WR* 122)—, but these characteristics in fact all apply to himself. The female cat levels a down-to-earth rebuke at her mate for neglecting his kittens on the pretext that he is immersed in scientific pursuits. Thus the women in this story function as a foil to the men's relentless pursuit of abstract chimeras. Men's sexual susceptibility to women further undermines their attempts to subordinate human existence to scientific control.

With the story "Self-experiment: Treatise on a Report" (written in 1972 and published in 1973), Wolf's contribution to Edith Anderson's commissioned anthology on the theme of sex change *Blitz aus heiterem Himmel*, Wolf's feminism takes wing. In this story about a woman who changes into a man, the differences between men and women become the central theme. Wolf's account of these differences is not what is remarkable about the story—for while presented with insight and nuance, it tells us nothing we have not heard before. Rather, the accolades she bestows on the feminine characteristics and her negative treatment of men testify to a new direction. Even after the heroine finds out that men have a better time of life, she opts to change back into a woman. The key concept here is "love"—an idea that will remain in the foreground of Wolf's thinking and with which she thinks femininity has a special affinity. In a question and answer period following a reading of *Cassandra* in 1983 Wolf clarified what she meant by "love": it means acceptance of the other; its opposite is fear, which leads to aggressiveness.[89] The heroine of "Self-experiment" concludes that the advantages men enjoy cannot compensate her for what she has lost—the ability to love.

The plot, as in earlier works when Wolf writes about differences between the sexes, plays in a scientific milieu, where Wolf, as always, equates the scientific with the male. Here the heroine herself is a scientist, but since she is a woman in a man's ballpark, with a twist: she wants to prove her worth as a woman by consenting to play the guinea pig in a sex-change experiment devised by her professor, in short by becoming a man. This, Wolf implies, is a wrongheaded aspiration. Men have conceptualized "equality" between the sexes as educating women to conform to masculine norms. But women have been foolish to make such assimilation their goal. Thirty days into her sex-change experiment the protagonist is eager to undo the process of becoming a man that she already initiated by becoming a scientist. She concludes her narrative, which is addressed to her professor, by saying: "Now we are facing my experiment: the attempt to love" (*WR* 228).

Wolf's protagonist becomes a man by drinking "Bepeter Masculinum 199." The psychological change is immediate: the new man Other (in German "Anders," which means "different"), feels good (a feeling that had been foreign to the woman). But the plot dictates that complete mental change must be gradual in this initially androgynous psyche. The heroine must retain enough of her feminine mind to be able to compare the masculine with the feminine mentality and to realize that she wants to change back into a woman. Through the privileged optic of Other, the reader discovers that the differences between a man and a woman encompass coenesthesia, attitude toward the world, and mood. A difference in intelligence between men and women is explicitly denied. Other discovers that a man regards the world as a place for realizing his ambitions. He is oriented on facts, things, and abstractions rather than on people. Consequently, what other people think about him does not matter to him. He is free of affect, hence indifferent, hence not vulnerable. Given all this, the story seems to ask provocatively, why would anyone want to be a woman? For women, the story says, come to the world with emotional baggage. A woman feels guilty. For her the world is a place of chiefly romantic hopes. She is oriented on people and emotionally dependent on what other people think of her, to the point of always watching other people for signs. She is sad, and prone to nervous complaints.

Wolf takes these stereotypical differences and turns them around into a set of positive attributes for women. Expressed positively, they mean that women see (the truth), while men are partially blind. Women are capable of love, while men are incapable of loving. These are men's secrets: they go through life "like in the movies" (*WR* 227). They may feel good, but they are not happy: "I . . . discovered that which must remain your secret in order that your comfortable privileges not be infringed upon: that the undertakings you lose yourself in cannot be your happiness" (*WR* 224).

Starting in 1973, Wolf made her position on gender questions explicit in a series of interviews, addresses, and essays. An early statement of her views appeared in her 1973 interview with Hans Kaufmann. Kaufmann notes a "certain bitterness" in Wolf's treatment of the theme of the sexes in "Self-experiment." Wolf responded that she is enraged over the fact that "women's liberation" in the

GDR is threatening to get stuck and is not asking new, radical questions. "Self-experiment" is meant to ask one such question: "Should the aim of women's emancipation be for them to 'become like men'? Would it even be desirable if they could do the same things, enjoy the same rights, and always get more—where men themselves so badly need emancipating?" (*DA* 799). Wolf is certain that men and women are different; women should not be forced to conform to the "masculine ideal," which, moreover, is out-of-date:

> As the material conditions allowing the sexes an equal start improve—and this must necessarily be the first step towards emancipation—so we face more acutely the problem of giving the sexes opportunity to be different from each other, to acknowledge that they have different needs, and that men and women, not just men, are the models for human beings. This doesn't even occur to most men, and really very few women try and get to the root of why it is that their consciences are permanently troubled (because they can't do what's expected of them). If they got to the bottom of it, they'd find it was their own identification with an idealised masculinity that is in itself obsolete. (*FD* 34–35)

Interviews in the following years give a clearer picture of what Wolf believes to be the differences between the sexes. She repeatedly uses the term "values" (*Werte*)[90] to articulate the feminine position and counterpose it to that of men, that is, to what she had called the "masculine ideal." Women want "friendliness, . . . a complete, fulfilled life" (*DA* 2: 859). Men are wedded to a treacherous "ratio"; they conduct the world's business as if humanity's problems could be solved by technology, whereby the world is still full of weapons (*FD* 76). According to Wolf, this rejection of the "achievement-oriented society" has been a trend among GDR women since about 1973, who after all had had to work like men since the inception of the GDR (*FD* 114).

At the same time, in the second half of the 1970s, Wolf, whose thinking is ever Marxist, that is, historical materialist, sought to give her assignation of certain pejorative values to men and positive ones to women a social and historical underpinning. In a 1976 interview she asserts that men have been deformed by social conditions, by the pressures of the world of work, which has caused them to become oriented on performance and success. Women, in contrast, have—perforce—historically been excluded from such mechanisms, and thus, by virtue of their very social oppression, escaped a more inexorable form of psychological conditioning. Where men's senses have been dulled ("abgestumpft," *DA* 2: 846), women have remained more "sensitive" and more "spontaneous." Yet women's "moral values" (*FD* 65)—their "more human scale of values" (ibid.) of affection, sensitivity, brother- (or sister-)liness, and above all self-realization— have the potential to "rescue society." In a 1978 interview she is historically somewhat more explicit: men have been deformed by the historical conditions of industrial society, by the pressure to compete and achieve (*FD* 75). Her thinking closely resembles that of Woolf in *Three Guineas*, a work with which she might already have been familiar.[91] Critics usually assume that Wolf drew on Critical Theory for her critique of instrumental rationality and her postulate that women escaped its worst consequences.[92]

Her search for the historical sources of men's "values" led her to the Romantics, to the period around 1800, the era of nascent bourgeois society in the wake of the French Revolution. In this period, Wolf believes, utilitarianism and the conversion of every relationship into exchange value began to reign supreme (*DA* 2: 532). A series of publications on the women Romantics resulted: the novel *No Place on Earth* (*Kein Ort. Nirgends*, 1979), on the legendary meeting of Heinrich von Kleist and Karoline von Günderrode in 1804; *Der Schatten eines Traumes* (The shadow of a dream, 1979), an anthology of Günderrode's works with a long introductory essay; and "Your Next Life Begins Today" (*AD*; "Nun ja! Das nächste Leben geht aber heute an," 1981), an essay on Bettina von Arnim. In these works "wholeness" becomes a catchword for her ideal: women demand wholeness instead of a separation of life, love, and work (*AD* 155, 165), while men succumb all too easily to the dissociation of sensibility already deplored by Schiller in *Über die ästhetische Erziehung des Menschen* (*On the Aesthetic Education of Man*, 1795) as characteristic of modern society, to division, fragmentation, and compartmentalization. In a 1979 interview she specifies that bourgeois industrial society, characterized by the division of labor, which was particularly apparent around 1800, is at fault; intolerant of people who wished to be "whole," it maimed men psychologically. Women escaped such deformation (*AD* 88). Yet at the same time, men determine what is "realistic"; women are silenced and marginalized.

This entire train of thought—a denunciation of the world as made by men; a scathing critique of the triumph of abstract, scientific, "rational," utilitarian thought, whose outstanding achievement has been to give us the weapons of our own destruction; praise of the humanistic values desired by the completely marginalized women; localization of the sources of the misery in the perversion of Enlightenment values that the rise of industrial society in the nineteenth century brought with it—reaches its vehement pinnacle in Wolf's speech "Speaking of Büchner," held on the occasion of her award of the Georg Büchner Prize in 1980. Speaking of Büchner's relevance for the present, and obsessed by the threat of nuclear war as the most urgent contemporary problem, Wolf gives a nutshell history of how the world got to be the way it is, and what happened to women in the process. She castigates the "instrumental thinking" and "utilitarian insanity" that took the upper hand in the nineteenth century and makes a particularly clear and vehement statement about how the triumph of the scientific ideal marginalized and silenced women in Büchner's day:

> Where are Rosetta, Marie, Marion, Lena, Julie, Lucile? Outside the citadel [of reason], of course. Unprotected in the foreground. No edifice of thought will shelter them. They have been made to believe that rational thinking is something you can do only if you are dug into the trenches! And they have neither the education nor any real inclination to do so. From a vantage point below and outside the citadel, they observe the strained mental activity of the male, which he directs increasingly toward safeguarding his fortress with exact measurements, calculations, and ingenious number and design systems. This activity thrives in the iciest abstraction, and its ultimate truth is a formula. How could Rosetta suspect that it is the fear of contact which causes the man to retreat from reality's abundance? That his fragility, and his fear of recognizing it, is what drives him to take refuge in his insane systems? That wounded and torn, and robbed of his wholeness by the ruthless division of labor, he is hounding himself, driving at reckless speeds, just to avoid having to make the "descent into hell" that is self-knowledge—even though, Kant says, reason cannot exist without self-knowledge? And how could Rosetta guess that a man who does not know himself cannot know a woman either? (*AD* 179–180)

Wolf explains the historical oppression of women psychologically: men, in Wolf's view, are afraid of anything that does not mirror them, hence of actual contact with reality, including feminine reality. They fail to know, indeed to see, women, except inasmuch as women conform to their preconceived categories. And she pours scorn on the "progress" that, in our own day, has tried to assimilate women to man's world:

During the wars, she replaces the man, proves her worth on his machinery of production and destruction. Her ultimate admission is that now she has become like him. She sets out to prove it to him. Progress, for her, is that she works like a man. And it *is* progress. She stands beside him, tending the machine, day and night. Sits next to him in the lecture hall and in the board room (although she is in the minority there, of course). She writes, paints, composes poetry like him—*almost* like him. Here one sees the first fine cracks in her performance. People attribute them to her oversensitivity and make allowances; or they don't make allowances. (*AD* 182)

References to war dominate this essay. Wolf adds militarism and war to the list of men's dubious achievements.

In the essays of 1978–1980 Wolf walks a fine line between asserting that women have been obliterated in the Western, male construction of reality; that women have been denied a voice, desire, history, and so forth; and according a positive identity to the feminine. Where do these positive characteristics come from? Wolf asserts them from "Self-experiment" on but never substantiates or accounts for them, except, starting in the second half of the 1970s, to imply that they are natural human characteristics that women have escaped losing on account of their marginalization in bourgeois society. For her mention of men's social "deformation" (*DA* 2: 845 and 859) implies that she thinks that a "natural," undeformed human identity was there beforehand. She likewise walks a fine line when she simultaneously asserts that economic realities have destroyed men, split them, and ruined them psychologically; and claims that only economic independence, such as GDR women know it today, will liberate women, set them up psychologically to rebel against the very system that they are being assimilated to (*FD* 114–115). Wolf's conceptual apparatus is not necessarily internally consistent. To give another example, it is hard to reconcile her invocation of a natural "wholeness" with her considerable commitment to psychoanalytically informed concepts like repression and selective memory.

Wolf on Matriarchy: *Cassandra*

At the start of the 1980s came a shift in Wolf's thinking. As is visible already in the Büchner essay, she began to see the worst social evil as militarism and war; her reflections are full of references to the danger of atomic war that threatened Europe. She plainly believed that this legacy of male domination most urgently needed to be combated. And at the same time she turned her sights from an orthodox Marxist explanation of the cause of alienation in the beginnings of industrial society to patriarchy itself as cause.[93] She dropped her study of the Romantics in favor of exploring the historical moment that had intrigued Morgan, Bachofen, Engels, and Bebel, the moment that marked the transition from "mother right" to patriarchy. Wolf focused specifically on the repression of the feminine that began, in ancient Greece, with the destruction of the Minoan culture by the Mycenean.

In her "Lectures on Poetics," delivered at the University of Frankfurt in May 1982, Wolf recounts the genesis of her interest in ancient Greek culture and of her novella *Cassandra*. Her interest in the Cassandra figure was kindled when she read the *Oresteia* in the context of a visit to Greece in 1980. Wolf takes Bachofen's interpretation of Aeschylus' cycle, that it is about the transition from mother right to father right, for granted. She recounts that she particularly wanted to visit Crete, the "cradle of the West" (C 180), the "country where women were free and equal to men" (C 200). Yet she studied Minoan culture carefully and seriously. She warns against overidealizing some prerational "feminine" and throwing all men's achievements overboard (C 260). She scrupulously avoids idealizing: she notes that Minoan culture probably actually had theocratic hierarchy, feudal classes, exploitation, and slavery. She also visited Mycenae, the representative city of patriarchy, where Cassandra, according to the *Oresteia*, was put to death as Agamemnon's slave.

For over a quarter of a century, since her laudatory essay on Ingeborg Bachmann "The Truth You Can Expect" (*AD*; "Die zumutbare Wahrheit," 1966), Wolf persistently paid tribute to the gift—bestowed invariably on women—of "sight." Wolf recognized in Aeschylus' Cassandra figure precisely what she had long admired: her seerdom, that is, her insight. Moreover, Wolf says, Cassandra seems to be the only character in Aeschylus' play who "knows herself" (C 145). Cassandra's proximity to Wolf's own paradigm of sexual difference in "Self-experiment," where a woman who "sees" and therefore speaks "the truth" is opposed to a man who is "blind" and can only talk "facts," is obvious. Persuaded that patriarchy repressed and distorted beyond recognition the matriarchal culture that preceded it, that aesthetics were an accomplice and prime agent in patriarchy's quest for self-glorification, and that Cassandra, in Aeschylus' representation, fell victim to this global reevaluation of values, Wolf by her own account became obsessed with the project of reconstructing the "real" Cassandra. "Who was Cassandra before anyone wrote about her?" (C 273) Wolf asks in the fourth lecture. After her return from Greece she read a great deal about classical antiquity, as well as a substantial number of contemporary feminist titles, which she lists in the bibliography included in the book edition of her Frankfurt lectures. At the same time concern about the atomic threat to Europe peaked in circles of East and West German women. In both Germanies women were terrified by the armament escalation of the late 1970s, when the Soviet Union and then NATO began stationing nuclear missiles aimed at targets in Europe. A conference in Groningen in April 1981 helped spread the fear that the United States would make Europe the theater of a nuclear war in perhaps three or four years (C 249).

Wolf adopts the historical argument of Engels wholesale—that private property, patriarchy, and class society came into being at the same time. Her writings of this time are spiked with direct and indirect quotations from Engels's *Origin of the Family*: "Patriarchy emerged with class society and private ownership of the means of production."[94] "The overthrow of matriarchy represented the defeat of the female sex in world history. The man seized control in the household, too; the woman was demoted, given menial status, made the slave of his pleasure and a mere tool for the procreation of his children."[95] She also cites Engels in her third Frankfurt lecture: "The first class conflict in history coincides with the development of antagonism between husband and wife in monogamous marriage, and the first class oppression, with the oppression of the female sex by the male" (C 230).

Nevertheless, Wolf becomes less of a feminist Marxist and more of a Marxist feminist. She writes that her study of matriarchal culture changed her way of looking at things comparable to the way her encounter with Marxism did thirty years previously (C 278). For her, the major event in the epochal change proposed by Engels and Bebel was the advent of patriarchy, the hegemony of men over women, and not the advent of private property, the division of people into property owners and have-nots. Nowhere does Wolf imply that socialism's abolition of private property will bring with it the solution of the woman question. Quite the contrary: Wolf writes that the "excessive arms race *on all sides*" (italics mine) relates to "patriarchal structures of thought and government."[96] She thereby expresses her opinion that patriarchy, which leads to war, rules in both West and East. Not only were sentences imputing aggressiveness to the Eastern as well as the Western bloc censored out of the GDR edition of the Lectures, but Wolf's ideological heresy was attacked in the GDR: Wilhelm Girnus, one of the editors of the GDR journal *Sinn und Form* (Meaning and form), castigated *Cassandra* for implying that "history is not at base a struggle between exploiter and exploited, but between men and women, or even more grotesquely, between 'male' and 'female' thinking."[97]

Since the 1970s Wolf had polarized the sexes, ascribing "instrumental reason" and its excesses to men and positive utopian characteristics to women. In *Cassandra*, her innovation is to align the masculine with war and the feminine with peace. She finds an intimate connection between patriarchy, objectification, and violence (C 259). In her Troy, which represents a society in transition, just over the brink of patriarchy, men's consolidation of their power evolves dialectically with the desire for war—and not with the desire for private property, which is elided as a theme. In her Büchner lecture Wolf had argued that a fear of everything that could not be systematized befell men in the early nineteenth century; hence they fail to see or know women, except as women flatter their self-image; women become objects. Now Wolf reperiodizes this argument and dates men's exclusion and repression of the feminine, and hence their fear of it, from the beginning of patriarchy.

Cassandra goes back to the "origins": the time when Clytemnesta killed Agamemnon, and thus when mother right, according to Bachofen, strikes its last blow. The novella shows how a peaceful matriarchal age was supplanted by patriarchy. In Wolf's interpretation Cassandra stands for women just beyond the brink of the transition from matriarchy, for the female voice as it spoke when women still had a social position out of which a genuine voice could come—before it was silenced, appropriated. Presented as Cassandra's interior monologue after she has been captured by the Achaians and taken to Mycenae, where death awaits her, the novel is about a woman's unavailing efforts to make herself heard. Karen H. Jankowsky has asserted that the novel was provocative in the FRG as well as in the GDR because it reached an "unsurpassed level of pathos" in discussing the origins and consequences of patriarchy.[98] Cassandra's most significant public word is "no." Her "no" is at once a "no" to violence (C 114) and a refusal of silence (C 127, 131).

Cassandra, presented as a seer who clairvoyantly sees the inevitable consequences of violence in the midst of those who blindly urge, naively assent to, or merely fail to oppose the war, who attempts to speak the truth amid a cacophonous abasement of language in shouting, orders, expressions of blind obedience, and whimpering (C 8), represents a construction of femininity prefigured by the heroine of "Self-experiment." But in *Cassandra* Wolf problematizes the uncomplicated logic of "Self-experiment," where femininity implied true seeing and true seeing implied true speaking, by inquiring into the dependence of perception and language on power. Power, it is said, blinds (C 42). Moreover, even if you do see, an attachment to power can keep you from speaking out about what you see. *Cassandra* is double-bottomed as a political allegory, with Troy representing the GDR. The idea that dependence on power tends to seal one's lips comments on the much discussed GDR phenomenon of self-censorship and could even, especially in view of Wolf's strategy of blurring the boundary between author, narrator, and character at the start of the text, be interpreted as Wolf's own self-criticism for excessive fidelity to the GDR regime. But it is perhaps also a cautionary message, in the spirit of Woolf's *Three Guineas*, to contemporary women, who are being tempted as never before in history to "buy into" the system, because of the material rewards such collaboration offers. More emphatically than Other, Cassandra turns from an initial envy of men, because they are promoted to more important positions, because within the Trojan priesthood her twin brother Helenos is chosen to be Haruspex, oracle speaker, instead of her even though he is not a seer, to not wanting to be a man on any account. It is violence, the killing of Hector, that changes her mind: "Never again, Hector, dear one, did I want to be a man" (C 111).

Critics have noted the importance of the theme of self-knowledge in the novel.[99] Cassandra is a daughter of the royal house; her affiliation with the powerful prevents her for a long time from speaking what she knows to be true, notably that the Trojan War is founded on a lie; that "Helena of Troy" is a fiction (C 69); and that the war in reality starts because the Trojans want war (C 70). It is only after Cassandra recognizes her ground, her blind spot, in the peripateia of the "heroes' grave," a tomblike prison to which she is confined and from which she arises as if reborn, spiritually disengaged from her father and from Troy, that she attains self-recognition, the position of enlightenment from which she delivers the interior monologue that constitutes the text.[100] Finally, the text suggests that even if you see and speak, and have no power, you will not be listened to. This is the fate of Cassandra's "no."

A skeptical verdict on language emerges from *Cassandra*. Few are its uses, many its abuses. A massive political manipulation of language by the Trojan war machine, which evolves with nascent patriarchy, precedes and overwhelms Cassandra's belated "no." The allusion to the Nazis' distortion of language is inescapable. Cassandra speaks of a "language war" in Troy (C 65), designed to fan the flames of passion for the war: the king suddenly becomes "our mighty king" (ibid.), new martial songs glorifying living warriors replace the tradition of revering only dead heroes.

The Greeks, representatives of full-blown patriarchy and of victory, hence of power, are the exemplars of entrenched blindness in the work. In Wolf's revisionist reading their blindness extends into classical literature's account of Cassandra's vision. Cassandra comments:

> It was the enemy who spread the tale that I spoke "the truth" and that you all would not listen to me. They did not spread it out of malice, that was just how they understood it. For the Greeks there is no alternative but either truth or lies, right or wrong, victory or defeat, friend or enemy, life or death. They think differently than we do. What cannot be seen, smelled, heard, touched, does not exist. It is the other alternative that they crush between their clear-cut distinctions, the third alternative, which in their view does not exist, the smiling vital force that is able to generate itself from itself over and over: the undivided, spirit in life, life in spirit. (C 106–107)

This passage makes Cassandra's own position clear. Truth is not in binary opposition to lie, as the Greeks would have it. There is, Cassandra, insists, a "third alternative," wholeness. Moreover, according to Cassandra (and Wolf), truth is not based on sense perception: Cassandra attains spiritual enlightenment when deprived of the light of sense in the hero's grave. Seerdom means being a conduit for "other realities" (C 106).

Wolf notes that Western literature began with a glorification of violence, with the description of battles and arms, and the "singing" of the "wrath of Achilles," and dissociates herself from it.[101] A feature of the *Cassandra* project that has undoubtedly helped make *Cassandra* not only Wolf's most popular, but also her most analyzed, most canonized work is her project of overthrowing Western aesthetics—because it is in league with the victors, that is, with patriarchy—and proposing a counterversion of its founding work, the *Iliad*.[102] In *Cassandra* she attempts to reconstruct the occulted woman's point of view. Cassandra's account of the Trojan War revokes Homer's: in her interior monologue the story of the *Iliad* becomes a dark story of slaughter, rape, treachery, perversion, abuse of power, and sheer bloodthirstiness. Achilles is not a hero but simply a beast, a murdering, raping, pedophiliac bully who joins lust for violence with violent lust. Cassandra fantasizes a chain of women, mothers and daughters, who will keep her woman's version of the Trojan War alive. She imagines herself begging Clytemnestra to give her a scribe: "But I implore you: Send me a scribe, or better yet a young slave with a keen memory and a powerful voice. Ordain that she may repeat to her daughter what she hears from me. That the daughter in turn may pass it on to her daughter, and so on. So that alongside the river of heroic songs this tiny rivulet, too, may reach those faraway, perhaps happier people who will live in times to come" (C 81). But of course, her version of things does *not* survive. Wolf's choice of historical allegory predicates that Cassandra, for all her dissident heroics, will end up in the victim role. Wolf gives her figure the choice between two kinds of victimhood: assimilation to patriarchal culture (possible if she fled with Aineas, whom she loved), or death. Cassandra chooses death.

The victory of the Achaians over the Trojans stands for the victory of patriarchy over mother right. Yet things are not so simple, not so black and white: the Trojans are willing accomplices in this epochal changeover. Wolf shows how the desire for war is gradually and insidiously instilled in the Trojans, principally by Eumelos, an upstart officer, and by Cassandra's ambitious brother Paris, whom the king wanted killed in infancy because it was prophesied that he would destroy Troy. And in the measure that the Trojans become obsessed by honor and military glory, Troy becomes a man's world; the old equality between the sexes vanishes. In Wolf's reading the war is only ostensibly between the Greeks and the Trojans; in reality it is between the old society, where women were still listened to and had a place, and the new male-dominated order. The losers of the war seem to be less the Trojans than the women: "All of a sudden it was no longer advisable for us women to be out alone. If you saw it properly—only no one ventured to do that—the men of both sides seemed to have joined forces against our women" (C 104).

Many details indicate this transition from matriarchy to patriarchy. In Troy, the worship of the Greek god Apollo (representing the male principle) has, at least officially, displaced worship of the mother goddess Cybele. Yet Cassandra's twin brother Helenus, the augur, puts on women's clothing to read the entrails of animals (C 28).[103] Utopia is figured in the cult of Cybele, which the Trojan women practice secretly in the caves on Mount Ida near Troy; Cassandra prays to Cybele for help. Cassandra wishes upon Achilles, who has killed a thousand people, that (mother) earth will spit out his ashes (C 83). Bachofen recounts that the worship of the moon is important in Amazonism and Demetrian matriarchy, as opposed to the worship of the sun or male power; Cassandra has a troubling dream in which she affirms that the sun shines more brightly than the moon. A direct echo from the Morgan-Engels tradition comes when the power-hungry intriguer Eumelos, who is responsible for fanning war sentiment in Troy, demands to know if Priam "consider[ed] blood ties more important than those of the state" (C 80)—playing on the supplanting of the matriarchal gens by the patriarchal state. Cassandra even feels a certain sympathy for Clytemnestra (C 41–42), symbol of matriarchy. Wolf adds details of her own. Cassandra finds that the Greeks stare at women: "In Troy men don't look at women that way" (C 81). But as the war progresses the climate in Troy changes. When Cassandra was a child, the queen, Hecabe, "often pregnant," sat in a seat resembling a throne, while Priam pulled up a stool next to her (C 13). During the war Hecabe is suddenly barred from council meetings, on grounds that war deliberations are "no longer the concern of women" (C 92). Priam's seat is raised, Hecabe's is not; the king now sits in state over the queen (C 100). Polyxena is "used" like an object to lure Achilles (C 125). Cassandra is married against her will to Eurypilos, a prospective ally of the Trojans (C 133).

In Wolf's Troy, peaceful matriarchal culture is represented as literally "repressed"—out of Troy into the surrounding mountains. Wolf's portrait of the women's commune is, as critics have complained, an idyll bordering on kitsch.[104] In fact Wolf seems not to be conveying her vision of a *future* utopia here but, rather, creating an image of *Urkommunismus*, primitive communism, which, as we have seen, Engels and Bebel associate with mother right. This community of Cybele worshipers, including mainly women but also including a few enlightened men, is significantly located in *nature*, as opposed to palace culture, and moreover is fraught with both

Freudian and traditional symbols of femininity and female fecundity (e.g., cave and willow[105]), so that Roebling calls it the "Mutterwelt."[106] Yet as she rightly argues, the community is not supposed to represent a woman's world, but the "third thing," the unrepressed state. Wolf makes a point of showing how expression and communication in this matriarchal context do not privilege language and reason, but also use the body and the senses.

The message to feminists? Wolf presents two points of view on the right strategy for women in a time of war: Arisbe's and Penthesilia's. Arisbe, a maternal Trojan figure, the "Great Mother," a witchlike wise woman and the center of the matriarchal "counter-world" (C 48) on Mt. Ida, argues against violence and for feminine "difference." The Amazon Penthesilea argues that the war is against women, that men *like* violence, and that women, in adopting violence, are not doing it for their enjoyment but because they must resist (C 118). The narrative avoids taking a clear position between the two. In the Third Lecture, however, Wolf distances herself from women's attempts "to integrate themselves into the prevailing delusional systems" (C 259). Moreover, she says in an interview of the same year that with Penthesilea she wanted to show "how this obsession with femininity can go astray" (FD 125). Wolf may believe in the moral superiority of femininity, but she rejects militant feminism. Feminism must *embrace*: for Wolf's ruling postulate is that *nothing may be rejected or repressed*. With its proper psychoanalytic explanation, everything, even Eumelos' warmongering, even Achilles' crimes, has its place.[107]

It is interesting to compare *Cassandra* and Wolf's much gloomier, less harmonizing novel *Medea*, written after unification. In *Medea* Wolf reuses the *Cassandra* blueprint, so to speak: it is similarly set at the point of transition from matriarchy to patriarchy. Eastern Colchis represents nascent and Western Corinth fully established patriarchy. Just as she sought the "real" Cassandra, Wolf sets out to redeem the memory of the Colchian princess Medea, who in her version becomes a persecuted innocent unjustly defamed in Corinthian legend and every subsequent patriarchal rewriting as the murderess of her children. Critics remarked and Wolf herself admitted that *Cassandra* was a political allegory.[108] In *Medea*, the allegorical dimension is too obvious to be missed. The rich, materialistic class society of Corinth represents West Germany, while mismanaged Colchis with its corrupt old king represents the GDR. If in *Cassandra* the theme of war and violence was central, in *Medea* the focus is the willful distortion of history and the repression of inconvenient memories generally, consonant with Wolf's view that life in the GDR was demonized by the West and left to disappear in a "dark hole of forgetfulness" after unification.[109] Perhaps in order to make this point forcefully, Wolf finds it necessary to make Medea a far more snow-white heroine than Cassandra was. She abandons the problematic of the corrupting influence of power. Unlike Cassandra, Medea is not divided between a desire for truth and an affiliation with power, nor does she undergo a process of self-recognition, but is cast as a courageous moral heroine who "knows herself" right from the start. Patriarchy supervenes not in tandem with the war spirit, as in *Cassandra*, but, seemingly, comes into being simply because men want hegemony. Wolf suggests that repression and oppression of the Other are devices for enhancing one's own self-esteem; one can reserve the designation "good" for oneself if the Other is assigned "bad." In a frightening passage Jason, who instead of helping Medea at her trial rapes her afterwards, concludes that male desire battens on the oppression of women: "We should take women. We should break down their resistance. That's the only way to root out what nature has endowed us with, the vile lust that spills over everything."[110]

Morgner on Matriarchy: Amanda

From the late 1960s women's time-honored role as mother, but yet more their potential for power in that role, captured the imagination of Irmtraud Morgner. The overwhelming, larger-than life reality of childbearing and childrearing as an activity (performed by women) that puts all other activities (performed by men) in the shade becomes a theme in *Trobadora Beatriz* that is continued in *Amanda*. But even in earlier novels Morgner purposefully moves women's lives from the wings into the brilliance of center stage, creating the impression that women's reality is anything but marginal. The charm of an image of women as important and self-sufficient explains Morgner's early interest in primitive matriarchy. The maternal context suggests to her the next step, that women, as mothers, do not need men. Thus in *Hochzeit in Konstantinopel* (1968) Bele tells a tale of parthenogenesis. She eats a clay figure of herself, becomes pregnant, and gives birth. The doctor writes a book prophesying a matriarchal future.

In *Die wundersamen Reisen Gustavs des Weltfahrers* (1972), a collection of tall tales, Morgner devises a feminist utopia in the form of matriarchal "Amazonia," although here she makes a mistake, associating mother right with Mycenae. In Amazonia women rule and are occupied with intellectual pursuits. They support themselves by writing postdoctoral theses for export. Men are kept on a reservation, where they do the washing, sewing, and child care. In contrast to the women, who run around naked, the men are clothed because they are ashamed of their genitals. The race is perpetuated by sperm banks, for which, for eugenic reasons, only 11 percent of the men are selected. War, a "male invention," is unconstitutional.

Amazonia is—if we can believe Morgner's footnote—intended merely parodistically, as an exaggerated counterexample to extreme patriarchy. To judge from a 1972 interview, Morgner had no intention of championing a feminism that sought to tip the scales of power in women's favor, but rather supported a "human" order that made no distinctions between men and women.[111] Her next novel, *Trobadora Beatriz*, corroborates this conclusion. She writes of Persephone and Demeter's attempts at "reinstating matriarchy" but does not affirm these attempts through assent by the heroine; Beatriz is "for the third order" that "should be neither patriarchal, nor matriarchal, but human" (*TB* 20). Persephone and Demeter, who for centuries have been trying to bring about a return of the matriarchy and dethrone "the Lord God," caricature feminists, or one radical feminist position, which Morgner herself did not agree with. Morgner adopts the standpoint, familiar from Bebel and Zetkin and dear to GDR ideology, that socialism is the precondition of women's emancipation.[112] Morgner's "feminism" is undeniable and trenchant, but it presupposes a foundation of existing socialism; it begins only where socialism, in her view, can go no further, where it runs up against the stone wall of custom. Thus Beatriz sympathizes with Persephone and Demeter's cause only so long as she experiences material exploitation as a woman in France. These experiences in the West also drive her to terrorism: "For your mother," she tells Persephone, "I could blow up Paris" (*TB* 61). But her meeting with the GDR communist Uwe Parnitzke seals her conversion from their radical feminism to socialism as the answer to women's as well as to the world's problems: "The last bit of sympathy for Persephone's legal party-liners, who wanted to replace existing injustice with a different injustice, left Beatriz" (*TB* 71).

Although in *Trobadora Beatriz* Morgner thus briskly begins by lampooning Western feminism disguised as "matriarchy," she nevertheless, in the further course of the text, glorifies women's maternal function. The character Valeska finds that her husband's function has exhausted itself with insemination; pregnant and thus "self-sufficient," "as a closed system," she files for divorce (*TB* 215). According to Valeska's "conjectural biography," which she dreams about at age thirty-eight, she forms a family the following year with Gerda and Marie; together the three women have a total of four children, two boys and two girls. They live in a communal apartment that has plenty of space for everyone. Each woman gains a lot of time through this *ménage à trois femmes* and is much freer than she was before. The only children are happy to have siblings. Raising the children in this fashion is easier for the mothers (*TB* 233). Two years after the publication of *Trobadora Beatriz* Christine Wolter would follow suit in this militant tendency to envision a utopia in the form of a women's "marriage" with her story "Ich habe wieder geheiratet" (I have married again, in *Wie ich meine Unschuld verlor* [How I lost my innocence], 1976).

Thus through the mouthpiece of Valeska Morgner entertains the idea that women are self-sufficient; men are more of a liability than an advantage for women and can be dispensed with. When Valeska changes into a man, she reflects about the consequences for her son: "Three fathers? Whether children need even one seems doubtful sometimes; but even patriarchal laws never question the need for a mother" ("Life" 137). These views cannot be written off entirely as Valeska's, for they echo Morgner's construction of a segment of the novel's plot. Laura, the book's second heroine, is a single mother. The novel loses no time in asking who the father might be, but dilates on Laura and her women friends' involvement with her infant son. It is an enormous compliment for Laura's new husband Benno that Laura's son Wesselin calls him "Mamma" (*TB* 378). Glorification of maternity also glimmers up in *Amanda*, where the character Konrad Tenner admits that men feel impotent in contrast to women and asserts that man's invention of science is just a substitute for women's natural gift of procreation (*TB* 219–220).

Like Wolf, Morgner early on shows a strong distaste for male scientists.[113] In *Hochzeit in Konstantinopel* the heroine's husband to be, Paul, is a stock male scientist type. While not wholly negative, he is certainly comical: he works constantly, travels abroad frequently, is fixated on his own immortality and at the same time obsessed with a scientific rival, and perpetually formulates "theories" about everyday life. In the "Rumba auf einen Herbst" portion of *Trobadora Beatriz* science is caricatured as a male religion (*TB* 77–78), self-important and distant from the real world. It is a question not of denouncing men, but conventional masculine ideals. Lutz's ideal of "reason" ("Verstand") is denigrated as incapable of dealing with everyday reality: "One couldn't praise reason enough. Lutz was in his element, he frolicked away up there, where it never smelled of diapers and a thousand trifles" (*TB* 153). Lutz, who reappears in the main body of the novel as one of Beatriz's lovers, retains his character there: "Lutz had fled. Because screaming children cannot be controlled by definitions" (*TB* 147). Lutz also becomes the target of a critique of the male orientation on success and superiority. Laura's disdain for these goals is shared by the ideal man who enters her life, Lutz's younger brother Benno, who criticizes Lutz for neglecting his children and calls him "an awareness dud" (*TB* 273).

In *Amanda*, a sequel to *Trobadora Beatriz* that appeared in the same year as Wolf's *Cassandra*, Morgner changes her mind about matriarchy. Primitive matriarchy appears in a positive light. Beatriz is reborn as a siren. We learn that "in the old days . . . there were many sirens. Then the men took control and introduced what people call history today: private property, class division, exploitation, government authority, wars" (*A* 12). This interpretation of the transition from matriarchy to patriarchy is, of course, based on Engels and hence falls within the penumbra of classic socialist theory, but goes far beyond Engels in placing the blame for the world's ills squarely on men. For Engels private property led to patriarchy. Morgner reverses the order: patriarchy brings private property and various other evils along with it. Some GDR critics duly criticized Morgner's version as an unwarranted attack on the male sex.[114] Like Wolf's *Cassandra*, *Amanda* aims to make a statement about the current danger of war and the necessity of pacifism. As in *Cassandra*, militarism is viewed as the legacy of patriarchy. Traditional women's values—nurturing ("Hegen")—must now gain the upper hand if the planet is to be saved from destruction.

Antimilitarism had already figured as a thematic strand in *Trobadora Beatriz*. This novel, whose loose structure allows Morgner to forsake the adventures of the Trobadora at will and dilate on a spectrum of current events, repeatedly reminds us that the Vietnam War is in progress. Morgner, whose message is urgently pacifist, vividly paints the horrors of this war. Peace, imaged by the Cluny tapestries of the woman with the unicorn, is presented specifically as a dream of women (*TB* 27).

Amanda springs directly out of the major political concerns of the early 1980s, peace and the environment. The novel cites a U.S.

general who declared that another war was expected in the mid-1980s, that this war would take place in Europe, that the war would use nuclear weapons, and that Europe would be destroyed (*A* 514–515, 292). Morgner also cites statistics about the exponentially increasing use of the earth's natural resources (*A* 515), echoing the West German Green Party's politicization of environmental questions in the late 1970s.

The problem in *Amanda* is named patriarchy, and the solution femininity, where femininity is conceived as a set of qualities that women have acquired culturally and that men also have the potential to acquire by culture, although most men do not have them now. The novel anchors its praise of the feminine and its claim for a feminine tradition in which the values of peace and nurturing are paramount in the assumption of a prehistorical age of mother right.[115] Like Engels and Bebel, Morgner identifies this "matristic" age as an age of primitive communism, but unlike Engels and Bebel, she interposes a new victory of femininity between the present day and a future communism. She speaks of the day when "Pandora will return and communism will grow up out of the tradition of primitive communism" (*A* 480).

In an interview of 1984 Morgner made clear that she was interested in myth for the sake of a primitive matristic communism that has left traces there, and that a future communism needs to build on: "The thread of tradition for communism must be taken up in primitive communism. Interest in myth is for me interest in this primitive communistic form of social being. Consequently, what fascinates me is less the ancient myths themselves, which after all have had patriarchal layers superimposed on them, hence layers of a class society, than their matriarchal substratum."[116] In *Amanda* she paints this age of primitive communism as a utopia in which the obscurity of prehistory—which she wisely leaves obscure—vanishes into a bright tapestry of myth and legend. *Amanda* is even longer than *Beatriz* and has an even more outrageous, fantastical, complicated, and allegorical plot. Morgner peoples the novel with deities and creatures from the pre-Olympic age: Gaja the earth mother; Arke the serpent, Gaja's daughter; sirens.

Morgner resurrects Beatriz from the grave to which she consigned her at end of *Trobadora Beatriz* because, she says, the state of the world made Beatriz turn over in her grave. Now, in her third life, Beatriz is a siren. Through the voice of the chatty serpent Arke, the reader is informed that in prepatriarchal times all wise women were reborn as sirens. But under patriarchy the wise women, and hence the sirens, dwindled. A *siren* in this novel seems to stand for an influential—persuasive, indeed irresistible, beautiful—female voice. According to Arke sirens' evil reputation was fabricated by patriarchy. The only trait of sirens that survived into patriarchy was the beauty of their voices, but, characteristic of such rewritings, it was cast as a dangerous attribute: in the *Odyssey* the sirens crouched among the bones of sailors that they had lured off their course with their song (A 41). Like all other sirens, Beatriz has *lost her voice* (where *voice* figures power) because the noise of battles makes sirens forgetful and silent. Nevertheless, Arke encourages her to try to sing, for sirens have an important mission: to persuade nations and governments of the necessity of compromise and peace (A 515–516). The woman's voice must now enter politics.

This novel registers a shift in Morgner's ideological position. Like *Trobadora*, *Amanda* is a concert of voices, women's and men's, who articulate a spectrum of political opinions on the world and on women. Many different views are aired in this polyphonic work. The forest of opinions is even less penetrable than in *Beatriz* because they are frequently attached to figures of uncertain credibility. In particular the character Konrad Tenner, who expresses admiring opinions on women, is suspect, because this one-time resistance fighter turns into a political opportunist and in the end proves a traitor to the witches' cause.[117] Yet if there is a principal message, if one voice is louder and more persuasive than the others, it is not one that, as in *Beatriz*, urges "megalomania," but one that speaks of world peace and ecological conservation and of the means to achieve these ends. The key word for this program is "nurturing." It is a feminine characteristic; men have lost it through culture but are capable of acquiring it again.

Three characters, the heroine Amanda, the daughter of Mother Earth Arke, and Tenner (before he turns negative) are the mouthpieces for this message. In Arke's formulation, which is only slightly varied by Amanda and Tenner (A 445 and A 528): "For several thousand years, the ruling specialist culture has highly developed the ability to nurture—a quality more or less given by nature to both sexes—in women alone. Suddenly the historical moment has come where the threat of annihilation makes this capability essential for the most important public goals" (A 306).

The trio of voices suggests that the matter is self-evident: every thinking person has to agree that the feminine virtues are essential for our survival. Morgner appears, with the Amanda-Arke-Tenner position, to have swung around, in this novel, to an ideological position close to Wolf's—except that she is carefully historical in her arguments, and explicitly eschews biologism. Woman's genius becomes her traditional role of nourisher, giver (Pandora), and harmonizer.

In *Amanda*, in contrast to *Trobadora Beatriz*, Morgner no longer glorifies a feisty, daredevil heroine—a heroine who is capable of laying bombs in Paris. Beatriz herself has changed utterly. No longer an activist, she has become a disempowered scribe who writes in hiding in a cave, then in captivity in a zoo cage. She is a siren who cannot sing and then has had her tongue cut out. We never find out who cut out her tongue, but as the siren Yetunde maintains that all attacks on sirens are performed in the style typical for the country, which in this case is the GDR, we are no doubt meant to infer censorship (chap. 61). Soon after being resurrected as a siren Beatriz has a change of heart. She distances herself from the inventive, outrageous ideas that were her trademark in the first novel: the flight of fancy, the sweep of ideas into limitless space, may be intoxicating, she reflects, but it is not what is needed in the world situation now, where weapons exist that could destroy the world twenty times over. Rather, what is called for is attention to the concrete:

> Evading the concrete belongs to the uncanny phenomena of intellectual history. There is a striking tendency to first head straight for what is most remote and to overlook everything else that one incessantly encounters in closest proximity. The verve of the gestures of striking forth, the adventurousness and daring of expeditions into the distance, deceive as to their motives. Not infrequently it is simply a question of avoiding what is closest, because it is too much for us.... It would be too narrow-minded to damn the adventurousness of the intellect, although it sometimes originates from obvious weakness. It has led to an expansion of our horizon that we are proud of. But the situation of humanity today, as we all know, is so serious that we must devote ourselves to what is closest and most concrete. (*A* 32)

These opinions are echoed by other voices, by Arke (*A* 200) and by a fictitious lecturer at Blocksberg University (*A* 375), and can probably by taken as Morgner's own.

According to an oracle, the mission of a siren, such as Beatriz now is, is to promote love and peace, to turn Prometheus—man—

from his destructive course (*A* 129). Prometheus, in Marcuse's words the "archetype-hero of the performance principle,"[118] occurred repeatedly in GDR literature as the figure for the technological, scientific producer. Morgner embellishes Beatriz's mission and ties it to her central idea of feminizing politics by invoking the Pandora myth (chap. 23). In doing so she draws on Goethe's play *Pandoras Wiederkunft: Ein Festspiel* (Pandora's return: a festival play), a humanitarian version of the legend in which Pandora brings culture, not ruin (*A* 78). This play, as will be seen, has evidently replaced Goethe's *Faust* in Morgner's affections. Through the voice of Beatriz, Morgner notes that in this play Goethe, remarkably, rejects the active Prometheus figure, whom he had represented as a hero in his early work, and instead validates the poet figure Epimethus, who married Pandora after Prometheus spurned her. In Morgner's own rewriting of the myth, Prometheus created the human race, but it was a human race conceived without love and incapable of loving. Pandora, Prometheus' intended spouse, is a benevolent figure, the "all-giver." Her box was not full of evils, but full of cultural gifts. Prometheus' loveless human race wanted only certain gifts in Pandora's box: the useful, measurable things. The other gifts—love of the earth, a sense of harmony and nurturing, the ability to compromise, and peace—escape. Only hope remains. Within the context of this legend, sirens have the task of helping Prometheus remember who Pandora was and ask her to come back, so that a peace-loving human race can finally be born (prologue, chaps. 22, 23, 41, 53, and 72).

Whereas *Trobadora Beatriz* was a book by Laura about Beatriz, this is a book by Beatriz about Laura, who becomes the main character. Beatriz's book, which she claims to be writing for Laura's son Wesselin so that he can read *Amanda* along with *Faust*, is, in contrast to *Trobadora Beatriz*, less a *second Faust* than an alternative to *Faust*, even in some ways a retraction of *Faust*. This second novel of Morgner's planned trilogy does not celebrate Faustian overreaching, megalomania, and genius; it regards with skepticism the related "Promethean" pursuit of "measurable riches and truths, increased knowledge, a sense of right and use, inflexibility, patriotism, conquest, victory, prosperity."[119] Beatriz is no longer Faustian. In a 1984 interview Morgner speaks of how she gradually came to see the sinister side of her "youthful identification figure," Faust, whom she still wholly affirmed in *Beatriz*: "Goethe's distance from the Faust figure, the figure's ambivalence, its dark side that makes perversions possible, even powerful perversions, all this I have gradually begun to understand during the work on my trilogy and in correspondence to global political escalations."[120] The text of *Amanda* suggests that a parallel can be drawn not between Beatriz and Faust but between Laura and Faust.[121] Like *Trobadora Beatriz* this text is stuffed with quotations, self-quotations, and allusions, including an abundance of allusions to *Faust*, which various critics have identified.[122] As a child Laura was attracted to the Faust figure despite admonitions that the role was unfeminine; as a young woman she emulated Faust by dabbling in alchemy. But at that point the career of this "female Faust" begins to diverge sharply from Faust's and in fact seems like a travesty of it. There are three major differences between Laura and Faust.

First of all, Laura pursues alchemy in a different spirit from Faust: she seeks what Morgner defines as the immemorial goal of woman, the "second order philosopher's stone" or "liquid silver," which has the properties of "transporting" one or "carrying" one "away" ("entrücken"), of making one undivided and indivisible, and of laying an island at one's feet. *Entrückung*, a concept implying being "carried away" in all of its senses and an El Dorado foreign to the feminist stock-in-trade, seems to represent Morgner's own original attempt to define an object of feminine desire. It already makes an appearance in *Trobadora Beatriz*, where Laura's sphinx-back ride from Berlin to Paris to view the Cluny tapestries of the Lady and the Unicorn by night was described as an "Entrückung" (TB 397). Morgner thereby ascribes to women an entirely different set of desiderata from the immemorial goal of men, which she designates, traditionally, as the philosopher's stone that will turn base metals to gold and promises to "lay the world at your feet." Moreover, the feminine ideal of a well-being defined as centeredness, inviolability, and the release from practical cares is very far from, indeed almost the antithesis of, Faustian striving and repudiation of quiescence.

Second, when Laura tries to achieve her goal through alchemy, the devil does not offer her a pact but simply punishes her by splitting her, thereby doing to her exactly what she sought to avoid. No deal needs be struck here, echoing a prior conversation between God and the devil; whereas Faust has a secret ally in "the Lord," for Laura the bosses of heaven and hell are simply two faces of male power, as Morgner's parodistic "Wager on the Blocksberg," where Archangel Zacharias and Archdevil Kolbuk bet over which of them will marry Laura, makes clear. In Laura's case the devil can simply crassly exercise his will.

Third and finally, Laura's further quest for her goal must, in order to succeed, take the immensely long detour of feminizing the government and society. Woman's temptation, which she must resist, is to opt out of the struggle for political reform and find an "individual solution." Inasmuch as Laura succumbs to that temptation—she sends Heinrich Fakal into the devils' citadel Blocksberg to steal the magical "drinking silver" for her—her story is a tragedy. The final chapter of the novel ends with a parody of the end of *Faust I*: Laura, seeking the disappeared Heinrich Fakal, cries "Heinrich," and a voice from behind responds, "Er ist gerichtet" ("He is condemned"). But in the short "Silvesternachspiel" (New year's eve epilogue), which suggests a more positive outcome for the plot, the witches sing optimistic feminist verses in the distinctive rhythm of the angelic choirs at the end of *Faust II*.

One of Beatriz's first tasks is to reread *Leben und Abenteuer der Trobadora Beatriz* and criticize it. Her main critique is that "Morgner's book stinks of inner censorship." Morgner falsely portrayed Laura as industrious, contented, cooperative, inconspicuous, and self-sacrificing, whereas in fact, Laura is a split woman—split between a woman (her tame half) and a witch named Amanda (her enterprising half). The metaphor of "splitting" is familiar from *Trobadora Beatriz*. "Witch" is part of the contemporary feminist imaginary: in the early 1970s feminists had become interested in witches as the outstanding example of patriarchy's vilification of women. Barbara Ehrenreich and D. English wrote in *Witches, Midwives, Nurses* (1973) that so-called witches had in fact been "wise women," women healers. "Witch" then rapidly became an honorific designation, an identification figure, for feminists.[123] In the GDR the Unabhängiger Frauenverband, which was founded just after the fall of the Wall, adopted the witch symbol, where the witch holds up her fingers in a V for "victory," on their most famous poster (see illustration).

In *Amanda* Morgner capitalizes on the new, popular, positive witch image and revamps Laura, so to speak, by having her born as a "clever witch." Her biography thus becomes paradigmatic for today's intelligent woman. In this new version Laura starts life as a peppy, intelligent little girl, a "troublemaker" ("Querkopf"). She balks at adopting passive female roles and takes male models—her father, Don Juan, and Faust. When a resistance fighter, a classmate's father, says that "woman is the hinterland of the soldier," Laura throws her full glass out of the window and leaves the party (*A* 112).

The Unabhängiger Frauenverband's first poster. The Unabhängiger Frauenverband (Independent Women's Association) was founded in East Berlin on 3 December 1989 during the Wende by twelve hundred GDR women. The poster says: "All women are courageous! strong! beautiful!" With permission of the artist, Anke Feuchtenberger.

Beatriz corrects the account of Laura's studies in *Trobadora Beatriz*: Laura did not study German literature, but matriarchal prehistory. This revision complements the antiwar theme of the novel: Laura, having read Heraclitus' phrase that strife is the "father" of all things, wanted to find out what the mother of all things is (chap. 35).

At this point patriarchy, disguised as the devil, steps in to lobotomize this all-too-free spirit. His excuse is a quarrel between Amanda and her lover over whether they should settle down and have children (his wish) or not (hers). The devil—who perhaps represents patriarchy as *socialism*—declares that there is a "secondary contradiction" ("Nebenwiderspruch")—SED jargon for the "woman question"—in Amanda that is threatening to become a "primary contradiction" ("Hauptwiderspruch")—that is, a full-fledged class antagonism—and therefore has to be operated out (*A* 118). He halves her so that she can make a husband and children happy: "Better precision work by Head Devil Kolbuk than the work of improvisation by customs. Ordinary ladies are served by any old men," chatters Kolbuk. But ironically, Tenner leaves Laura, as her housewifely half does not appeal to him. The other half becomes the witch Amanda.

The plot of the novel consists of Laura's and Amanda's quest to become reunited, which in turn, according to Amanda, presupposes getting rid of the rule of the male devils and changing the world into a utopian place. For Amanda instructs Laura early on that their hope lies in politics, not alchemy: "Distillation is not possible—we must conqueror Orplid" (*A* 223). The "Silvesternachspiel" is guardedly hopeful; it implies that the latter goal has been accomplished. Additionally, Beatriz gets a substitute tongue. But nothing is said about whether Amanda and Laura are reunited.

Whereas in *Trobadora Beatriz* splitting was implicit and had Faustian implications, here it is explicit and is represented, as in Wolf, as purely negative, disempowering, crippling: "No original inventions can be expected from split beings," says Amanda (*A* 222). What does "split" mean? When Morgner applies it to woman as well as to an occasional male character in *Amanda*, it implies the repression of a strong desire. Apropos of women specifically she also seems to use it precisely in its Beauvoirian sense. Woman is split between her enslavement to the species versus her commitment to herself, to her transcendence.

Morgner fancifully rewrites world history in order to show how men came to be in power and women divided. Dividing, Morgner proposes in *Amanda*, is foreign to women by virtue of their historical mode of being, for in ancient days, "the women, occupied as they were with farming and children, and thus constantly dealing with totalities, found it difficult to divide. The men became specialized first"(*A* 91). If this beginning at least flirts with the Marxist idea that being determines consciousness, the rest of Morgner's account drops a materialist mode of explanation and simply becomes the history of male egotism and broken promises to women. Thus the men, the early experts in "specialization," took the concept of "good" for themselves and gave women the concept "bad." Wise women began to seek to disrupt this "order" through magic and science. Men followed them, but took over the project themselves and assigned women the role of onlooker. The devil got wind of these endeavors and imprisoned all the "troublemakers," male and female. He then devilishly offered amnesty to one sex—either sex. In an exchange for a promise to the women to re-create the magical "drinking silver" they wanted, the men achieved their release. Women remained imprisoned. But then, in Morgner's myth, men pursued the "gold" philosopher's stone. Thus they took up alchemy, chemistry, mathematics, and all the other analytic sciences, and got so interested in these things that they forgot everything else. They did not keep their promise to women by which they got the power initially, to re-create the "drinking silver" and thereby free them. Indeed, Laura reflects on another occasion, echoing a common feminist complaint, that in all the revolutions men and women have made together, the women got the short end of the stick afterward (chap. 34). As things progressed in early history, women's sorry lot was to be "halved"—that is, exploited for their use value, by "custom" (*A* 95). The useless half just withered away. The devil—whose referent here seems to be patriarchy as state power—then halved all the ones that were left, the resistant ones, the "troublemakers," and kept the useless halves as "witches" (presumably, smart women who collaborate with patriarchy, who "make it" in a male world).

The Laura/Amanda duo resembles the Laura/Beatriz duo of the earlier novel: Laura is her old practical self, but apolitical; she mainly just wants to give herself and her son a better life. Amanda is the enterprising, political, theoretical one with ideas. Yet Amanda is not the old Beatriz. She is less quixotic and more of a peace activist than Beatriz was. Her projects are in the realm of political allegory. Her politics are prefigured by an incident in Amanda/Laura's childhood: on the day of Germany's unconditional surrender Laura and a friend captured the forbidden bleaching yard as a playground, taking advantage of the fact that the grown-ups, who all had some past involvement with the Nazis to hide, didn't dare stop these innocents. Now, in present time, Amanda's plan centers on capturing Castle Blocksberg, the devil's domain, which stands for the high echelons of power and is also a kind of intellectual beehive or think tank. Currently, Castle Blocksberg is exclusively in the hands of men. The novel recounts a series of legendary male power grabs that started when Mother Earth's male consort imprisoned her in ancient days. The only women in the devils' citadel are the "witches," the useless halves of the feminine "troublemakers" in the devils' keep, and these witches are relegated to a brothel in the neighboring Hörselberg. Amanda favors taking over Castle Blocksberg in order to experimentally develop feminine values in usable form there. She finds that Castle Blocksberg with its double standard is currently not useful. Here Morgner's critique seems aimed at "patriarchy as socialism": Castle Blocksberg is figured as a political organization within a socialist context, for it is said: "A double standard as a place of refuge also has to more than damage socialism. Castle Blocksberg with the annex Hörselberg sees to it that patriarchal customs do not die out. But a socialism that does not abolish the predominance of men cannot develop communism" (*A* 446–447).[124] Amanda also observes elsewhere that on earth women may be getting somewhere, but "all portals in the castle are still barricaded against us" (*A* 240). It is well known that there were no women in the upper echelons of the GDR government.[125]

Turning from the question of feminist goals to the issue of feminist means, Morgner caricatures contemporary feminist positions through witches' "factions." There are three factions, which are succinctly described by the Walpurgisnacht commentator in each Walpurgisnacht commentary: "The WUU or Redskirt faction with Isebel at its head values the art of war developed by men for its own use and is hostile towards men. The Greenskirts or Holle's daughters led by Hulle only know what they don't want, namely: to be like men. In other words, they don't know what they want. The Owl faction headed by Amanda is androgynous and in a position to instill dangerous tendencies in their raven customers" (*A* 329–30, 410). Monika Meier points out that the male commentator simplifies the positions of the three factions and probably plays up their differences.[126] The leaders of the two principal factions, the Redskirts and the Owls, also articulate their own positions, however, and it becomes evident that they disagree about how women should take over Schloß Blocksberg. Amanda, the leader of the Owls, is antihierarchical, communistic, and pacifistic (*A* 231, 406, 233). An upturned pyramid, symbol of reversed hierarchy, hence utopia ("Himmelreich," "paradise," *A* 16), is her sign. Her basic strategy for taking over the castle is ideological infiltration (*A* 330). She adumbrates her role as follows: "I shall play through the conquest of the golden pot in my head, in the sandbox, and on the drum in many different variations" (*A* 132). Use your imagination, influence children, and make your position heard: this is presumably the same strategy that is articulated more clearly by the siren Sappho, Gaja's favorite siren, who recommends feminine infiltration ("Unterwanderung") of male culture, on the model of Greek culture's infiltration of Roman culture (*A* 481). It is hinted that the "Greenskirt" witches agree with this position, since one of Frau Holle's daughters voices it early on (*A* 107).

The Redskirts, or Isebel faction of "witchist" (feminist) witches hates men, but wants to appropriate their militaristic methods for their own ends (*A* 436–438). Early in the novel the wise serpent Arke warns against this strategy, observing that if women adopt a male style in order to assert themselves successfully, if they use men's means and grab for power, they will arrive at men's ends (*A* 80–81). Toward the end the heroine Amanda, who becomes president of the Blocksberg in the "Silvesternachspiel" and whose political position the end thus seems to underwrite, discredits the Isebel faction and criticizes radical feminism as follows:

> But the WUU [witches' underworld's underworld, *A* 436] movement would not only simply take over the sexism of the average raven under a different sign. It would also take over their instrumental reason and their concepts of power. And what would be the worst and downright catastrophic for the impending battle: by battle, Isebel could only imagine a pitched battle. Instead of utilizing thousands of years of female experience, the leadership of the WUU would disciple itself to a male "military art" that presupposes power apparatuses. Against this "art of war"—the word itself could only be said unwillingly—witches could only accomplish something if they got out of it. Isebel's strategy, however, did not differ in principle from that of the head devil. (*A* 444)

Despite her sharp critique of militant feminism Morgner does not back off completely from Valeska's dictum that "one would have to be a man" in *Beatriz*. That position is articulated by Catherine the Great of Russia (in her reincarnation as a siren) as a serious pragmatic consideration. The siren Katarina, in a conversation with Arke that sounds as if it could have been a conversation between Christa Wolf and some more practical thinker like Morgner herself, and in fact sounds like the conversations between Arisbe and Penthesilea in Wolf's *Cassandra*, laughs at Arke's declaration that women must not enter politics. She observes that women can't simply get political power—not even where they have the right to work and talk. The right to work is not the same as power. Women who want to rule are *forced to become like men*. "Being permitted to talk and work does not automatically lead into the control centers of power" (*A* 307). Katarina continues: "As czarina and androgynous person—all talented people are androgynous—I had to hide my feminine qualities and cultivate my male ones. The few women who operate in higher political positions today also do not have any other choice. They are coworkers. As in the lower positions. The farther the distance from the summits of power, the greater the proportion of female coworkers" (*A* 307).[127]

The glorification of women's peacefulness nevertheless carries the day. The end of the novel speaks, albeit vaguely, of an ultimate positive ending sometime in the future. Morgner's feminism remains faithful to socialism. Thus Laura's quest for "drinking silver," condemned by Beatriz as an "individualistic strategy" (*A* 533), fails. Yet the feminization of Castle Blocksberg, a utopian goal that is implicitly compatible with socialism, happens. But we are not told how: it is a "long story."

Women and Peace

Thus in 1983, the rapprochement between Morgner's and Wolf's thinking is close. It testifies to a centering of feminisms in the early 1980s around the issue of peace, an issue on which there was widespread agreement among women and transcended factionalism. Both Wolf and Morgner connect woman constructed as mother; primitive matriarchy as extolled by Bachofen and Bebel; the traditional feminine virtues of loving, caring, and nurturing; and peace. Wolf's feminist strategy is, as ever, moral. Cassandra is a courageous dissenter who has morality on her side, but who is ultimately a victim rather than a positive model for identification. Morgner manages a better match between her return to turn-of-the-century domestic ideals and present-day feminism, since her plot stages a power grab and thus suggests that pacifism and femininity can forge an alliance with activism and success rather than being eternally married to passivity and victimhood.

It should be evident that Wolf's and Morgner's praise of the feminine, for all its nineteenth-century roots, cannot be evaluated as regression to nineteenth-century essentialism or domesticism. Wolf and Morgner cannot be seen to have made their peace with traditional domestic values but, rather, are trying to infuse them with new energy under changed circumstances. They appear with a strong "alienation effect," to use Bertolt Brecht's term, in the GDR context, where women were not at home, but at work; where the party line on gender was that men and women are essentially the same; and where women felt in danger of being coopted by an achievement-oriented work ethic and frustration at the cold war remilitarization about which they had no say.

Wolf and Morgner found followers among other GDR women writers of the 1980s in their reinforcement of the connection between women and peace. In her short novel *Respektloser Umgang* (Disrespectful company, 1986) Helga Königsdorf turns to the improbable topic of science in order to forge more securely the link between women and pacifism: the narrator, a woman scientist, fantasizes that the woman atomic physicist Lise Meitner (1878–1968) tried to forestall the discovery of the atom bomb, while Meitner, appearing to the present-day narrator as a phantom, bequeaths to her the mission of averting the nuclear threat.[128] Renate Apitz in *Hexenzeit* (1984) stages a mythic appeal to the Norns from "the Realm of the Mothers" as an episode in the novel.[129] The women of Europe—thousands of women from all historical periods and all classes—issue forth for the first time in history from the Realm of the Mothers and march for months toward the Norns. Their message: death threatens Europe; the Norns must wake up and weave peace! Interesting here is the identification of the peace movement with women construed as *mothers*, that is, the creators of life and hence opposed to all destruction. Will the hand that rocks the cradle indeed be the hand that rules the world? Perhaps, because the Norn of the Future, Skuld, listens to the women sympathetically. No understanding of GDR feminism is complete without understanding its reideologizing of the maternal.

4 Writing Women's Images

> The truth is that when we write of a woman, everything is out of place—culminations and perorations; the accent never falls where it does with a man. . . . A porpoise in a fishmonger's shop attracted far more attention than a lady who had won a prize.
> —Virginia Woolf, *Orlando*

> As flowers turn toward the sun, by dint of a secret heliotropism the past strives to turn toward that sun which is rising in the sky of history.
> —Walter Benjamin, *Illuminations*

It is a commonplace of Marxist thought that the material relationships of an age condition its intellectual production. The class that enjoys economic supremacy spontaneously and naturally confirms its power by producing an ideology. It propagates this ideology, which serves to justify its government and its laws, as a law of nature, as eternal truth. Marx and Engels wrote in *The German Ideology*:

> The ideas of the ruling class are in every epoch the ruling ideas, i.e. the class which is the ruling *material* force of society, is at the same time its ruling *intellectual* force. The class which has the means of material production at its disposal, has control at the same time over the means of mental production, so that thereby, generally speaking, the ideas of those who lack the means of mental production are subject to it.[1]

Not only does the ruling class itself labor nolens volens under a "selfish misconception"[2] about the nature of things, but, because of its hegemony, it universalizes its own false consciousness, so that even the underclass ends up believing in the ideology of its oppressors. The oppressed are thereby persuaded that their oppression is given, justified, and natural instead of contingent and changeable.

The early-twentieth-century "crisis in historicism," initiated by Benedetto Croce and further theorized by Karl Heussi, Charles Beard, and others, asserted vis-à-vis an earlier ideal of objective history that all history is contemporary and subjective. According to the new insight there is no objectively given past. Each age reinterprets the past to suit its own purposes. Marxists responded to this historical relativism not by relinquishing their claim to the validity of their own version of history, but by emphasizing that history has traditionally been written by the rulers to the exclusion of the oppressed. Twentieth-century social history was born of the insight that the lives of ordinary people had been dropped out of historiography and hence consigned to oblivion. As E. P. Thompson famously put it in *The Making of the English Working Class* (1963), the agency of working people needed to be rescued from "the enormous condescension of posterity."[3] Writers who were part of the immediate intellectual heritage of GDR writers, Bertolt Brecht and Walter Benjamin, eloquently formulated the idea that history has been written by and for the victors, that the powerful sought written commemoration of themselves and their deeds in the interest of their own propagandistic self-imaging, and that the oppressed classes were thus persuaded that they had no history. In his 1934 poem "Questions from a Worker who Reads" Brecht has his reading worker ask a string of "naive" questions, which begins:

> Who built Thebes of the seven gates?
> In the books you will find the names of kings.
> Did the kings haul up the lumps of rock?

Brecht's worker comes to the conclusion that historiography tells the stories of great men and their victories, to the exclusion of those who actually did the work:

> Every page a victory.
> Who cooked the feast for the victors?
> Every ten years a great man.
> Who paid the bill?[4]

In his 1940 essay "Theses on the Philosophy of History" Walter Benjamin stages a confrontation between two schools of historiography, between so-called objective history or what he calls "historicism," which he designates as the losing position, and its victorious challenger, "historical materialism," or partisan, Marxist history. Benjamin eloquently accuses the former of inevitably siding with the victors and excoriates the historiography and the cultural canon that result:

> With whom [do] the adherents of historicism actually empathize [?] The answer is inevitable: with the victor.... Whoever has emerged victorious participates to this day in the triumphal procession in which the present rulers step over those who are lying prostrate. According to traditional practice, the spoils are carried along in the procession. They are called cultural treasures, and a historical materialist views them with cautious detachment. For without exception the cultural treasures he surveys have an origin which he cannot contemplate without horror. They owe their existence not only to the efforts of the great minds and talents who have created them, but also to the anonymous toil of their contemporaries. There is no document of civilization which is not at the same time a document of barbarism.[5]

In a discussion group on "Literature and consciousness of history" at the Seventh Writers' Congress of the GDR in November 1973, participating GDR writers echoed these ideas of Brecht's and Benjamin's. Thus Volker Braun noted, citing Benjamin: "The consciousness of history is self-consciousness. The reality we deal with is working history, and what we customarily call history, is 'the object of a construction' loaded with 'present time' (Benjamin)."[6] Claus Küchenmeister said: "Every ruling class or every class trying to gain power prepares history.... Oppressed peoples—also classes—were and are always made to believe that they don't have a history, that they are devoid of history."[7]

Writing Women into History

The application of these ideas to women is abundantly familiar today. It is a standard complaint of the Western women's movement that written history is *men's* history, that women have been excluded from history, and that it is therefore imperative to write the history of women now. These points were made forcefully by Mary Beard in *Woman as Force in History* (1946). Surveying histories and works of literary criticism written by American men, she finds that they tend simply not to mention the significant achievements of women.[8] The same argumentation was already advanced by the turn-of-the-century socialist Lily Braun. At the beginning of her extensive history of women *Die Frauenfrage* (The woman question, 1901) she criticizes historiography from a Marxist point of view that anticipates Brecht's poem:

> Natural human egoism invested historiography with class character. The rulers and educated people did not see beyond their own sphere; just as people speak only of the leader of the army as the victor in campaign reports, dedicate all the laurels to him alone, and build monuments to him, little noticing the thousands who actually fought the battles, in the same way the common people, the carriers of human history, were almost forgotten over those who, favored by good fortune or by talent, towered above the masses and were visible from afar.[9]

The consequence for women's history is obviously that "the history of women's development takes up an infinitesimal space in the general history of humanity as it is transmitted to us from childhood on. It is above all a history of wars and therefore one of men that we have had to commit to memory."[10]

In the present day no woman has insisted on the necessity of women's history more outspokenly than Irmtraud Morgner. Asked in a 1972 interview whether she had a central theme, she replied: "Yes: the entrance of women into history."[11] In statements and publications of subsequent years she lost no opportunity to speak for the importance of women's history and to explain why she considered it essential. For Morgner history is the sine qua non for present-day women's self-confidence. She believes that having a history gives people courage, and that, conversely, not having a history robs them of the confidence necessary for action. She reiterates again and again, both *in propria persona* and through the mouths of fictional characters in *Die wundersamen Reisen Gustavs des Weltfahrers* (1972) and *Trobadora Beatriz* (1974), that anyone who wants to accomplish something great needs the support of history. In the discussion group on "Literature and Consciousness of History" at the Seventh Writers' Congress of the GDR on 15 November 1973, just alluded to, she said: "When you want to set about doing something significant, you cannot do without the support of history."[12] The characters Bele in *Gustav* and Uwe Parnitzke and Bele H. in *Trobadora Beatriz* echo this idea with only slight variations in phrasing.[13] Morgner's standard illustration of her thesis is a member of the nobility, whose poise rests on the knowledge that his family tree reaches back to the Middle Ages. It is clear that when Morgner says "history," she means image rather than fact. She is calling for role models, factual or fictional, for precedents that women can have recourse to, for inspiring precursors that women can emulate.

In the same discussion group "Literature and Consciousness of History" Morgner made a remarkable statement. Before Morgner spoke up, the topic of discussion had wandered from socialism's respect for history and what the attitude of present writers toward literary tradition should be, to history and class consciousness, to the recent Nazi past and the right of today's youth to learn the facts, to the necessity of building a socialist consciousness in today's youth through historiography. There was an extensive debate, with many participants, about the "fathers," the positive models in German history as well as the often less positive actual fathers.[14] Morgner's contribution exploded into this discourse: "The whole time the discussion here has been about the fathers. The largest part of the male half of humanity, the powerless men, has been historically expropriated for thousands of years; but the other, female half of humanity, the slaves of the slaves, has in this sense been doubly expropriated."[15] More eloquently and forcefully than previous speakers, she spoke of the psychological importance of having a history. Echoing Benjamin and Brecht, she affirmed that written history is the history of the rulers. But she took issue with Brecht's "Questions from a Worker who Reads" for leaving women out of account. The workers, the nameless slaves, she countered, were expropriated from history for thousands of years, but they at least left visible monuments behind. Women, as the slaves of the slaves, left behind no record at all—yet the great artistic, intellectual, and technical achievements of history were based on their labor. The phrase "the slaves of the slaves" was to become another leitmotiv in her works and interviews. She declared that writing women's history—which must necessarily take the form of legend—is one of the great missions of literature: "To reverse historical expropriation after the reversal of economic expropriation, to make palpable to the people who bear the burden of carrying our state forward that their legendary history is their advantage—that is what I consider a great mission of literature."[16] In 1977 she observed that being expropriated from history is *as bad as* being expropriated from the means of production.[17] The implication of such a statement is that it is as important to change consciousness as it is to change economic relationships, and that the historical mission of literature is therefore as important as the communist revolution! In *Amanda* Morgner extended the analogy between literature and economics by speaking of men's "monopoly" on explanations of the world (*A* 79, 287). Through the persona of the witch Isebel she announces that it is important to build myths, because power is gained not only militarily, but also ideologically (*A* 49).

As early as *Die wundersamen Reisen Gustavs des Weltfahrers* (written 1967/68, published 1972), we find out that when Morgner says "history," she means "fiction." If no so-called historical record of the past was written, then legends must take its stead. This novel does not yet foreground gender consciousness or play it off against class consciousness. Gustav, the fictive author of the tall tales that make up most of the novel, drives a garbage truck. Therefore, he "was by culture a liar, not by nature. The creative forces of the powerless were working in him."[18] His tall tales realize his dream to be a locomotive driver and see the world. His son profits from his father's fictitious past to become a real locomotive driver; his granddaughter advances to university study. Bele H., the granddaughter and also the fictitious author of the novel, criticizes history as it issued from the mouths of professors and from books, noting that she experienced it as a "threat"[19]—though whether on account of her working-class background or because she is a woman is left open. The afterword by Bele's double, the "editor" Beate Heidenreich, makes clear, however, that women specifically have been been distorted by history.[20]

Morgner's *Trobadora Beatriz* presents not only the problem but also a solution to the problem on a grand scale. With the fantastical story of Beatriz, Morgner makes good her word to write women into history, through legend if necessary. Explicit theorizing accompanies the story of Beatriz and clarifies the author's intentions in creating the character. An array of different characters protests that existing history has been written by and for men, and that women need their history. Laura Salmann speaks of "historiography" as "this male sea of egoism" (*TB* 26). Beatriz presents herself as the poet who will ask the question of women's history. She runs into Bele H. (the heroine of *Die wundersamen Reisen Gustavs des Weltfahrers*) in Split, who tendentiously mentions Brecht's poem of the reading worker: "'In it, the poet has the question raised of the creativity that was not recorded in books. Of the slaves who built the cities for example, who left nameless but visible traces of their abilities; about the men. I am waiting for the poet who could have a reading woman worker pose the questions,' said Bele H. 'Questions about the slaves of the slaves who were not able to leave visible traces of their abilities.'—'You are probably waiting in vain for a male poet,' I (Beatriz) said; 'the female poet is near . . .'" (*TB* 194). Even more important, Beatriz herself is meant to be women's history personified. The Irmtraud Morgner character in the novel calls her "a typical case of creating a legend by correcting history" (*TB* 28). More explicitly still, Morgner herself says in an interview of 1977: "In a certain sense history appears in person in this figure of Beatriz."[21] In Beatriz women's history appears in heroic guise: Beatriz stands for women's genius, desire, and quest for subject status throughout history. With her revolutionary ideas, zany actions, resourcefulness, and erotic freestyle, Beatriz is meant to be an inspirational model for today's women.

In *Amanda* Morgner approaches the same topic from a different angle. In an interview in 1976 Morgner had said that women's history as it exists consists almost only of black chapters.[22] In *Amanda* she takes on some of these chapters in both history and legend and undertakes to de-demonize them. Reflecting on the figure of the siren, she remarks (through the mouthpiece of the character Arke) on the mechanism by which old legends are subverted: an original trait is exaggerated until it comes to have the opposite value. Arke postulates that the sirens of matriarchal prehistory were wise women reincarnated, who had the capability of "bringing forth beauty" (*A* 41). In patriarchal Homeric times they kept this attribute, but were restyled as dangerous temptresses who lured and ate men. Morgner also looks critically at the legend of Walpurgisnacht on the Brocken—a legend that led to thousands of women being burned as witches—and asserts that it is the distortion of a historical reality: in Charlemagne's time the Saxons used to retire to lonely places in order to celebrate their religious festivals secretly. Conversely, Morgner observes in *Amanda* that the unrecorded history of women is a history of crimes against the female sex (*A* 184). In her fanciful rewriting of the history of creation and of the world, which explains how women came to be split beings, she humorously, if maliciously, ascribes a sequence of such "crimes" to men.

Starting in the late 1970s Christa Wolf also began explicitly to deplore women's exclusion from history. In her 1979 essay on

Karoline von Günderrode "The Shadow of a Dream" Wolf speaks of women's "historyless state" (*AD* 138). Two years later, in her speech "Speaking of Büchner," she expressed herself more forcefully: "It is Rosetta's fate to live invisible to herself and to Leonce, speechless, stripped of reality, in a space that is denied, soundproofed, manipulated away, and which the rest of her world cannot see no matter how hard they try.... She lets her own history be taken away from her" (*AD* 181). In her fourth Frankfurt lecture Wolf says that the history of women has yet to be written: "Woman as an intellectual has existed in appreciable numbers only for the last sixty or seventy years. We know stories of her and about her, but *her* history—a history of incredible exertion and courage, but also of incredible self-denial and renunciation of the claims of her nature—has still to be written. It would be, at the same time, the history of one of the undersides of our culture" (*C* 294). From her investigation of the women Romantics through *Cassandra* to *Medea* (1996) Wolf's writing represents an attempt less to reconstruct than to re-create women's history, to foreground the presumptive role of women in the historical process, to forge a hypothetical feminine response, "from below" and inevitably oppositional, to history as made by men, and, most important, to justify her own construction of the feminine by giving it historical roots and motivations. While her interest in giving women a history is more recent and less theoretically elaborated than Morgner's, she has done as much to create women's history (or women's legends) as the former.

Wolf's most thoroughgoing work on women's history to date is her recent novel *Medea*. Here Wolf, tacitly affirming the theses of Brecht and Benjamin, demonstrates how memory, and hence historiography, are controlled by the interests of the powerful. In her rewriting, the Greeks in the period of burgeoning patriarchy are driven by a compulsion to fuel their own self-regard at the expense of an "other" comprising, in particular, women. The Corinthian king Creon literally kills (in the person of his daughter and heiress to the throne) and represses the possibility of woman's power. Seeking a scapegoat, the Corinthians then successfully transform the innocent wise woman Medea into a model of depravity for posterity. Like *Cassandra*, the novel doubles as a political allegory of East and West, so that the demonization of Medea by the Greeks is meant to suggest the postunification demonization of the GDR by the West.

Writing Woman's Images

The project of writing women into history, whether through historiography or literature, immediately raises the question: How should it be done? In what role should women be cast? History and literature purport to mirror, but they also model. While writers turn to life for characters whose stories merit the telling, people, under pressure of self-definition, turn to history and literature for examples of congenial and successful personalities who can serve as models for their own life stories. When a writer writes about a woman, therefore, an image, a possible model for imitation, is at stake. Until recently women as subjects of history have been all but submerged. The historical image of women arising out of artistic representations seems, from the vantage point of the second half of the twentieth century, to be a quaint and antiquated distortion, if not an actual "job" emanating from suspect ulterior motives. It demands to be stripped off. For a feminist writer the question then becomes how to redo women, how to push them onto stage as new characters, how to give them a more strategic role. This is not an innocent, but a political enterprise. For specific contextual reasons, as will be seen, GDR "feminism" revolved around the issue of redoing women's images, of creating a new feminine identity, to a much greater degree than its Western counterpart.

We live in an age where the *media*tion of the self-image by literature, film, photography, and so forth is particularly strong. In the twentieth century young people no longer expect or are expected to tread in their parents' footsteps, but to "choose" their own path in life. No one was more aware of the importance of the image (*Leitbild*) and of the modeling role of literature than politicians in the communist countries. The existence of a doctrine of "socialist realism," which impresses literature into the service of ideology, attests that the communist countries, far more than the capitalist West, seriously believed that literature, by constructing a collective imaginary and playing on "identification, communion, sentiment,"[23] could guide young persons down the right path. Particularly since Stalin co-opted literature as a propaganda tool and told writers that they were the "engineers of the human soul"[24] in 1932—the date when socialist realism was prescribed to writers in the Soviet Union—communist aesthetics has viewed literature as an ideology machine to help build communism by changing consciousness. The dominant strategy involved constructing positive models for imitation.

In such a climate, literature was a priori political. Every literary work was written in the awareness of conforming or failing to conform to the scheme the government prescribed, to the works it held up for praise or blame. Although the idea of producing literature according to a scheme initially met with resistance in the GDR, an impressive number of novels was nevertheless produced in the 1950s and 1960s that incorporated the requisite characteristics and attempted to tailor their message to the party's goals. These include the *Betriebsromane* (factory novels) and *Entwicklungsromane* (novels of development), as well as the *Ankunftsromane* (novels of arrival) of the 1960s.[25]

With regard to gender characteristics, communist psychology believed that they too were largely socially acquired and that art and the media played an important role in determining them. The GDR psychologist Heinz Dannhauer writes of "the great significance of mass communications media and art, in particular literature, in propagating the gender-specific image."[26] The objective of GDR educational policy was to reduce as much as possible the traditional sex roles, mainly by raising girls to be more like boys, but also by teaching boys to be more helpful around the house.[27]

Patricia A. Herminghouse has documented the image of women in socialist realist literature of the 1950s and 1960s in her 1976 article "Wunschbild, Vorbild oder Porträt? Zur Darstellung der Frau im Roman der DDR" (Ideal, model, or portrait? On the presentation of woman in the GDR novel) and expanded the picture in her 1985 article "Schreibende Frauen in der Deutschen Demokratischen Republik" (Women writers in the German Democratic Republic). Far from mirroring the lives of actual women of the period, this literature, she points out, constructs an imaginary ideal, a model life, which is intended to raise readers' consciousness.[28] The GDR had to replace the traditional image of femininity with an image of woman as resolute and capable, and moreover employed, a mother (though not necessarily married), and of course committed to the socialist cause. The first project the GDR had to accomplish vis-à-vis its female population in the immediate postwar period was to persuade women that they could do "a man's job" and get them into the factories. Thus female factory workers, crane operators, and tractor drivers dominate in the fiction of the 1950s. In the 1960s, after the closing of the border to the West, the emphasis changed to educating women and qualifying them for professional careers. The Politbüro communiqué of 16 December 1961 "Die Frau—der Frieden und der Sozialismus" (Woman—peace and socialism) calls for more women in managerial positions and for the qualification of women especially in technical and scientific fields. Consequently, professional women populate the fiction of the 1960s. Until the 1970s there was little difference between the image of women in fiction written by men and the image of women in fiction written by women.

Whereas talking about the "image of women" in Western literature politicizes terrain in which gender implications had hitherto for the most part slumbered unconsciously, performing the corresponding operation on GDR literature is like treading into a previously mined field. By the 1970s, the era of liberalization, writing the image of woman was, in a context where the function of literature had until very recently been ordained from above, doubly politically charged. Women writers who wrote in this decade were necessarily aware of writing in conformity or in tension with the "socialist image of woman" that had been prescribed in the extremely recent past, and they were also aware that this new model had broken sharply with the (now discredited) image of woman from the literature of the (otherwise highly regarded) bourgeois "inheritance," in short with the victim image conjured up by such heroines as Gretchen, Emilia Galotti, or Luise Millerin.

We have seen that in *Trobadora Beatriz* Morgner pursued a conscious strategy, betting on the idea of the impossible, legendary, Faustian woman as her principal ploy, but not neglecting other registers, such as a tone of outrage at women's historical ill-treatment. The remainder of this chapter will show some of the ways in which other GDR women writers, in the post-1971 period of liberalization, addressed the crucial problem of identity by rewriting the role of women. Several works in this period take their cue, as will be seen, from Wolf's celebrated and controversial novel *The Quest for Christa T.*, which appeared in 1968, before the liberalization. Two distinctions must be drawn.

First, I focus on fiction rather than on historical portraits or fictionalizations of historical women, because the fiction chronologically preceded and set the tone for the historical writing rather than the reverse. The novelists of the first generation whose ideas can be considered feminist, that is, the generation born in the late 1920s and early 1930s, had all attempted to cast images of women in fiction by the mid-1970s. Feminist historical fiction, initiated by Wolf's work on the women Romantics in the later 1970s, became a popular genre only in the mid-1980s.[29] Such historical novels can be regarded as part of the feminist wave of the 1980s, when feminist ideas, including Western ones, were well known and had become popularized. They include such works as Renate Feyl's volume of eleven portraits *Der lautlose Aufbruch: Frauen in der Wissenschaft* (The soundless start-off: women in science, 1981) and her historical novel about the brilliant but oppressed Victoria Gottsched, wife of the Enlightenment author Gottsched, ironically entitled *Idylle mit Professor* (Idyll with professor, 1986); Sigrid Damm's *Cornelia Goethe* (1987), a reconstruction of the life of Goethe's sister that floods its eighteenth-century subject with twentieth-century feminist sympathy for the female victim; and Brigitte Struzyk's *Caroline unterm Freiheitsbaum* (Caroline under the freedom tree, 1988), a fictionalized retelling of the eventful life of Caroline Michaelis-Böhmer-Schlegel-Schelling.

Second, I am not interested in the image of women that simply "arises" from fiction written by women, but in fiction that is written with the more or less conscious intention of presenting an exemplary case. Image-building is also different from "showing the real" or the exposé, which often has the intent of complaint and which will be the subject of the next chapter.

Literary tradition offers two principal roles for women, each of which has its own strategic potential, that of the successful heroine and that of victim. The success story is a useful option where literature is believed to have the power to furnish models for imitation. Casting women as victims expresses women's sense of outrage at their own deprivation. Assuming that readers will bring moral standards to the text with which they will contrast the victim's plight, it seeks to arouse sympathy and the desire to right wrongs. Far more frequently than in the West, where the victim role has been preferred, GDR women writers took the route of portraying women as heroines.[30] The reason, I believe, was that this option was predetermined by the expectations and practice of socialist realism, a doctrine that exercised a formative influence on this generation of writers and whose legacy continued to make itself felt in GDR fiction even after the imperative to write according to its prescription had been dropped and writers consciously rejected this "antiquated" style.[31] Socialist literary theory actively promulgated the modeling role of literature. It called for positive heroes. GDR women writers ingested this logic. While the feminine victim figure is not missing in GDR women's literature and in fact became increasingly prevalent in the 1980s (Wolf's *Cassandra*, as seen in the last chapter, is an example), the strong, successful woman dominates in the 1970s. Morgner's argument for the necessity of writing women into history is a logical outgrowth of this theory, as is her decision to write her heroine Beatriz as a feminine Faust, to devise a model of femininity that transgresses everything normally thought of as feminine. The image of the strong woman, which I take to be peculiarly a product of its socialist context, is one this chapter will particularly pursue.

The literary tradition provided a genre, the novel of education (*Bildungsroman*), whose function it was to present an exemplary life by showing how an individual could chart his (for the protagonists are overwhelmingly male) course through society's options in an age when no single path was prescribed and ultimately find the right choice for himself. Since the philosopher Wilhelm Dilthey introduced the concept in *Das Leben Schleiermachers* (Schleiermacher's life, 1870), Goethe's *Wilhelm Meisters Lehrjahre* (Wilhelm Meister's apprenticeship years) has been considered the paradigmatic novel of education, the work that founded the genre.[32] In his 1936 essay on *Wilhelm Meisters Lehrjahre* Lukács upheld this work as a model for socialist literature in the present. In the late 1950s the GDR turned to a cultural politics that stressed socialist repossession of the bourgeois "inheritance."[33] The novel of education, which in the GDR was more frequently called the "novel of upbringing" (*Erziehungsroman*) or the "novel of development" (*Entwicklungsroman*),[34] was the preferred, officially sanctioned novel type in the GDR. As of 1957 the party encouraged writers to produce novels of development according to a particular pattern. The novel was to show the hero's successful adoption of a party perspective, his assimilation of socialist values, and his integration into socialist society.[35] The resulting novels of development of the 1950s and 1960s that more or less conform to this prescription include such works as Dieter Noll's *Die Abenteuer des Werner Holt* (The adventures of Werner Holt, 1957–1959) and Max Werner Schulz's *Wir sind nicht Staub im Wind* (We're not dust in the wind, 1962). Herminghouse has documented and analyzed the "female novel of education" of the same period.[36] Most of the novels I shall discuss in this chapter are in the "novel of education" tradition.

Within the corpus of fiction written by women from the late 1960s through the 1980s, amongst all the diversity, two trends are discernible. The first, taking its cue from Wolf's *Quest for Christa T.*, bristles against the "socialist image of women"—but also against the traditional image of women and indeed against any other-imposed "image" of "women." It questions the socialist recipe for women's "emancipation" and urges that "fulfillment" is a personal, private, subjective affair, which is not to be had by leading one's life according to a prescribed pattern. It manages to construct a heroine who, in the state socialist context at least, is inspiring by virtue of her very nonconformism. This trend reaches a first peak in the original novels of Monika Maron, destined never to be published in the communist GDR.[37] It reaches a second peak in the work of Gabriele Stötzer-Kachold, the only full-fledged dissident among GDR women writers, which angrily tears at all received opinions and prefabricated definitions of what "reality" might be.

The second trend has no fundamental quarrel with the socialist formula. In conformity with the socialist ethos it views work, whether creative or scholarly work or work for the social good, as the sphere of women's self-realization. The heroine typically has highflying dreams and ambitions and no serious doubt that she has the potential to do everything a man can. The "antagonist" here that the woman must assert herself against is not the social fabric or received ideas, but the snares that life holds out specifically for women, chiefly lovers, husbands, and even children, but to a less dangerous degree, workplace sexism. While these works rarely sing the praises of socialism as the best social system for women as loudly as Morgner in *Trobadora Beatriz*, they tacitly affirm the socialist context, presenting heroines who are not noticeably ideologically or socially maladjusted. Above all, these women live up to the socialist ideal of the strong, competent, working, professional woman. If the first trend objects to the socialist image of woman as yet another objectification, this second trend could be seen to represent the feminization or subjective appropriation of the image, which women writers carried over into a period when it was no longer mandatory to contrive "positive heroines" in order to build socialism and when "nonantagonistic contradictions" between women's lives and the socialist system could, at least to a degree, be aired in fiction.

Particularly the works in the novel of education tradition that appeared through the first half of the 1970s—Wolf's *Quest for Christa T.*, Gerti Tetzner's *Karen W.*, Brigitte Reimann's *Franziska Linkerhand*, and Morgner's *Trobadora Beatriz*—have been seen to constitute a breakthrough in East German women's writing and have received considerable critical attention.[38] Within this criticism a tendency exists to identify the more "rebellious" works—works of the first trend—as more "feminist," and to express disappointment, in the name of feminism, with works that are affirmative of socialism.[39]

I find that this assessment is amiss, first because I do not favor defining "feminism" in oppositional terms, or indeed aligning it with imagination or even subversiveness, but rather see it purely as having the goal of empowering women. Secondly and by way of qualification, there can be no "feminism" where women are not perceived to constitute an interest group. For an individual woman, this means waking up to a sense of being a *woman* and feeling solidarity with other women, instead of, say, viewing them primarily as rivals, or as disadvantaged beings whose lot one personally wants to escape. The trouble with the socialist solution to the "woman question," therefore, was above all its historical refusal to admit that women as a group had interests that socialism could not solve and that might not mesh harmoniously with what was perceived to be the general social good. Precisely the advent of this insight among GDR women marks, to my mind, the beginning of "GDR feminism." This coming to consciousness, which is present in the work of Irmtraud Morgner much earlier than in any other GDR woman writer, emerges in the genre of the female novel of education only in the latter half of the 1970s and is more marked in novels of the second trend, that is, in the feminine success stories. The works involving nonconformist heroines, and particularly the earlier ones, for all of their saying "I," rather disappointingly show little or no sense of solidarity with other women. The heroines assert their own interests *as* women, but not the interests *of* women.

The Nonconformist Rebel

Christa Wolf's *Quest for Christa T.* is usually considered, in the formulation of Sonja Hilzinger, the first GDR work with "emancipatory tendencies."[40] This novel certainly set a genre in motion, the GDR women's novel of education, where the woman's education pointedly fails to conform to the party line on women. The work not only breaks with the officially sanctioned image of the socialist heroine, but overturns the entire paradigm of the socialist novel of development that cultural politics had been at pains to set in place since the mid-1950s.[41] In its context a provocative and transgressive work, from a literary historical point of view it represents a breakthrough.[42] It is interesting that the trend it started, which includes such maladjusted heroes as Ulrich Plenzdorf's Edgar Wibeau, was initiated by a woman writing about a woman.

To a Westerner reading the book today it may well be not at all immediately apparent what is feminist or even "emancipatory" about *The Quest for Christa T*. Aside from an episode of wife battering—Christa T. tells her narrator of her hospital acquaintance's abuse at the hands of her husband and her psychological dependence on her abuser (Q 132)—and a sensitive but not highly critical representation of the phase of Christa T.'s life in which she was a housewife and mother, it is not concerned with women's issues. It thematizes self-finding, the infinite self (for example, Q 166 and Q 167), and the deceptiveness of names and labels (Q 35). One finds the same thing, earlier and more abundantly, in the work of Max Frisch. In Wolf's novel, of course, these premises are applied specifically to a woman. The significance of the work arises principally from the context in which it was written, the regimented East. In *The Quest for Christa T*. Wolf transgresses the prescriptive literary codes of her day both thematically and formally, creating an uncomfortable heroine who refuses social adjustment and a difficult, meandering, porous text out of which it is impossible to extract a conclusive political message, much less one affirmative of conditions in the GDR. Wolf explicitly challenges the precepts of socialist realism when she has her narrator—whom criticism sometimes identifies with Wolf herself [43]—say that writing means to furnish examples, and that Christa T. is indeed an example. But (here is the twist) she is not exemplary, in the sense that not "a single one of the laudatory words which our time and we ourselves have quite justifiably produced" (Q 45) can be applied to her. She is not a "Vor-Bild," a model; she cannot be used (N 57, Q 45). The narrator repeatedly emphasizes, meaningfully, that she was "real" (for example, Q 44). It is difficult not to conjecture, as most commentators on the novel do, that Christa T.'s death of leukemia is "political," given that the narrator attributes to Christa T. the insight that "before long people won't still be dying of this disease" (Q 182)—whether she dies, in the anti-GDR reading, of stifling conditions in the East[44] or, in the pro-GDR reading, because she has isolated herself and broken off all productive connections to society.[45] Bashed in the East and celebrated in the West, the book immediately became a battleground for critics, a site of conflicting ideological appropriations.[46]

The apparently reliable narrator, mustering an elegiac tone designed to maneuver the reader into an empathetic response, encourages the reader from the start to regard Christa T. as a special, exceptional person. "She doesn't need us; . . . we need her" (Q 5):

this pronouncement is usually read to mean that Christa T. represents the type that GDR society must learn to accommodate if socialism is to live up to its utopian aspirations.[47] What does her specialness consist of? Although Christa T. grew up against a background of successive regimes and prescriptions for behavior, including the Nazi period, the war, and finally the Stalinist period of the GDR, she refuses to be regimented. She is dreamy, imaginative, observant. She is not outwardly rebellious, but her attitude is questioning, sober, and critical. An insightful person, she sees through things and is immune to the intoxication of mass demonstrations and jubilations (Q 56). The image of Christa T. that arises out of the narrator's memories and reflections is that of an individualist, a nonconformist, a person who simply finds it impossible to fall in with what is expected and be like everybody else.

But far from being a nonconformist with a program, Christa T. is in perpetual quest of herself "inside and outside" (Q 55). The second sentence of the novel tells us what is most important about her: that she attempts to be herself (Q 3). The second to last chapter of the book makes this clearer: She is embarked on "this *long and neverending journey toward oneself*" (Q 174; italics Wolf's). Outwardly, this means that she is unstable, always unable to orient herself on a single goal. A repeated pattern in her life is *leaving*: in the narrator's interpretation, she leaves what she knows too well, what no longer represents a challenge (Q 41, cf. 169–170). The notion of an inner life inexpressible in words is driven home by the figure of the narrator, Christa T.'s friend, who hovers diffidently around her subject, perusing her diaries, letters, and unpublished fiction, juxtaposing these testimonies to her own memories of Christa T., her own conjectures, her own vision of what Christa T. was like, constantly criticizing the impulse to write a "story," to find the "key" to the dead woman, to make falsifying sense out of things. In fact, this unusual narrator-protagonist relationship was, in Myra Love's pathbreaking reading, the first aspect of the novel to be labeled feminist, inasmuch as it established a model of intersubjectivity not based on the patriarchal norm of dominance.[48]

Christa T.'s quest, which seems to be motivated by a sense of malaise in a society that pushes her to be a certain way, is legible against the backdrop of the transition from Nazism to state socialism, in which GDR Germans of Wolf's generation were swept along. Having witnessed violence as a child, having glimpsed chaos beneath the daylight order, she cannot take placative and restrictive social orderings seriously. Throughout her life she broods about the human propensity for violence. Her most positive traits are her deep seriousness, her morality, her idealism. We are told that in the first years of the GDR, when everyone was afire with ideas of utopia and perfection, Christa T. joined in, for she had found a match for her own idealism. According to the narrator, the question that motivated her was: "What does the the world need to become perfect?" (Q 53). Yet deeper, thinks the narrator, was her need to understand herself as necessary to the perfectibility of the world. This is perhaps what is meant when the narrator asserts—as the most important thing about the story—that "Christa T. had a vision of herself." (Q 117) But as the initial euphoria in the new state ceded to organization, order, and doctrine, Christa T. embarked on a quest for self that led her to reiterate the insight of her childhood: "I am different" (Q 57 and 22). Her passionate moralism remains with her to the end. She will later, as a teacher, oppose violence and oppose her pupils' facile bandying of the expected socialist phraseology.

Christa T. accomplishes nothing unusual in her life before she dies of leukemia at age thirty-five: she works as a teacher, writes some fragments, completes her studies in literature with a thesis on Theodor Storm, gets married, has three children, has an affair. Yet the narrator constantly assures us that Christa T. was extremely significant, insisting: "You haven't understood a thing if you shrug your shoulders, turn away, turn from her, Christa T., and attend to grander and more useful lives" (Q 136). Christa T.'s significance lies precisely in her *not* being a positive hero, in her *not* being a "model," in her *not* being one of the "frightful beaming heroes of newspapers, films, and books" that people in the GDR have, distressingly, internalized as their models (Q 56). Her value is essentially negative: it it lies in her *putting into the question* the normative, in resisting the pressure to become a "little screw" in the social machine (N 72), in failing to adapt, in insisting on "attempting to be herself." It was perhaps even significant for the identificatory reception of this text that Christa T. was a remarkable person with an unremarkable career—a person who had the talent to be a writer but too much doubt in her own gift to pursue that path. Here at any rate was a challenging novel written by a woman about a challenging woman—even though it presents no positive solution to the predicament of women and does not even propose, as a premise of the narrative, that there is such a thing as women's predicament.

The Quest for Christa T. has been read as a successful and as an unsuccessful feminist text. It has principally been Christa T.'s "feminine" solution of marriage and motherhood that has provoked criticism.[49] It has also been proposed that the novel has nothing whatsoever to do with feminism, indeed that Christa T. could as well have been Christian T.[50] Recent critics with the benefit of hindsight argue that Christa T.'s sex is not fortuitous. Thus Katharina von Hammerstein, writing from the perspective of 1987, rightly points out that Wolf genders the ostensibly sexless theme of self-realization in post-*Christa T.* texts like "Self-experiment," "Berührung" (Touching) and the *Cassandra* lectures as a specifically feminine demand.[51]

A sense of feminine solidarity enters Wolf's work in two stories she wrote after *The Quest for Christa T.* Like *Christa T.*, "Unter den Linden" (written in 1969) and "Self-experiment" (1973) are about a woman's self-finding, but unlike *Christa T.*, these stories swerve in a recognizably feminist direction. They set the tone for all of Wolf's later writing on women. In both stories, the heroine seeks and arrives at a conception of herself that involves rejecting dominant male norms in favor of adopting what Wolf construes as a different, specifically feminine identity. "Self-experiment" has been discussed in chapter 3. The earlier story, "Unter den Linden," while quite different in genre, is similar in theme. It musters the same repertoire of ideas, that is, it polarizes "truth" and "fact" and is about the importance of "love," coupled with men's inability to love.[52] Two stories run parallel in "Unter den Linden." First, there is the story of the first-person narrator, who, through the medium of a dream, works through and comes to terms with a failed love affair in her past, which is traumatizing although "nothing happens." Second, a girl, younger and more vulnerable, has a similar relationship and a disastrous affair with a man, which ends catastrophically, with her abjection, and leads to her expulsion from university. In both cases the woman abandons herself to her love for a man who, himself incapable of loving, withdraws from, and trivializes, the affair.

The device of the parallel case has three functions: it generalizes the model, thus ensuring that the story's problematic cannot be written off as merely the narrator's psychological problem; concomitantly, it intimates, as *Christa T.* never did, that there is a commonality among women, which is framed here in terms of a superior but more vulnerable sensibility; and it shows that the experience of having one's love answered by coldness is far from being trivial. The story not only has absolutely nothing good to say about either man, but also, in the narrator's dream, identifies the girl's lover with the opportunistic careerist Peters, who abandons his first wife in order to marry a young blond, thus upping the number of male miscreants to three. The story affirms the women's position, their demand for love. When the heroine's lover (in her dream) tells her that she (as usual) is going too far, and that really nothing at all happened, and that she should not take things so tragically, she ripostes:

> Perhaps we are in some way still fighting the binding agreement not to make a tragedy out of the absence of love. A man like you is beyond all that. He rationalizes everything and refuses to suffer. For us, unfortunately, the only connection to the world is through love. For the time being. We will have to suffer a short while longer. But we are prepared to learn. Have no fear, even our sorrow will atrophy. . . . But we are showing reason. Are already beginning to voluntarily withdraw from ourselves. Don't worry, soon there will be no one pouring out his troubles to you. Soon there will be no connection left between us but the blindness of our souls. (*WR* 116)

The story's resolution is wishful: it takes place in the narrator's dream. In the dream the narrator works through her disappointment and ends by finding *herself* in the guise of a happy woman who is well-dressed. Her attractive outward appearance suggests self-esteem. It seems to signify a refusal to be victimized, a refusal to be harmed by something that is in fact merely shabby, men's inability to love.

A line of GDR women's fiction following *The Quest for Christa T.* involves women who rebel against social norms and constraints and embark on the quest for a life congenial to them. Examples include Gerti Tetzner's novel *Karen W.* (1974) and short stories by Helga Königsdorf written in the late 1970s and early 1980s.

Karen W.—as its title already suggests—follows the pattern started by *The Quest for Christa T.* Like *Christa T.*, this is the story of a woman who is seeking to be herself, who rejects the various roles that society offers her. The first-person narrative, whose dominant tense is present, begins *in medias res*: we find Karen in the act of deciding to leave her lover Dr. Peters. But this event proves by no means to be conclusive. The peculiarity of the plot is that it perpetually skips between tracks: just when it seems about to settle into the genre of the novel of self-finding, it skips into the groove of the love story. Karen oscillates between two impulses: a hungriness for life, a centrifugal urge for ever more experiences; and a search for a center that will give meaning to her life, for which the only reasonable candidate is her relationship with Peters, even though Karen hates Peters's workaholism and careerism and the life-style they force her into.

Karen puts into practice the kind of rebellion that remained latent in *The Quest for Christa T.* It is characteristic of her story that she never does the obvious, prescribed, or easy thing. Born and raised in a village, she defies her father and becomes the first girl from her locality ever to attend high school. At university, where she studies law, she meets the radical communist Peters. In her relationship with Peters Karen W. spurns the conventional options. When she gets pregnant, she decides that she does not want to marry him. Yet presently she also gives up her job as a lawyer, for the birth of her child makes this career too difficult. Initially *happy* as an (unmarried) housewife and mother, she later feels that life is passing her by with Peters, who is devoured by his academic work as a professor. All his thoughts revolve about his work, his job, his career, and academic politics. She too finds herself being sucked, against her inclinations, into the life of "naked goal-oriented thinking."[53] So Karen returns to the village she came from, where she at first just "lives" (with her daughter Bettina), and then, when she runs out of money, works in the fields. Eventually she returns to Peters, but soon she finds that she really cannot stand the kind of life he leads. He tries out life in the village, but finds, in turn, that he cannot stand that. They separate. She has an affair with another man. The end of the novel leaves open whether she and Peters will get back together.

Schmitz-Köster rightly observes that this novel goes farther than any previous one in rejecting the life model for women officially propagated in the GDR.[54] However, while this novel is certainly about a woman's self-finding and her emancipation, it has no feminist message. It offers no prescription for women, nor even a sense of feminine solidarity: the heroine "prefers the company of men to women," since, in her view, women get weepy or calculating quicker.[55] The heroine's personal solution essentially involves an opting out rather than an opting for. Undeniably, the central experience of Karen's life is her relationship with Peters. Her life pivots around him: she is never able definitively to leave him, for the end of the book finds her leaving the village and moving back to the city where they used to live just when he said he would come home from abroad. In short, the novel sketches the heroine's self-finding quite naively in traditional "feminine" terms: a relationship with a man; time to "live"; rejection of careerism.

Karen W. construes women's self-finding in terms of a rejection of "the system" not unlike that of the hippie movement of the late '60s. That is, the heroine looks at the traditional feminine life-style and doesn't like it; and she looks at the traditional masculine lifestyle and doesn't like that either. What she rebels against is the bourgeois inheritance—and of course any remnants of the fascist past—in favor of an ideal communism, which actual socialist society fails to live up to. A critic from the former GDR has admiringly called *Karen W.* "courageous."[56] For it is an outstanding example of the fiction of the 1970s that breaks radically with the literary norm of the 1950s and 1960s by asking, for the first time, what society can do for the individual instead of what the individual can do for society.[57] If there is tension, it exists more between the younger and the older generation than between men and women. The solution involves giving up any kind of conventional life-style, blithely disregarding people's opinions, and following the dictates of one's own idealistic inner dream. But it is unclear to what extent the espoused life-style is not self-indulgence in traditional feminine fantasies. It has no political perspective; it has no system-building potential or even aspiration, but is merely antisystem. From the perspective of a later feminism, there is only a fine line between this solution and one of the traditional feminine life-styles—indeed, one that is perennially upheld as a defense of difference, as "the luxury of being a woman."[58]

The life-style that women rebel against in GDR women's literature is typically construed as "men's life-style." The mode of existence attributed to men could be summarized as the onesided pursuit of professional goals to the detriment of one's growth as a human being as well as one's sensitivity toward others. Wolf's stories "Unter den Linden" and "Self-experiment" as well as her published statements set the direction for this identification. Tetzner in *Karen W.* follows suit in associating careerism with the main male figure.

Whereas Karen W. draws the radical consequence of abandoning her own career, other women, starting with the narrator of Wolf's "Unter den Linden," experience the same crisis but opt for a different solution, that of severing their emotional dependence on the less-than-understanding man. From the 1950s on GDR fiction had, in keeping with government policy, glorified the image of the working woman. In the late 1970s and 1980s it took women's professional lives for granted. Abandoning one's career is only rarely advanced as a solution to conflicts between personal life and career. This is not because women realize that careers offer a kind of security that relationships do not, so that come what may, they must give their careers priority over their personal lives—a train of thought a woman in the West might follow. East German women had no fear that if they left a job they would be unable to find another one.[59] Stories about women frequently see them leaving one job—sometimes for a relationship—only to take up another one later on. Instead, most heroines of East German women's fiction believe, in accordance with the Marxist conception of the meaning of work,[60] that their self-realization lies in their work, sometimes in a career but more often in some kind of creative vocation.

In "Hochzeitstag in Pizunda" (Wedding day in Pizunda) in her debut volume of stories *Meine ungehörigen Träume* (My improper dreams, 1978), Helga Königsdorf has her diarist narrator resolve her crisis by leaving not her job but her husband. The diarist is a middle-aged woman, married for twenty years, a successful professional, with two children, who seriously rethinks her life: "I have lived hastily. I have accepted patterns of behavior that have been foisted on me. I have demonstrated talent in doing everything that was expected of me. I forgot only one thing along the way. I no longer know who I am."[61] She starts to write stories. Believing her husband unsympathetic, her solution to her crisis is to leave him.

Even if women rarely drop their careers in later GDR women's fiction, questioning the career-oriented life-style nevertheless remains a theme. In the story "Unverhoffter Besuch" (The unexpected visit) in her second volume *Der Lauf der Dinge* (The course of things, 1982) Königsdorf questions the image of the successful professional woman. Is this really enough? Is this really life? The story itself does not ask these questions, but forces the reader to ask them after reading the last sentence, when it becomes clear that the confrontation between a successful mature woman and a teenage girl who is pondering the "big questions" and wondering what life holds for her is one between mother and daughter. The mother is "successful" on account of her superb organization: the right man, the right child at the right time, degrees, successes. But the teenager surfaces like a repressed part of herself. The daughter had opted to live with her father at the time of divorce. Now she is dissatisfied with him, which apparently prompts her visit to her mother. The story seems to ask, at what price success? Hasn't her mother—who lost her daughter; whose boyfriend is fearful because of the role she has assigned to him, permitting him to visit only every Friday night; who is about to have a quick abortion before a lecture series—organized all the humanity out of herself?

Among the most profiled progeny of Christa T. are Monika Maron's rebellious, all-questioning heroines. Essentially champions of the rights of the imagination, these women fight against its oppressors, who are identified in *Flight of Ashes* (*Flugasche*, 1981) with state socialism and in *The Defector* (*Die Überläuferin*, 1986) with social norms generally; the scientific spirit, in which men seem particularly invested; and the heroine's own moral domestication, her interiorization of these social values, or what she summarily calls her "head."

Maron's first novel *Flight of Ashes* records a woman's existential crisis, provoked by her abortive attempt to publish in a GDR magazine an exposé of the polluted, unsafe conditions in Bitterfeld, casually disguised as the industrial city B. The novel itself thereby becomes an exposé of state socialism, which is presented as a self-validating social order that fails all tests: of honesty, perceptiveness, imagination, enterprise, livability, and fairness to workers, individuals, and not least women. The exponent of this view is the volatile Josefa Nadler, a journalist who wants to help society—indeed, workers—by publishing "the truth" about an unsafe power plant. Josefa is a party member, but she is also a flaming radical from the GDR point of view. Rebelling against the self-censoring, hypocritical mode her professional life demands from her, she spouts iconoclastic ideas. For example: the distance between intellectuals and workers is unbridgeable; factory work is dehumanizing; socialism represses individuality ("they are cheating me out of me, out of my qualities," she fumes.[62]) Inasmuch as she reflects on women's issues—and these play a relatively small role in the novel—she attacks, in an imaginary speech she holds on Women's Day, socialism's "false" emancipation of women that forces them to work—and for less pay than men—and to conform to male-dictated sexual mores. She stubbornly refuses to conform and play by the rules, even though her own rebelliousness severely rocks her equilibrium. Finally she walks out on her job, resolving never to return: a truly unheard-of desertion of work in the GDR context. Small wonder that this novel was not published in the GDR until 1990. The West German publisher Fischer Verlag originally published this and all of Maron's subsequent works.

Maron's next novel *The Defector*, using the Wall as a metaphor for whatever real or metaphysical constraints confront the heroine in her quest for her own desire,[63] displaces the brunt of its subversiveness from a political to a psychological plane. The plot takes the reader through surreal vistas of dream and fantasy, where the heroine meets embodiments of other, buried aspects of herself, or what one of her alter egos, reminiscent of Christa Wolf, terms the *useless* in herself.

Neither of Maron's novels flies under a feminist flag, but both pursue, more energetically and extensively than any GDR work hitherto, a liberation of the repressed and a rejection of all restrictive concepts of identity. Following Christa Wolf, GDR tradition identified such liberation and rejection with the feminine.[64] Maron's novels are outdone only by the work of the ultraradical Gabriele Stötzer-Kachold, whose work started to be published in underground literary magazines of the GDR "scene" in the '80s[65] and appeared in book publications only in the West after the fall of the Wall. With her "stylization of the body and, more specifically, of the vagina as a source of truth and self-knowledge,"[66] Stötzer-Kachold mounts a violent, radical attack on patriarchy.

Strong Women: The Neopositive Heroine

The other recurrent female type in GDR women's fiction of the 1970s and 1980s is the strong woman. Whereas the nonconformist rebel type could be seen to have infiltrated the socialist novel of education, following the lead of *Christa T.*, the strong woman type had a firm footing in it. What is interesting for feminism about this type is the way women writers adopted it as a model for feminine success, detaching it from its socialist-realist political affiliation and reattaching it to a variety of feminist purposes. The result is a feminist heroine type that is specific to the state socialist context and that has no counterpart in the West.

This type, which might be called the "neopositive heroine," does not rebel against the (male) system but, rather, assimilates to the male model. The successful fictional heroine is thus often gendered male. Her characteristics are intelligence, strength, energy, courage, and resourcefulness. She is ambitious and competent, not supportive and accommodating. The barriers that life erects for her—pregnancy, children—seem merely to be there in order to be surmounted. She makes the same choices as men, opting for career over relationships, public recognition over private felicity, profiling herself over helping others. She knows, or at least comes to know, what she wants from a relationship with a man, both casually and in terms of partnership, and demands it. Typically, she has several relationships and does not suffer long in unsatisfactory ones. If married, she is not a faithful wife.

This is not to say that there are not also some female protagonists who at least start out as victims. In the novel of self-finding, their development involves rehabilitation, finding their own strength. An example of such a novel is Doris Paschiller's *Die Würde* (Dignity, 1980), whose working-class protagonist, immature when she gets pregnant, married because of the pregnancy, trapped in a loveless marriage, downtrodden and demoralized, with no sense of wanting to be where she is or knowing where she wants to go, runs away, asserts herself, lives through an inner rebellion, lives on her own, and arrives at a sense of her own worth. Other examples include stories by Hannelore Lauerwald, "Die uralte Geschichte" (The age-old story) and "Eines Tages . . ." (One day . . .) (both in *An einem Donnerstag oder Der Duft des Brotes* [On a Thursday or the aroma of bread], 1975), in which women wake up to their own oppression and break off their relationships with the men who are its cause.

The strong woman type occurs both within and independently of the novel of education. In the novel of education, "flight from the feminine role/fate" would be a good way to convey the plot dynamic: it is as if a success story cannot be conceived other than in masculine terms. Outside of the novel of education, in novels about issues, the type is used to justify a certain kind of decision, for instance, the decision to abort, the message being that such a decision does not signify weakness or helplessness but precisely the opposite. In the remainder of this chapter I shall describe the vicissitudes of the type in works of the 1970s and 1980s, starting with four novels of education, and moving on to works by Charlotte Worgitzky and Maya Wiens where the strong woman type comes "ready-made."

Brigitte Reimann's unfinished novel *Franziska Linkerhand* (1974) is a pivotal work in the making of the GDR neopositive heroine, inasmuch as it fuses the idea of a woman's self-finding with a positive, even politically correct heroine who lays claim to a man's career. This huge work, which was ten years in the making and published posthumously, is another feminine novel of education after the model of *The Quest for Christa T.* It is devoted more to probing and unfolding Franziska's psychology, to recording the nuances of her reactions to the world and of her impulses, than to setting a finished role model before the reader. Although an omniscient narrative voice occasionally intrudes, Franziska herself is the principal narrator. She writes in an associative, confessional style, often proximate to stream of consciousness, addressing herself to an imaginary confidant and lover Ben and continuously switching back and forth between the first and the third persons. The novel billows with episodes. Much attention is given to Franziska's relationships with men, in particular to her relationship with Wolfgang Trojanowicz (whom she calls "Ben"), which has largely psychological interest. Beyond this, Franziska is endowed with an idealism and a courage that would inspire admiration in either sex and that allow her to be received as a role model. *Franziska Linkerhand* is an autobiographical novel—but one that, as one commentator remarks, makes order out of the chaos that Brigitte Reimann's life actually was: in Franziska, Reimann "lives out her principles and her ideas of decency and morality."[67] Reimann, a writer who followed the "Bitterfeld Way" to the new workers' city Hoyerswerda, transposes her own experiences onto the persona of the young architect.

This novel bears no explicit feminist message. Nevertheless, several aspects inspire feminist interest. The first is the characterization of Franziska as an independent, rebellious, indomitable woman. The second is Franziska's vehement rejection of a traditional feminine role, her refusal to be "one of them," and the contrast between Franziska and other female figures, who, with certain exceptions, are consistently portrayed as victims. Finally, the conflicts inherent in the situation are dramatized by the contrast between Franziska's unsubmissive personality and the sexual norms prevailing in her environment. The novel captures very well the sexualized atmosphere in which a young woman under thirty constantly has to function. Not only do the men in Franziska's world regard her above all as a woman rather than as an architect, but she herself has an antenna for the sexual tension latent in virtually every encounter she has with a man, as well as a swift grasp of the gender issues implicit in other interpersonal configurations (even though she frequently does not side with the woman).

Franziska is first and foremost a free spirit. In early adolescence she imagines herself as a wild running horse. When she is beginning to see Ben, she wants to maintain the independence of her opinions: "She became obstinate from fear of seeing the world through his eyes."[68] In this regard she is like Karen W. But she is totally unlike Karen W. in the way she insists on realizing herself, in the style of a man, in the public sphere. She exhibits an energy and a toughness that could serve as a model for a man. When Franziska insists that she is feeling wonderful even though she has the flu, a doctor says to her: "Men like you made Prussia great."[69] It is a feather in her cap—though it is meant as a criticism—when her boss accuses her of "arrogance and ambition" and declares: "You want everything and want it immediately."[70] Whereas Karen W. drifts, Franziska Linkerhand demonstrates commitment. The plot testifies to her courage. An architect, she opts for a job in the desolate Braunkohle-area project city Neustadt instead of staying in her attractive home city—at first in order to put distance between herself and her ex-husband, but finally by choice. Raised in a safe, wealthy, privileged bourgeois home, in Neustadt she plunges into a proletarian milieu. The ideals she cherished as an architecture student are bruised on the realities of her job, which consists in seeing that workers' quarters, apartment buildings made of prefabricated parts, are put up as quickly as possible. She is instructed that there is no hope of being creative; the city has to be built economically. She nevertheless argues her viewpoint, that the socialist architectural style does not take the real needs of people for community into consideration, and eventually at least succeeds in winning the respect of her boss. Unable to find another outlet for her creativity and her desire to help people, she enterprisingly opens a free consulting office for interior decoration. She is all "passionate engagement."[71] She becomes a heroine among the workers. What Franziska finds in her search for an identity is her commitment to realizing her ideals. She says in the book's last, unfinished chapter: "It must, it must exist, the intelligent synthesis between today and tomorrow, between dreary block construction and the cheerful, lively street, between the necessary and the beautiful, and I am on its track, proud, and oh, how often, hesitant, and one day I will find it."[72]

Franziska is a woman who, although she never says as much, wants the freedom and the subjecthood *of a man*. From the beginning Franziska feels no sense of identity, much less solidarity, with other women. She never has anything good to say about her mother, a narrow-minded traditionalist who airs bourgeois pretensions and mouths admonitions. The mother-daughter relationship here is one familiar from other novels such as Wolf's *Divided Heaven*: an idealistic daughter confronts a materialistic mother or mother-in-law. But here it is not just a case of generational conflict. Franziska also goes through school without having a close girlfriend. In early adolescence she rebels against becoming a woman: "I didn't want to surrender, not to the female pain, not to the mindless everyday world of women that my mother practiced in front of me."[73] Getting her period is a crisis for her:

> *They got me*, thought Fransziska, panic-stricken. She felt trapped and delivered over to the sphere of women, to their cycle that subjected them to the moon, and to the carousel of their duties that forced them to wipe the insidious, never to be conquered dust from

the furniture every morning, to dip greasy dishes into the hot dishwater every day at noon; plagued with nausea for nine months, to drag a foreign body around with themselves, one that nurtured itself from their body fluids, their blood, and to scream in a delivery room.... A container, she thought, I have become a *container*.[74]

She goes to her doctor and weeps: "I don't want to be a woman."[75] Later she rejects what she conceives as the feminine role, the feminine virtues, and the feminine fate. She is uncritical of men and highly critical of women who take the easy route, who "rest on the chest and the wallet of a man."[76] It is implied that such women lack imagination and courage. She views this role as a gilded cage, comfortable yet confining.

The secondary female figures are an unenviable lot. After spending her student years in a man's world, Franziska meets a number of women in Neustadt and finds out about their lives. In contrast to Franziska herself, these women are by and large portrayed as victims. Franziska shows some sympathy for some of them but little inclination to identify with any of them. Thus the sulky secretary Gertrud, raped at age eleven, alcoholic, single, won't let a man near her; she has a suicide attempt behind her and finally does commit suicide. Frau Hellwig, a waitress, took care of five children whose mother died in 1945 for a total of twenty years. Their father, a farmer, lived with her for years and then finally fled over the border. Franziska is appalled when she hears this story: "No, she doesn't want to learn all that now, patience, self-sacrifice, the old-fashioned virtues that people handcuff women with."[77] She resolves never to sacrifice anything to any man or any children.[78] She wants independence, and nothing that will diminish it, including friends or love. Other women's life stories are equally uninspiring. Frau Bornemann, Franziska's neighbor, sent by her mother to work in a factory at age fourteen and pregnant by her boss at age seventeen, had to work for a living although she would have liked to continue her education. Sigrid is abandoned by Trojanowicz (for Franziska) after she followed him to Neustadt and they lived together for five years. The wife of her boss Schafheutlin, a "professional housewife and mother,"[79] gave up her profession as an engineer for her husband and four children. Franziska despises her, especially because she plays the martyr.

Franziska, desirous of being happy and in control of things, wants to dissociate herself from other women, whom she considers to be complainers. The closest she comes to any sense of feminine solidarity is by reflecting about how women are yoked by custom even though they are emancipated by law. She realizes that even in a country where women have equal rights and earn equal pay for equal work, custom persists in treating them very differently: "Only later [i.e., after her studies] did I understand that in a society that pays women the same wages for the same work (on that issue there is nothing more to be said), that in our country other unwritten laws preside, laws that have been made in a world ruled by men."[80]

Franziska's panicky withdrawal from everything she associates with "woman" may seem to be the opposite of feminism, especially since the novel presents her viewpoint without criticism. Yet this very attitude was widespread among intelligent women of Franziska's generation both in the GDR and in the West. The desire *not to be like one's mother* is an impulse that GDR women writers like Morgner share with American writers like Sylvia Plath.[81] Morgner's Amanda says: "My decision to become a train engineer was indisputable from my third year of life on. . . . Since my mother could not exemplify anything except obedience and my father was the only train engineer that I knew, I took him as a role model" (*A* 83). The narrator of *Amanda* glosses: "Only by way of exception can an adolescent girl identify with her mother. Normally the mother is the disadvantaged parent even today. . . . Adolescents however—male or female—, who are just beginning to feel how forces gather and collect and move in them, do not choose a self-effacing person to identify with, but instead one that is entitled to move ahead" (*A* 279). For lack of reasonable female role models identification with the "strong sex" was the first step for many feminists. The next step was the disappointed jolt at realizing that men were not prepared to accept a woman as an equal. Then came the recognition that life held something else in store for oneself, a woman, than for a man; that men in fact were not as similar to oneself as one had perceived oneself to be similar to them; and finally that one actually had more in common with women, even with the hated mother, than with men.

Later novels find their way to the male-gendered heroine more unproblematically than *Franziska Linkerhand*, without becoming mired in feminine self-hatred, and offer a more straightforward feminist message. It is the same message that energizes Morgner's call for female megalomania: women should give up on traditional (losing) feminine positions and imitate the first sex, so as to achieve happiness and self-esteem. Undeniably, these larger-than-life heroines, with their adventures and successes, exercise a fascination and power of suggestion over the female reader: "You can do it too!" they seem to whisper. The plots of Brigitte Thurm's *Verlangen* (Desire, 1981), Lia Pirskawetz's *Der Stille Grund* (1985), and Christine Wolter's *Die Alleinseglerin* (The solo yachtswoman, 1982)—three novels of the 1980s that are in other respects very different—are all cut from the same template: a strong heroine finds her way from an initial position of flawed strength to a final one of enhanced strength.

Compared with Reimann's *Franziska Linkerhand*, Brigitte Thurm's *Verlangen* takes a giant step in the direction of having a woman make decisions which, at every turn of the plot, mimic those of a man. Gina Vermeer, initially outwardly successful and reasonably happy, goes on a trip both literally and figuratively. An overwhelming experience puts her in touch with herself; she sees her earlier existence in a new perspective; she rethinks her life and decides to change it. Thurm's protagonist is a surreally successful career woman, an art historian who is about to be named a professor, who at the time the story is told is on a nine-day lecture tour in the Soviet Union, where she is received in various cities by official welcoming committees and treated as a very important person. Her professional identity and her success are entirely unquestioned. Work and career are not the arena of her struggle to find herself. Indeed, at the end of the story she realizes that they have become an essential part of her life and that she cannot give them up. Instead, as with Wolf's, Tetzner's, and Königsdorf's heroines, the locus of her self-finding is the intimate sphere. Her personal life, her feelings, are at stake. What Gina discovers in the course of her Soviet tour, during which she falls in love and has an affair with her Russian interpreter, is that her emotional life is important and that it is imperative for her to divorce her husband, though not to trade him in for her Russian lover. For she realizes that her Russian lover is not transplantable to Germany, whereas she cannot visualize moving to the USSR: she cannot live without her work, and she does not want to give up her children. This is a woman who, contrary to the traditional model, gives up nothing for love.

Gina is not alone in the world of fictional heroines in the early 1980s who find their basic self-definition in their work rather than in their relationships. The forty-five-year-old heroine of Renate Apitz's story "Das Jahr der Wibke Winter" (The year of Wibke Winter, in *Evastöchter* [Daughters of Eve], 1981) for example, walks out on her marriage to a wealthy farmer and returns to her old editorial job in the city when she discovers she cannot stand to be "Albrechten seine" ("Albrecht's old lady"), as the villagers call her.

Verlangen borders on popular fiction, especially in its repeated references to Gina's attractive appearance and sexy clothing. This makes it all the more interesting for the image of women that it presents. Gina is thirty-six years old and a mother of two. Her children, shadowy figures who are mainly the accoutrements of a successful woman and do not appear as psychological characters, appear to have interfered neither with her appearance nor with her swift, successful career. The dark spot in her life is her husband Hartmut, essentially because he refuses to fall into place as "wife" to Gina's career. Consumed by professional envy (he's in the same field) and personal jealousy (he can't forgive his wife for once having had an affair with an older, famous professor), Hartmut makes Gina's life more difficult by not doing his share at home and with the children and constantly implying that she should be more of a homebody, wife, and mother. The conflict for a woman between family and housework, and career is explicitly thematized; in fact, Gina and Hartmut have a screaming argument over it.[82] But housework and child care are invoked as factors that merely complicate, and do not pulverize, Gina's life. Intelligent, energetic, competent, and hardworking as she is, she manages to deal with them.

The novel purposefully contrasts the figure of Gina with the traditional female role. Gina follows in the footsteps of those GDR novel heroines who, like Franziska Linkerhand, want everything now: "Addicted to happiness, greedy for life like many people in her generation, she wanted the impossible: everything together, completely and at once."[83] Women's role is represented as given over to reproduction, which leaves no time for productive creativity:

> Every Sunday Gina saw the rich world of men and the poor world of women. From her own and other people's experience, from that of her family, friends, and neighbors she knew: Whether mechanic or office employee, physics professor or railway gateman, whether farsighted thinker or narrow-minded pedant, they had their worldly hobbies, they planned, designed, tested, built, they were—without effort—small-scale creators. But their women, whether intelligent or not, and with whatever talents they might have, remained locked into a cycle of small and petty duties, worries, and care-taking that was always the same, and that all amounted to the same thing: to maintaining that which was.[84]

This novel is remarkable because it completely remakes the woman according to the nonvictim model. To be sure, Thurm has her heroine experience, pro forma, the perennial conflicts of women in GDR women's fiction. Thus, for example, the novel shows how Gina has internalized the traditional feminine nurturing role, even while ardently pursuing her career; it thematizes her constant busyness. Yet this conflict is not crippling in this story. To give another example, this novel asks, like previous works by Tetzner and Königsdorf, "At what price success." Yet Thurm affirms the importance of emotional happiness without in the slightest disconfirming the satisfactions of a successful career. What is extraordinary about the novel is that it shows a successful career woman who has the power to dump a husband at will, not because he is horrible, but *merely* because he fails to live up to her ideal. Gina is in a position where she can, and does, act exactly like a man.

Lia Pirskawetz's *Der Stille Grund*, a long, entertaining adventure story with a fantastical strain and humorous tone reminiscent of Morgner, is narrated with an irony that is foreign to *Verlangen*. The novel combines the story of a woman's self-finding with an ecological issue, saving the picturesque southern region of the GDR, called "Saxon Switzerland," from creeping industrialization. Of the three 1980s novels of self-finding under discussion, this one constructs the most appealing heroine, one who satisfyingly opts for her ideals over mere personal comfort and security. At the start the twenty-three-year-old Carola Witt is well-positioned: she is Secretary to the City Council and likely successor to the major in Lachsbach, a town in the endangered region. But she faces a professional dilemma and a personal problem. Her professional dilemma is how to prevent a factory from expanding into the wilderness area called "Stiller Grund" and yet secure the economic future of neighboring Lachsbach. Her personal problem is how to free herself from her parents' negative influence, namely from their orientation on success coupled with their almost complete neglect of her, which has left her with a craving for affection. She wishes to become, in her formulation, "master of my life."[85]

Pirskawetz is sensitive to the sexism that pervades the German language in a seemingly ineradicable fashion. Carola, as an intelligent and competent young woman, seems to have no option but to gravitate toward positions on which usage has bestowed the masculine gender. The word that denotes Carola's job, for example, Secretary (*Sekretär*, male secretary), cannot take a feminine ending on the model of *Lehrer/Lehrerin* (male/female teacher) or *Professor/Professorin* (male/female professor) without changing its meaning so that it designates an entirely different profession. A *Sekretärin* is not a female *Sekretär*, but a secretary, a person who takes dictation and types letters. Hilariously, the *Sekretär* Carola has a male *Sekretärin*. This surly and unhelpful young man, whom she privately dubs "the icon," is a source of constant low-level frustration to her: "I had to struggle for every bit of assistance from him," she notes.[86]

The plot moves the heroine with geometric precision, in the course of a year and a day, from an initial position of cowardice and emotional neediness to a final position of strength, from which she confirms her commitment to ecology. Thus at the beginning of her story, too cowardly not to do what everyone expects of her, she sacrifices her favorite rabbit to the knife in honor of one of her ambitious and loveless parents' rare visits. In the end, in contrast, she breaks off a romance and rejects marriage with a man who gradually, in his thirst for success, reveals himself as the mirror of her parents. This man, the "beautiful aristocrat" Albert Schönherr, as his name reveals, energetic and intelligent, initially strikes the less attractive, less elegant, less well-educated Carola as a dream man. It enhances his appeal that he seems to offer her the love and security she always wanted. But she finally realizes that his entrepreneurial thinking does not tally with her mission of saving the wilderness area called "der Stille Grund." She has firm principles, whereas his goal is selfish: he will do whatever it takes to rise. Whereas at the beginning of her story Carola was still a slave to her need to be loved, at the end she shakes herself free and opts for principle over emotions, thereby becoming what is generally understood by the phrase, "master" of her life.

Carola's "education" takes her back in time to the turn of the century. The main purpose of the time machine is to illuminate the origins of the ecological issue. But the return to the turn of the century has a second function, namely, to stage a confrontation between the heroine and feminine roles of the past. Pirskawetz successfully uses consonant first-person narration to establish Carola Witt as a model woman: Carola tells her story engagingly, humorously, analytically, and perceptively, without self-deception, and with a good deal of sympathy for herself of one year ago. One of the novel's feminist accomplishments is to have this model woman consciously and pointedly break with women's past, both literary and historical. On her arrival at the turn of the century Carola thinks about what she knows of women's roles at that time, and comes up with the female victim role from the German literary past: "Full of horror I mentally reviewed the female roles of the German [literary] past. . . . Gretchen—abandoned, Emilia Galotti—stabbed, Luise Millerin—poisoned, Maria Stuart—executed, Käthchen von Heilbronn—a slave to love, Maria Magdalena—jumped in a well, Rose Berndt—driven to infanticide, Wendla—a victim of quackery. But I didn't feel the slightest desire to become a victim. I was in the mood neither for a heroic nor a tragic death; I wanted to live, work, and accomplish things."[87] The thought of this victim role, which she always scornfully rejects, returns to Carola several times throughout her process of development. In the end, affirming her decision to leave Schönherr, she reflects: "I have something against feminine naïveté. I have something against the Gretchens who let themselves be seduced and the Maria Magdalenas who jump in the well. I wouldn't like to be a sacrificial maiden."[88]

The author also has her heroine reflect on the actual condition of turn-of-the-century women, which she discovers is different from the literary representation of women, but nonetheless unenviable. Around 1900 a woman is forced either to come up with tricks to please a man or to work under poor conditions for little money. The mirroring-with-a-difference continues in the juxtaposition of past and present: at the turn of the century Carola is of course the mayor's secretary (*Sekretärin*), while the Secretary (*Sekretär*), a character not unlike the "icon" in appearance and personality, is male. Carola's persistent struggle not to succumb to turn-of-the-century expectations for women is important for her development. Thus she is able, by dint of her competence, seriousness, and modern self-confidence, to win the mayor's esteem and become a relatively influential person in local politics. The novel adopts the Morgner-like conclusion that a self-confident self-presentation is indispensable for women: "Girl, a confident demeanor should be your rule of thumb."[89] Men at the turn of the century are not in the habit of speaking to women about serious topics, but she manages to overcome the problem. Even in the erotic sphere, which according to Morgner is men's "last domain," she seems fully in control of the situation: with Schönherr she takes the initiative; later she decides—and the decision is portrayed as entirely hers—in favor of the worker Ekkehard.

The implications of Carola's adventures at the turn of the century, which she carries back into the present as insights, are that in gender relations as in politics, there is *always* another way of doing things; but to carry it off, one must vigilantly resist the temptation to conform to the expectations of others. It is in the past that she becomes a heroine, definitively transcending the feminine fate of the period by deciding not to marry Schönherr even though she is expecting his child. At the end of her story, when she returns to the present time, she *dismisses* her pregnancy, saying she isn't pregnant and never was, as if pregnancy were a symbol for the victimization she has combated and rejected. On the last day of her story, on her way to the special City Council meeting that she called and at which she will successfully defend the wilderness area, she asserts her feminine personhood by counterposing it to a masculinity that has shrunk to the anonymity and conformity of the impersonal pronoun. In German, the impersonal pronoun "one," *man*, is derived from, and sounds identical to the word for "man," *Mann*. Carola says: "*One* ('man') *is punctual*. I am no longer *one* ('man'). I am *Carola Witt*."[90]

My fourth example, Christine Wolter's *Die Alleinseglerin*, is an exception among women's novels of education, first in its sustained use of the metaphor of sailing for leading one's life and second for its gritty, sometimes even bitter tone despite its positive ending. It is a story about a woman and her boat, told by a first-person narrator as the story of her youth with great self-consciousness, explicit fictionalizing, and much irony. Like Wolter herself at the time of writing, the narrator lives in Italy. The story of self-finding she narrates takes place in the GDR.

The novel makes abundantly clear that the world of boat-owning, boat-fixing, and sailing is a male world. When the heroine Almuth buys her father's boat, therefore, she can be seen as a woman trying to make it in a man's world. In the guise of the boat story Wolter delivers an unusually acid exposé of men's sexist attitudes in the GDR. In pointed contrast to Morgner, Almuth compares her own life in the present-day GDR unfavorably with that of historical women in the "early bourgeois" period, who, according to her research, were in the process of successfully liberating themselves. Her professor duly warns her to avoid imitating "feminisms determined by other social orders" in no uncertain terms: "Beware of the faddish women's libber attitude."[91]

An aspect of sailing that is crucial for Wolter's allegory is that it classically requires a minimum crew of two. If the story has one message, it is that a woman can forget about "smooth sailing" with a male "mate." A woman who has the temerity to acquire a boat must learn to sail it alone. After innumerable troubles having to do with the reluctance of men to form relationships, single parenthood, overwork, lack of money, and spending all her spare time fixing the boat, Almuth's moment of triumph comes when she succeeds in sailing her boat alone. She is then "rewarded" by a satisfactory love affair; indeed, in the narrative present, she is conducting another one.

Not all novels that attempt to remake the image of women are novels of self-finding. Charlotte Worgitzky consistently wrote fiction that dispensed with the trope of inner development in favor of making its point more directly, through the interaction of static characters who represent different positions. The image of the strong woman dominated in her work from the beginning. Her volume of stories *Vieräugig oder blind* (Four-eyed or blind, 1978) anthologizes stories dated as early as 1970. The two earliest stories, "Quäze" and "Leben wie im Paradies" (Life as in paradise) already feature energetic women. The heroine of the fantasy "Leben wie im Paradies" cannot stand and escapes the lazy man's food paradise ("Schlaraffenland") into which her husband has eagerly tunneled through a rice mountain. The heroine of "Quäze" is a woman with ambitions, a writer who is leery of marriage and yet more so of children because they might derail her from her vocation. Yet it is in her first novel, *Die Unschuldigen* (1975), that the nature of Worgitzky's feminist vision becomes clear. The novel is peopled with strong, talented, ambitious women who have no use whatsoever for any of the feminine virtues. To judge from this and from her later novels, Worgitzky was the main proponent of "sameness feminism" in the GDR. This work is a *roman à thèse*, written to make a point, and all of her subsequent novels have been similarly programmatic. The point here is that women can and should be men's equals in the world of work and careers, while men can be just as talented as women at caring for children.

The epigraph of *Die Unschuldigen*, quoted from the heroine's diary, already sets the tone: "Only then will they really be free and be able to do both without prejudice—to perform intellectually creative work *and* bring children into the world—, when it has become clear even to the very last male that the difference between the sexes is not one of intellect and that men are capable of bringing up children just as well as women."[92] Worgitzky is intent on clearing the path for women's liberation, conceived as self-realization in intellectual or artistic vocations. To her mind, motherhood is the main obstacle in that path. Her solution is simple: men should take over a large portion of the work. So she argues that men are not, as a sex, any less endowed with family feeling or natural talent for childraising than women. Society, she argues, is myopic to insist that children belong with women, to privilege mothers over fathers and by the same token condemn them to a life of child care. It is similarly foolish to make fun of men who take over parental duties. The novel additively presents cases that prove her point, parading before the reader women who are competent, intelligent, talented, and career-oriented, and men who are warm, loving, and maternal.

The principal female figure is the radio journalist Leonore Wicki, born in 1929. Leonore is an intelligent, rational, unsentimental, strong-willed, emancipated woman who is preoccupied with feminist issues. She makes it her business to present interesting women to the public through radio interviews. She has had many affairs but no interest in marriage. Her diary tells us that she cannot imagine anyone being happy who merely runs a household and raises two children. She speaks out for abortion, becomes upset over patriarchal locutions in everyday speech and patriarchal attitudes in socialist journalism, and fumes at the GDR's system of classifying children by their father's and not their mother's profession. She has an affair with a married man and wants his wife to know about it. We are meant to like her. Her decision, at age seventeen, to give her son up for adoption at birth, proves to have its excuse: she was a war orphan; the year was 1946; she was unmarried. In present time, at age forty-two, she does want a child—and moreover, as a single parent, so that the father will not interfere too much in its upbringing.

Worgitzky's other main female figures are cut from similar cloth. They include the interpreter Anne Helmholtz, a generation younger than Leonore, a strong-willed woman who leaves her five-year-old son at home with her husband while she travels extensively on the job; the actress Maria Kamnitzer, who once thought of adopting an orphanage child (the protagonist of the novel) but then found he interfered too much with her career and gave him back to the orphanage; and the brilliant composer Karoline Schlesinger, a married mother of two whose family drives her crazy because it leaves her only the mornings free for her work.

Worgitzky's second novel, *Meine ungeborenen Kinder* (1982), a work about the importance of legal and easily available abortion, features a heroine made of even sterner stuff. The actress Martha Trubec is ambitious and energetic, a successful, even indestructible forty-five-year-old career woman, on whose psyche her six abortions leave barely a scar. Readers accustomed to associate abortion with psychic anguish for the woman are ill-prepared for an iron heroine at the center precisely of an abortion story. She is so impervious that many readers have found it easy to dislike her.[93] As in *Die Unschuldigen*, Worgitzky reverses the conventional sex stereotypes. Martha is more dynamic, more career-oriented, and far less maternal than, for example, the father of her first aborted child: "Heinrich was more accommodating, also less energetic than I. Probably I often overwhelmed him with my loud enterprising spirit."[94] The actress freely acknowledges, in retrospect, her sexual desires: "At any rate, I believe that the main reason I fell in love with another man was because my sexual needs were not satisfied by Heinrich for so long. In the long run I couldn't take it any more."[95] Heinrich is one of the many men in GDR women's literature who leaves for the West, but in this novel of 1982 his desertion of the GDR is not politicized, and Martha remains in the East not out of political commitment, like Wolf's Rita in *Divided Heaven*, but rather, like Gina Vermeer, out of concern for her career: "I wouldn't have followed him because I was too attached to my career, which I would scarcely have had a chance to pursue at that time in West Germany."[96]

Worgitzky's latest novel, *Traum vom Möglichen* (Dream of possibilities, 1991), which is about a love affair between a middle-aged man and woman, again presents a woman who outshadows her male counterpart in vitality, courage, and psychic stability. The man, nicknamed "Bang" (a play on the German adjective *bange*, "afraid") is ultrasensitive, in fragile health, and quick to perceive slights to himself and to punish them by withdrawing emotionally. The woman, a psychologist, is strong, understanding, and patient; she has to "manage" Bang, who on the whole seems less like her lover than her patient, as if he were a child.

I choose as my final example of a novel with a strong woman heroine Wiens's *Traumgrenzen* (Dream limits, 1983), because the protagonist is precisely at the watershed that divides GDR from Western feminism. *Traumgrenzen* is another novel about abortion that, like Worgitzky's *Meine ungeborenen Kinder*, defends a woman's decision to abort. The protagonist Nina is a motherless, runaway, unmarried, unskilled teenage mother who is pregnant for the second time. From the Western optic, therefore, she has the profile of a victim. In a Western feminist context it is hard to imagine that this girl could function as anything other than a negative example, as testimony to society's failure to serve women. In this GDR novel, in striking contrast, she figures as a strong woman, a heroine who can do it all—or almost all. An energetic and decisive young woman, Nina, upon finding herself pregnant in the eleventh grade, leaves the home of her neglectful, sexist, and repressive father, a medical doctor, in order to have her baby and make her own life. Rejected for study, she works: "But I wanted to bring up my child alone, not in father's house and not with his money."[97] And when on her own: "After all, I wanted it this way. I was away from home and did not always just do what other people told me."[98] In short, Nina is portrayed as a heroine—and moreover, as one who completely contradicts the Western stereotype of the passive product of state socialism, since she is willing to undergo hardship for the sake of independence.

But a woman's strength has *limits*, the novel tells us. The stumbling block for Nina is her second pregnancy. Her dream is to keep the child, but she understands that two small children would make her other dream, university study, unrealizable. Her regretful decision to abort is the meaning of the title *Traumgrenzen*: "She has the feeling of being worthless. Her energy is not even enough for two children and university studies. She didn't even try. Gradually, she is using up all her dreams. For a piece of reality. Then resign yourself, she says to herself. Learn to resign."[99] Yet the novel ends optimistically: "Nina does not want to stop dreaming. She will have a year's time in the day-care center. [This refers to her new job.] She will fill out a new application. She will make an effort. She will love. And be loved. Maybe she will have a second child. What is lost at the beginning, anyhow?"[100] Thus as in Worgitzky's *Die Unschuldigen* and *Meine ungeborenen Kinder*, the strong woman type is invoked to justify a choice some might call selfish.

Despite her "limitations," Nina cuts a much better figure than the father of her second child, to whom Wiens strategically contrasts her. In an interesting plot twist, Wiens justifies the heroine's decision to get an abortion on the grounds that a man would have done no differently. Before deciding to abort, Nina takes the unusual step of offering to have the baby and give it to the father to raise. The father declines, since he feels that bringing up a child would limit his possibilities. There are several implications of his refusal. For one, the reader is meant to ask: Why should Nina have a more modest conception of her life and career chances than a man? Why should she be any less ambitious? For another, Wiens implies like Worgitzky in *Die Unschuldigen* that a large portion of child care could devolve onto men; that men are not naturally unfit for the job, but that society and custom, reinforced by laws that privilege the mother, have given them the luxury of not having to entertain the idea or to learn anything about the subject. And finally, the contrast with the child's father confirms Nina as a heroine, because she, unlike him, is at least capable of raising one child and pursuing a career.

It has been observed that GDR women's literature of the 1980s resembles FRG autobiographical women's literature of the 1970s in its tendency to represent women as victims, its use of identificatory mechanisms, and its narcissistic self-absorption.[101] While psychological themes and a tone of complaint do increasingly come to the fore in literature written by women in the 1980s, as will be seen in the next chapter, the image-building function of GDR feminism that was prominent in the 1970s nevertheless persisted into the next decade, as has been demonstrated here. Ricarda Schmidt's study of the concept of gendered identity in four sample works of fiction, two East German and two West German, written by women and appearing in 1988 or 1989, supports this conclusion, showing that the East German works (Maron's *Defector* and Wolf's *Sommerstück* [Summer piece]) press for a concept of feminine identity, whereas the West German works (Helke Sander's *The Three Women K.* [*Die Geschichten der drei Damen K.*] and Uta Treder's *Luna Aelion*) do not.[102] GDR novelists of the 1980s availed themselves of both preferred types of the previous decade: the rebellious nonconformist who, if not exactly a "model," at least invites the reader's approval, and the frankly identificatory positive heroine. While the state socialist context was ultimately responsible for inspiring the image-building project, the implementation of both types increasingly disengages the heroine from any partisan message: Maron's and Kachold's defiant heroines verge on the dissident, while the positive heroines of Thurm, Pirskawetz, Wolter, Worgitzky, and Wiens become more feminist, intent on advancing their own cause as women, and less builders or defenders of socialism.

5 The Reality of Women's Lives

We may safely assert that the knowledge which men can acquire of women, even as they have been and are, without reference to what they might be, is wretchedly imperfect and superficial, and always will be so, until women themselves have told all that they have to tell.

And this time has not come: nor will it come otherwise than gradually. It is but of yesterday that women have either been qualified by literary accomplishments, or permitted by society, to tell anything to the general public. As yet very few of them dare tell anything, which men, on whom their literary success depends, are unwilling to hear.
—John Stuart Mill, *The Subjection of Women*

Predictably, I was angriest at the men I felt closest to, the ones I knew really did care—about me, about having good politics; so often they simply *didn't get it*, a solid, dumb lump of resistance masquerading as incomprehension of the simplest, clearest demands for reciprocity....

Part of being oppressed was having one's perceptions negated; part of being an oppressor was doing the negating.
—Ellen Willis, *No More Nice Girls: Countercultural Essays*

For women the measure of the intimacy has been the measure of the oppression. This is why feminism has had to explode the private. This is why feminism has seen the personal as the political.
—Catherine A. MacKinnon, *Feminism Unmodified: Discourses on Life and Law*

In "Die kleine Seejungfrau" (The little mermaid, in *Schattenriß eines Liebhabers*, 1980), a story about relations between the sexes, the GDR writer Rosemarie Zeplin takes Hans Christian Andersen's tale of the little mermaid as a paradigm for women's failure to communicate satisfactorily with the men with whom they are on intimate terms. In Andersen's tale, the mermaid is allowed to become a human being who can walk on land and dance at the ball only at the price of giving up her voice. She therefore forgoes the crucial possibility of telling the prince that it was she who saved him from drowning. She must rely on *his* ability to recognize and acknowledge *her* instead. She hopes in vain, for the prince believes that a princess, who moreover would be an advantageous match, rescued him, and marries her instead of the mermaid.

Andersen's tale might be read to mean that the prince represses a reality—his debt to the little mermaid—that is no longer useful to him. He relegates the little mermaid to the "aquatic depths" of the unconscious. Zeplin seems to understand the tale this way, since in her own story she has her "little mermaid" character, Angelika, whose husband has fallen in love with a young student and left her, tell it. Thenceforth Angelika—who finally commits suicide—is completely incomprehensible to him. From the perspective of the main character Lisa: "He simply acted as if Angelika were completely incomprehensible to him, too incoherent and simple-minded to be able to figure her out. He, who knew her better than any other person, denied her and the intimacy of his knowledge. I don't understand her, you won't understand her, Lisa read in his face."[1]

Complaints arising from the disempowered meet a strange fate: they tend simply not to be heard. They fall into a psychological space whose equilibrium they would upset, and into a public space that has no room for them, whose smooth functioning they would disturb. By a trapdoor mechanism of individual and collective psychology, the problems of the disempowered therefore fall right through these spaces and into the cracks of oblivion. Zeplin's treatment of the little mermaid story suggests that the more inconvenient it is for those who hold the power to become aware of these problems, the more inexorably the denial mechanism that bars their entrance into consciousness operates. The more these problems are limited to the disempowered group or individual and do not extend into the ranks of those in power, the more they are nullified. Women as a historically disempowered group have suffered from the misrecognition or denial particularly of such "women's problems" as men do not share. As

Christa Wolf says in "The Shadow of a Dream," men have determined what reality is. The problem has been exacerbated by a secondary mechanism of self-censorship: what woman dares articulate a complaint that is predestined to be trivialized, distorted, or even completely disregarded? Charlotte Worgitzky writes: "It has become such a matter of course to look at the world with the eyes of men that women often have a hard time comprehending that their often decisively different experiences are important enough to name aloud."[2] One of the greatest barriers to women's advancement has surely been the difficulty they have experienced in securing an audience, in the consciousness of men, for the reality of their lives.

The solution to this dilemma lies in making public what had been private, in speaking out. Originality here is far less important than critical mass. What counts is hearing something over and over again, from as many voices as possible. Once the problem is recognized and articulated as a common problem, a class problem, it cannot be so easily ignored. Above all, the sufferers themselves can then no longer be so easily intimidated into believing that their problems are mere personal failings, deviations from the norm, cause for shame. Zeplin's story shows to what extent men have the word. Alongside the story of Angelika, the narrator shows how the heroine Lisa is talked out of her self-esteem by her husband Eckhard, a theater director who is always "casting" her in unfavorable roles. He belittles her research in mathematics to the point where she also feels compelled to belittle it when speaking to him about it: "She mentioned this research at home, with Eckard, only with the adjective 'so-called' in order to forestall his scorn."[3] Lisa is by turns "emotionally impoverished" or "blindly given over to her feelings and completely incapable of thinking logically," depending on the situation.[4] The same kind of experience of being talked down, talked out of what you think you are and into some other role is testified to by interviews Alice Schwarzer conducted with West German women and reproduced in Der "kleine Unterschied."[5] Schwarzer shows persuasively that the courage it takes to talk back comes with power, and that power comes above all with a job and the resulting financial independence.

After the liberalization of what could be said in literature under Honecker, the 1970s and 1980s brought a tidal wave of GDR fiction written by women that gave voice to the reality of women's lives. In tandem, a large amount of documentary literature was published. In 1973 Sarah Kirsch published *Die Pantherfrau* (*The Panther Woman*), a volume of interviews with women. Maxie Wander's *Guten Morgen, du Schöne* (1977), another volume of interviews with women, was a milestone. It was the first time that German women, chosen from every age group and from every walk of life, had talked openly about every aspect of their lives from politics to sex. To judge from its success, there was an interest in women's lives, in contrasting the biographies of older women who had grown up under Hitler with women who had grown up partly or entirely in the new state, and in how the GDR "new woman" was coping with the new life that socialism had prescribed for her. The majority of the women in Wander's volume give the impression of being in control of their lives, if not contented. None call themselves feminists, although some of the younger women have feminist ideas. Following Wander's bestseller, a flood of published interviews appeared, for instance, Irina Liebmann's *Berliner Mietshaus* (Berlin apartment house, 1982); Gabriele Eckart's *So sehe ick die Sache* (The way I see things, 1984); Christiane Barckhausen's *Schwestern* (Sisters, 1985); Christine Müller's *Männer-protokolle* (Male statements, 1985); Christine Lambrecht's *Männerbekanntschaften* (Male acquaintances, 1986); and Erika Rüdenauer's *Dünne Haut. Tagebücher von Frauen aus der DDR* (Thin skin: Diaries of women from the GDR, 1987).

This chapter will give an overview of the major themes and contentions of the large body of GDR women's literature that presents the day-to-day reality of women's lives, inasmuch as these themes and contentions bear a feminist message. What the literature treated in this chapter has in common is the intention of breaking entrenched social taboos. It testifies to the authors' impatience with pretending that things are not the way they are, with choreographing relations between the sexes according to timeworn patterns of propriety and shoveling "exceptions" under the rug. It expresses irritation with men's lack of awareness of women's oppression.[6] Some of the fiction that was published was written with emancipatory intent, to prove a point. Some is milder, but a feminist agenda nevertheless shimmers through. Some is mainly psychological.

The Double Burden

One of the earliest themes that inspired feminist fiction in the GDR was the double burden. It was a topic that, as of the mid-1960s, was in the forefront of government concern in the area of family politics. No aspect of women's lives was more thoroughly documented and studied. Women were officially recognized as suffering from the double day. In an era when American feminists urged that combining motherhood and a career was eminently doable, called for child-care facilities, and encouraged middle-class women to get out of their suburban homes and return to the professions,[7] the GDR government, after twenty years of putting the superwoman model into practice, was obliged to acknowledge its shortcomings. Small wonder that it became not only one of the earliest, but also one of the most enduring, most ubiquitous themes in GDR women's literature: it was a subject where feminism and *Parteilichkeit*, party spirit, coincided.

To recapitulate the facts: by the early 1970s, 82 percent of women in the GDR worked or were being trained; the working day was 8¾ hours long; according to a study performed in 1965, 47.5 hours per week per household were spent on housework. Another study of 1970 showed that 47.1 hours per week per household were still being spent on housework, and of these, women did 37.1 hours while men did 6.1 hours.[8] Growing numbers of women were opting for part-time work because of household responsibilities. The government expressed its concern by funding labor-saving conveniences such as commercial laundries and cleaners and shopping centers and by calling on men to do their share of the housework.[9] Here it did not meet with any great degree of success. By 1971 so many women had been driven into part-time work—nearly one-third of all who worked—that the government felt it necessary in 1972 to reduce the workweek to 40 hours for mothers of three children in order to attract them back into full-time jobs.[10] Irmtraud Morgner, who had already thematized the double day in *Rumba auf einen Herbst* and *Hochzeit in Konstantinopel*,[11] sums up the matter in *Trobadora Beatriz*: "Most women were forced to have the second or third shift as their hobby: household, children" (*TB* 260).

Some of the earliest feminist stories focused on the inequitable distribution of housework and child care between the sexes and chalked it up to the housework-shy man. The GDR granted women equal rights and equal education; work was less a right than a duty; yet men's attitudes toward women, especially in the home, remained as traditional as they had been when women were condemned to "children, cooking, and church." Although such works as Wolf's *Divided Heaven* document that women had trouble being accepted as useful equals by male colleagues in the workplace, the theme of men's voluntary uselessness in the household, which proliferates in women's fiction of the 1970s, testifies that men in the GDR grew used to the working woman far more quickly than to the idea that they themselves should do their share of the child care and housework. Five feminist stories of the 1970s by Renate Koetter-Johnschker, Worgitzky, Morgner, Hannelore Lauerwald, and Christine Wolter reveal a male mind-set that may strike today's American reader as a local historical curiosity, but that in fact existed and was also the norm in West Germany during the same period. The American woman's status as "homemaker," as Queen of the Home, was never part of the German tradition.[12] Rather, men came home from work and expected to be waited on like "pashas." In an era when West German women accepted men's failure to do housework and child care largely uncritically, as "the way men are," and fell in with the "feminine," domestic role that men expected of them—that is, were oppressed without realizing their oppression—, the East German women who wrote these stories recognize it for what it is and mercilessly satirize it.

Most of the writers in question are of the generation born in the 1930s. The key to their coming to consciousness was presumably the mass entry of women into the labor market. Whereas West German women accepted being housewives and being treated like housewives because they *were* housewives, East German women worked all day; the government encouraged them to think of themselves as men's equals. In the *Familiengesetzbuch der Deutschen Demokratischen Republik* (Family statutes of the German Democratic Republic, 1965) it was actually written into law that "both spouses contribute their share in bringing up and caring for the children and running the household."[13] Government communiqués insisted that housework and child care should be shared.[14] The contrast between official emancipation and the servant role women were expected to play at home was too crass to be passed over in silence.

Feminist fiction portrays women rejecting the housewife role with a vengeance and suspecting men of trying to maneuver them into it so as to further their own careers. The word used by Koetter-Johnschker in an early story, "Im Kreislauf der Windeln" (In the diaper cycle, 1971), is "exploitation."[15] In this story a woman takes a baby year off from work at her husband's behest. As the days go by her husband retreats from housework and child care more and more and treats her increasingly like a housewife. This story demonstrates how important paid employment is for women and how not working deprives her of a bargaining chip in the family. The man progresses in his career at the woman's expense. On her child's first birthday the disgusted heroine informs her husband of her decision to return to work. The author plays on the famous toilet scene in Heine's *Deutschland. Ein Wintermärchen* (*Germany, a winter's tale*): "And then she let Robert take a glance into the witches' cauldron, out of which the musty vapors of a bourgeois marriage steamed up. No shout of I-don't-believe-it could stop her. She elucidated her future plans to him unwaveringly: Beginning the next day she wanted to go straight to work. In other words: That's it for the diaper cycle."[16]

Another story at the vanguard of this assault is one of the earliest GDR feminist works, Worgitzky's novella "Quäze," published in *Vieräugig oder blind* in 1978 but dated 1970 by the author. It is a humorous, but actually bitter, story about how society pushes women into the housewife-and-mother role, and how their ambitions founder on the demands of that role. The plot shows how the heroine Quäze, who wants to be a writer and in particular wants to write about women's issues, which she thinks about constantly, is cornered into becoming a housewife. Quäze is emancipated; she does not want to get married and particularly does not want children, which she thinks would spell doom for her vocation as a writer. Her downfall starts when she has a romance with Bem, also a writer. Bem wants to marry her, or failing that, at least to live with her. Since Quäze loves Bem, she acquiesces: they move in together. What can go wrong, she thinks, if she makes it a condition that housework be shared? Quäze sets up a strict division of labor. The irony of the situation is that Bem is an "emancipated man": not only does he initially appeal to Quäze because of his liberated views on women's emancipation, but he willingly agrees to do the domestic tasks Quäze allots him. But the gap between theory and practice is enormous. Once they are living together Bem never thinks of doing any housework on his own initiative, but constantly has to be reminded. In the end Quäze does it. Bem doesn't know how to do anything around the house; without directives, he does everything wrong. The shopping lists Quäze has to write for Bem can never be explicit enough. If none of the vegetables on the shopping list are in the store, Bem buys no vegetables at all. Bem asks how much sugar and what kind of oil to buy and whether to put the oil in the fridge. It never occurs to him to clean. He doesn't think of washing his clothes and never has a clean shirt. He has no idea how to remove a spot from his tie. When

Quäze tells him to use spot remover, he can't find the bottle. He never answers the doorbell: Quäze has to do it. And so forth. The predictable result, a commonplace in GDR "double-day" fiction, is that the man's career flourishes while the woman's withers: Bem gets lots of writing done and Quäze nearly none.

Whereas Bem figures in the story as a lovable but infuriating buffoon, the novella directs the brunt of its critique at social norms. Society at large pressures Quäze into the traditional feminine role. When the neighbor woman has to take her child to the hospital and leaves her baby with them, she automatically hands it to Quäze, not Bem. To her mind, Bem does a lot of housework for a man. When Bem and Quäze get married after all, supposedly for convenience, Quäze, who used to rail against the masculinity of German last names (many end in the masculine *-er* or *-mann*), finds herself taking Bem's last name, for by law the couple must take one name, either the husband's or the wife's. The story climaxes in a scene where Bem invites his lectors to dinner after his book is published. In the course of the evening they manage to treat Quäze like "the lady of the house," that is, like a housewife, a sex object, and a dilettante who dabbles in literature. These are the fruits of marriage for a woman writer, Worgitzky implies.

Morgner's story "Gospel of Valeska," published in *Trobadora Beatriz*, starts with the same trope of the housework-shy man. Valeska dreads moving in with Rudolf because she fears it will mean that she will have to do all the housework. Rudolf, a scientist, does not dream of doing any himself. He does not shop and even takes his breakfast in a restaurant. Yet he is unprepared to accept a similar attitude from Valeska, who is also a scientist—because, after all, she's a woman. When she excuses herself on grounds that she's a scientist for not having made dinner for the academic friends he invites to her place, he reacts frostily.

In "Unterwegs im Regen" (On the road in the rain, 1975) Lauerwald has her heroine contemplate the fate of a woman whose husband blackmails her emotionally into giving up evening classes in order to become, in effect, his domestic servant. The heroine "feels ashamed for the other woman. . . . She sees herself standing in this corridor, hears a male voice demanding the evening meal, or a fresh handkerchief, or a bucket of water for a footbath. At the same time she realizes that she will never stand in such a corridor."[17]

Wolter presents a novel solution to the problem of the unequal distribution of housework between husband and wife in her story

"Ich habe wieder geheiratet" (1976). The first-person narrator, a scientist, divorces her husband, also a scientist, because he stops doing housework, insists on "creative leisure time" for himself, starts bossing her around, and acts in a condescending fashion. Thereupon, she enters into a new "marriage": she moves in with a woman. Rosa is a supportive "spouse." Each of the two women has one young child, who gains a friend and playmate through the new living arrangement. The narrator finds her new union ideal.

Later stories continue and expand on the theme of the housework-shy man. In the story "Pi" (in *Der Lauf der Dinge*, 1982) Helga Königsdorf records from a little boy's naive perspective life with his divorced mother. She has a boyfriend she met at work—indeed, she is his superior, a fact that seems to upset him. But at home she is, in the boy's eyes, tantamount to his servant: "Women are really strange. In her work she's the big boss. She's in charge. Earns the money. And at home she cleans up junk after a character like that."[18] Morgner in *Amanda* presents a street scene that shows that shopping is still a woman's job: "The male employees stroll about, smoke, converse. The female employees rush from shop to shop with shopping bags, shopping nets, and lists, dragging together food and other merchandise" (*A* 454). Mathilde's life with her Egyptologist husband Dr. Seydel in Renate Apitz's *Hexenzeit* falls into the familiar pattern. Mathilde's existence is a veritable treadmill of housework and child care, punctuated by her full-time museum job: Apitz gives a step-by-step account of every day of her week, whose monotony rivals its stressfulness. Her husband, who had had the reputation of a confirmed bachelor before they married, retreats into his work and his pleasures when he gets home. One evening Mathilde is listening to Seydel play music; a scream comes from the bathtub; Mathilde runs to find that a glowing red heating element has disengaged itself from its socket and is about to fall on her little son in the tub. Mathilde deals with the emergency; her husband continues to play music. When she asks him later why he didn't help her, Seydel says "with his voice filled with willingness to oblige that Mathilde would just have had to ask him."[19]

While these stories on the double burden aim to place the blame on men and on the social customs that allow men to shirk all domestic responsibilities, others were written with the objective not of pointing the finger, but of depicting the double burden in all of its tedious detail and conveying to the reader a sense of its crushing weight. Two works by Brigitte Martin are cases in point. Both thematize the double burden on the example of the single working mother. The first, *Der rote Ballon. Geschichten um Brigge Bem* (The red balloon. Stories about Brigge Bem, 1977), consists of a series of seven stories narrated in the first person over a period of years by Brigge Bem, the single parent of two school-age daughters.[20] Before their father, to whom she had not been married, left her after nine years of living together, she had worked as a typist; afterwards she went back to school and finally to *Ingenieurhochschule*, where she is when the stories begin. She has a job, and she wants eventually to study sociology. Bem is crushingly busy: her "second shift" with the children runs from 6:00 P.M. to 10:30 P.M. "When they say: Have a good one, I say: Off to second shift."[21] She is never finished with anything. The novel offers no solution to a case like Bem's. While one has the impression that a life companion would alleviate Bem's loneliness and give her more of a sense of family, the novel never suggests that a man would make her life easier or solve the problem of the double burden. She has occasional lovers. The men all have basically nothing to offer her; Martin gives all of them last name "Em." The novel pointedly ends when her relationship with her latest lover-for-a-night fizzles. Bem, who has dreamed, against her own better knowledge, of romance and family, notes: "'For you', that's the children, that's the career, the household, the university studies, the relatives you have to 'please.' This 'for you' does not mean anything more than that."[22] Yet a feminist message shimmers through the lines: it is that men's lives are, in general, simpler, easier, and happier.

Martin's second volume of fiction, the novel *Nach Freude anstehen* (Standing in line for happiness, 1981), similarly portrays the hectic life-style that falls to a single working mother. Like its predecessor, this novel does not appear to be constructed at the service of any particular point or point—except perhaps to suggest that women's lives are complicated and difficult—but rather seizes the reader with its trueness to life. The heroine's job in a computer center keeps her out of the home for eleven or twelve hours a day. Thereafter she returns to an evening during which she tries to accomplish, rarely successfully, what is most pressing: "housework and services for the children."[23] She virtually never has any leisure time in which to regenerate herself, nor the time or energy actually to play with the children. Everything is her responsibility: in the evening she is responsible not only for doing the housework, but also for maintaining the mood. In sum, "the evening begins with more duties that have not been carried out than those that have, and this determines the atmosphere, for which she alone is responsible."[24] Men are not portrayed as the villains in this novel either. Their casual attitude toward housework is taken simply as a fact of life. Edith states matter-of-factly about her steady boyfriend: "He is not bothered by undarned pantyhose, grayed curtains, clouded bookshelves, missing tumblers, children's pants that are too short."[25] We are not to assume that a husband would solve her problems: her married friend Marianne dismisses that idea with the remark that "with a man, you have one more child."[26] As in Martin's previous novel, the double day is seen simply as a woman's problem.

Neither here nor in any other East German fiction written by a woman is it suggested that the solution might be for the woman to give up work. Giving up employment is literally never advanced as a solution to women's double day. It is, however, gently suggested here that women would be helped by more flexible working conditions. In *Nach Freude anstehen* it helps greatly that Edith manages to get herself a sick leave for a couple of weeks. Simply having a little free time proves the key to finding a solution to her problems.

Vignettes of the harried days of working women became a little genre of their own, which dot women's fiction starting in the late 1960s. Thus Morgner writes ironically of the benefits of work for a mother of three in *Hochzeit in Konstantinopel*:

> Mrs. Konstantin, mother of three children, occasionally would have been overcome with sadness if she had remained a housewife and thought about her life. Ever since she started working in the lightbulb factory, she no longer had time to reflect. She felt fabulous, the work that accumulated was doable if it was well-organized. Mrs. Konstantin's schedule planned for the following: Monday window washing, Tuesday washing, Wednesday ironing and mending, Thursday mopping and waxing, Friday grocery shopping for the whole weekend, Saturday baking or canning, hair salon, Sunday gardening.[27]

Similar day-by-day accounts occur in Helga Schubert's "Mondstein" (Moonstone, 1982)[28] and at great length in Apitz's *Hexenzeit*.[29]

A string of stories treat the problem of the double burden humorously, by suggesting that it might be helped through magic. Thus Worgitzky in "Karriere abgesagt" (Career canceled, dated 1972 in *Vieräugig oder blind*), lets her heroine ask a wish-granting angel for the power to do without sleep. When she can work through the night as well as the day, she manages to become a school director, though when she has a third and then a fourth child, she also has to economize with her nights. Morgner's story "Das Seil" (The tightrope, in *Trobadora Beatriz*), is especially clever in its use of a magic trick that is at the same time a concrete metaphor: Vera Hill, a scientist with a three-year-old child, literalizes the idea of a balancing act by traveling to work on a tightrope. This saves her two hours of commuting. The idea of using magic to solve the problem of the double burden became a joke that GDR women writers seemed never to tire of telling with new embellishments. In Monika Helmecke's "Lauf weg—kehr um" (Run away—turn around, in *Klopfzeichen*, 1979) a woman asks a good fairy for a second, parallel life so that she can have time to compose music. In Maria Seidemann's "Der hilfreiche Rabe" (The helpful raven, in *Der Tag an dem Sir Henry starb* [The day Sir Henry died], 1980), a magic raven—a play on the expression "Rabenmutter" ("raven [=neglectful] mother")—comes and plays nanny to the dramatic producer Silvia's two noisy, rambunctious sons so that she can get her work done. Morgner herself uses the trope repeatedly, suggesting that it would help if women could live one-thousand-year lives (*TB* 372), or could invent a potion to make sleep unnecessary (*A* 135 passim), or could fly like witches (*A* 497).

Motherhood

Much GDR women's fiction centers on *children* as the main source of women's double bind. Woman as mother dominates in GDR women's writing. The contrast to the tradition of women's literature and also to contemporary Western fiction is striking. Motherhood has never been and is still not a major literary theme in the West. The heroine of the past was a young, unmarried, childless woman. Today the field is broader: themes of ambitions, study, and careers join those of relationships, love, and marriage, not to mention rape, sexual harassment, and abortion; but women's life with children is all but elided. In contrast, the typical GDR heroine is a mother, chances are a single mother. In fiction written by women in the GDR children became a huge topic, encompassing every conceivable aspect of mothers' lives with their children. These include, in the order treated below, the exhausting nature of small children; the conflicts that children create for women in terms of career and work; the problems of single motherhood, including those of child care and relationships; and women's and children's psychological interdependence and conflicts.

Many women writers recognized that children were *the* problem for women. The oppression that motherhood created for women was Morgner's earliest feminist theme. In "Notturno" (1964), Karla, pregnant for a third time, reflects how motherhood has robbed her of her artistic dreams, prevented her from pursuing her original career goal of pediatrician as well as every subsequent one, ruined her appearance, and reduced her to dependence on a patronizing husband whom the children adore because of his scarceness, while taking her for granted. "I'm not a baby factory," she protests.[30] In *Rumba auf einen Herbst* (completed 1965; published 1992) she reworks the same story. Here, the housewife Karla is even more clearly tagged as a victim, for her husband Lutz, vacationing without her, starts an affair with a woman who is virtually her opposite. Ev, professional, ambitious, feminist, rebellious, is the successful woman type, the prototype of Bele and Beatriz that Morgner in *Beatriz* will come to associate with "megalomania." She resists having children, arguing: "Talent is above all the ability to concentrate. A mother is always at least subconsciously with her children."[31] Moreover, Morgner drops the tacked-on happy ending of "Notturno," presumably written in deference to socialist-realist demands, where the heroine unconvincingly dismisses her complaints as a mere bad mood. The demands of the mother role are made apropos of Karla heavy-handedly: "The children were the most important thing, the children were hungry. . . . A mother always had to have ideas. . . . A mother always had to come up with something new . . . a mother always had to clear the table."[32]

Worgitzky's story "Eva" (dated 1976 in *Vieräugig oder blind*) makes the point that woman is, to speak with Simone de Beauvoir, the victim of the species. This Eve does little other than have six children and two abortions before succumbing to a gynecological disorder that might, ironically, terminate her life at the same time as it terminates her ability to bear children.

Whereas in the United States the media have created an image of mothers who want to be with their children all the time, of mothers going to work guiltily and wishing they could stay at home with their children, GDR women's literature, without giving the impression of being against children, produced a corrective to this vision of the parent-child idyll. Many stories illustrate how exhausting the task of raising small children is. Helga Schubert's "Die Ausnahme" (The exception, in *Anna kann Deutsch* [Anna can speak German], 1975), shows how a mother gets a child ready for school in the morning and listens to the child's nonstop talk when he comes home at noon. Monika Helmecke's "September 30" (in *Klopfzeichen*, 1979; translated in Lukens and Rosenberg, *Daughters of Eve*) looks at the problem on the microscopic level: she describes a housewife's exhausting day. It is written in the style of Natalya Baranskaya's novella "A Week Like Any Other" (1969; pub. in German in the FRG in 1979; in the GDR in 1980), a celebrated work on women's double duty that chronicles a hectic week in the life of a working mother in the Soviet Union. Helmecke's story is a first-person narrative by a woman writer—who, however, rarely gets to write. She gives an hour-by-hour account of her day with her two children, a baby and a preschool-age child, from 5:30 A.M. till past midnight, while her husband is on a business trip and the preschool is closed. It is a day of constant work. The children are mind-deadening. She counts the hours until the children go to bed and finishes the day by getting drunk.

Of the stories that show how exhausting small children can be, Helga Königsdorf's "Heimkehr einer Prinzessin" (Homecoming of a princess, in *Meine ungehörigen Träume*, 1978) is among the most inspired. I reproduce the beginning of the nonstop speech with which Katrin assails her mother upon her return home from work:

> Mommy, how come you're so late? Are we still going swimming? Grandma made us sandwiches. Martina forgot her sandwiches today. Martina got a hamster for her birthday. She didn't invite Stefan cause he beat her up. We decided he couldn't be in the brigade any more. Everyone wants me to be in the brigade. Martina too. Mommy, can Martina come swimming with us? Martina's hamster is cute. Mama, let's us get one too. Oh please, Mommy![33]

The child's uninterrupted chatter goes on in this style for over a page.

Children and Careers

East German women writers were by virtue of their vocation particularly sensitive to the issue of how children can be combined with demanding creative or intellectual work. Morgner, mother of one, said that she adapted her writing style to constant interruptions and that her work came to a dead stop during school vacations.[34] In the same vein, in *Trobadora Beatriz*, where Morgner admits her writer colleagues into the fictional world of Beatriz's adventures, she has Sarah Kirsch turn down a request to write a love poem for Beatriz because Kirsch's two-year-old son has caused her to get behind with her work (*TB* 200). Wolf (mother of two daughters) reflects in *Parting from Phantoms* in an essay on Grace Paley:

> A woman with small children is bound to write differently than a man does, or than a woman without children does. Her time gets broken into small segments; her ability to concentrate, which may never have let her down before, wears thin, and she may never regain it. She must get used to feeling that the intensity and time she devotes to writing is time taken away from her children; and she must endure the ongoing feeling of guilt and resist the ongoing temptation to give up.[35]

Many East German women writers recognized that raising children and having a career are basically incompatible and if there is one reason why women fail to advance in their careers, it is because they bear and raise children. In *Trobadora Beatriz* Morgner has Laura tell the story of "shoes," which illustrates how all of a woman's talents and ambitions are undermined by motherhood.[36] Walli and her husband can wear the same clothes: they are "the same size." They can even wear the same shoes—symbolizing going places. But it is the husband Sigmund who goes places, not the wife Walli. As in the double-burden stories, the woman's stasis or even regress is measured against the man's progress. Walli has three children. From child to child, her career goal shrinks from doctor to a degree in Slavic studies to elementary-school teacher; finally she becomes a secretary. When her husband is not wearing them on trips and when Wally is not wearing them, symbolically, in little social gatherings of Sigmund's colleagues and their wives in her home, she keeps them, also symbolically, with the wedding presents, in the cupboard in the living room with the crystal and porcelain. In *Amanda* Morgner tells a similar story. Hilde Felber, married mother of four and a dynamo of a woman, occupies an important government position: she is a section head in the cabinet council. But, the narrator observes, she would probably be secretary of state or deputy minister if she had succeeded, as she wanted, in having an abortion instead of a fourth child at age forty.

Some fictional heroines draw the consequence that it is better not to have or to defer having children. Of all the East German women writers, Charlotte Worgitzky is the one who presses hardest for a solution to the child problem and frequently advocates this one. Worgitzky's heroines are usually gifted women with artistic or intellectual ambitions. These women's attitudes toward having children resemble Kafka's fear of having a family: work demands all their energy and concentration; their time must be conserved for work; children would be a distraction as well as a major responsibility; therefore, they will not have children. In her story "Quäze," the heroine Quäze regards with dismay the example of her friend Hanne, a gifted pianist who sacrificed her career for her four children, while her husband, a violinist, became famous. The conflict between children and career then becomes the central theme of Worgitzky's full-length novel *Die Unschuldigen* (1975). Here, two professional woman abjure having children because raising them would wreck their careers. One gave a child up for adoption in pre-GDR days and aborted a second. Another, an actress, adopts a child, but decides differently and gives it back to the orphanage when her rehearsal schedule gets heavy.

The counterexample of a woman *with* children who tries to do creative work is given in the minor character Karoline Schlesinger, a composer. Her response to a radio interview question about the number of her compositions voices how difficult it is for her, as a mother, to find the time to compose at all:

> I have two children and a husband who is the financial director of a large enterprise. It took me years to get myself my mornings for my work—I really had to fight hard for them, because everyone says: But you do have time, you're at home, what do you do anyway, a little plunking on the piano. . . . The children come home from school at noon, in the evening my husband comes home from work, everyone wants to eat, and everyone works off frustrations on me. When I've worked the whole morning I'm so exhausted that I first need to rest—to take a walk or to lie down for an hour—, instead of dealing with completely different kinds of problems that actually require all my attention.[37]

Worgitzky's professional women who do have children suffer in the measure that they fail to shift the childrearing burden onto their husbands.

Whereas Worgitzky's ambitious heroines unsentimentally unload their children in one way or another—whether onto husbands or orphanages or through abortion—other authors represent the career woman's decision not to have children as painful. In Wolf's "Self-experiment" the heroine, a scientist, realizes that she has repressed a desire for a family and children. Beate Morgenstern's "Das Mädchen Mirka" (The girl Mirka, in *Jenseits der Allee*, 1979), is a delicate story that tacitly thematizes the problem of combining family and career for women and of being a woman in a man's world. Elke has a career as her journalist-husband's assistant ("Sachbearbeiterin"). She travels with him on his many international assignments. But there are three problems: she is and will forever be his subordinate; in the world at large she is an anomaly among women; and she is and will remain childless, because a child does not harmonize with her career. Such stories invite the reader to reflect on woman's insoluble double bind: a woman can strive to emulate a man's career, but she will never be able to combine a career and children as unproblematically as a man.

Elfriede Brüning, an older-generation writer, presents a summa of the family-career "contradiction" for women in her novel *Partnerinnen* (Women partners, 1978) by juxtaposing the life stories of four women who make different choices. One woman subordinates her children to her career, another forgoes children to advance her career, another puts her three children first, and a fourth chooses to be a stay-at-home housewife and mother. The story shows that both the childless career woman and the traditional housewife are headed for the rocks, each in her own way. Of the remaining two, only the traditional, family-oriented, unambitious mother of three who puts loving and nurturing first is really happy, but the novel is far from prescribing this role as a sovereign remedy for happiness, since not every woman is blessed with such a personality, nor is this route bound to turn out right. The last portrait, that of the traditional housewife, counterbalances the portrait of the happy mother: this housewife renounces a career for husband and family, only to feel that she is treated like a doormat and to be disappointed by her daughters, who aggressively assert their independence from her. The message is that it is nigh unto impossible for a woman to find precisely the right balance between family and work. No good solution exists.

Maya Wiens's *Traumgrenzen* points up the conflict between having a child and having a career in an interesting and novel way: by placing a *man* before the choice whether to keep or abort a child. Nina, a young single mother of one child who is pregnant again, realizes that she cannot raise a second child by herself. Before deciding to get an abortion, she makes the father an offer, possible under East

German law: if *he* will take and raise the child, she will bear it. The narrator glosses: "She confronted him with a decision that for women is part of life."[38] Thomas felt "overtaxed" by her offer. "Her offer simply did not belong to what was for him the realm of the imaginable. He could have sooner imagined himself living like Robinson on an island for twenty-eight years than living in Berlin with a child, and on top of that with an infant."[39] After Nina makes her offer, Thomas represses the whole topic. Then he slowly and gradually makes himself think about it, only to come to a negative conclusion: "If he had the child he himself would be limiting his own possibilities. And when he finally knew what he had to be, what he had to do, then he might not be able to do it any longer."[40]

Single Motherhood

The fictional mothers whose children interfere with their careers are frequently married. Since part of the purpose in these stories is to show how children obstruct a woman's, but not a man's, career, a male contrast figure in the form of a husband is expedient. The conflict between motherhood and employment where employment is conceived simply as a normal full-time job rather than as a particularly demanding one is, in contrast, usually illustrated on the example of women who are single parents. In such stories single parenthood itself is not presented as the problem. The single working mother was a widespread social phenomenon in the GDR. In the years after the Second World War many widows raised their children alone. Before 1961 the attrition of men to the West was high; frequently these men left their wives and children behind. The divorce rate climbed. The social stigma attached to having a child out of wedlock decreased as the state increasingly prioritized single mothers for child-care spaces and for subventions, such as sick child leave starting with the first child and financial support if no child care was available, which enabled them to combine motherhood and employment.[41] Single motherhood was dignified to the extent that mothers had the option of recognizing the father of their child, in which case they were entitled to child support from him; if he did not pay, the state took over the payments.[42] According to a 1992 microcensus 20 percent of families in the New States were headed by a single mother (a total of 431,000 women); of these, 44.2 percent had never married.[43] Especially in a context where husbands were viewed as not especially helpful around the house, the single mother came to stand for the typical woman. Her problem of combining job, housework, and child care was not seen as that of a small, deviant minority, but, in Marxist parlance, as a "contradiction" basic to the lives of women in socialist society.

It may seem peculiar, in a state that prided itself on making employment and motherhood compatible for women by providing an extensive child-care net, that women nevertheless complained about how difficult it was to combine both. Yet child care, as a service for women, never equaled the child-minding service women used to perform for men. In the days when a woman's family was her career, the wife was there, twenty-four hours a day, for a husband who worked. For today's woman who is trying to work or pursue a career, child care does not represent this kind of backup. GDR child-care centers had generous hours, from 6:00 A.M. until 6:00 or even 7:00 P.M., but these hours did not necessarily tally with every work shift. Then as now, parents had to coordinate their working hours with child-care hours rather than being able to count on child care that suited their work schedule. Morgner shows in *Amanda* that a single mother tram driver would be obliged to work night shifts for the sole reason that both day shifts cut across child-care drop-off and pickup hours. Spontaneous deviations from the child-care center timetable were out of the question. Wiens's *Traumgrenzen* makes the point that the doors of the child-care center are locked at 8:00 A.M.; after that, the personnel fusses if a parent arrives with a child.

Child care for infants and toddlers (*Krippe*) remained consistently unpopular in the GDR. Sending a child there was never a preferred solution. Jutta Menschik and Evelyn Leopold report that only one-third of 0–3-year-olds were in public child care, and that these were mainly the children of single mothers.[44] Most mothers tried to stay at home or send the children to a grandmother. Gerda Szepansky, interviewing women in 1993, reports the continued unpopularity of the *Krippen*.[45] In contrast, most parents of preschoolers (ages 3–6) sent their children to child care (*Kindergarten*). Yet the solution was not perfect. Child-care centers did not take sick children, although child care is precisely where children picked up colds and other infectious diseases. The methods of training children were often at odds with those the mothers would have liked to see used. Children usually preferred to be with their mothers and sometimes rebelled at going to child care at all.

The notorious weekly child-care centers (*Wochenheime*) that existed in the 1950s and 1960s were generally felt to be a recourse of last resort. Worgitzky in "Hänsel und Gretel. Kein Märchen" (Hansel and Gretel. Not a fairy-tale, dated 1976 in *Vieräugig oder blind*) implies that sending a child there is the modern-day equivalent of setting a child out in the woods. Christa Müller's "Candida" (1979) tells a similar tale about a *Wochenheim*.

Working mothers of school-age children (ages 6–10) were frequently under even more pressure than mothers of preschoolers, since the GDR, like the BRD, had half-day schooling (school let out in time for lunch) and afterschool (*Hort*) places were harder to get throughout the 1970s and 1980s than preschool (*Kindergarten*) places.[46] For school-age children, after-school care was never available in the GDR for children beyond the fourth grade.

Some of the problems encountered by women in raising children alongside working at a full-time job are shown by Morgner's Laura figure and by Brigitte Martin's Edith Michael in *Nach Freude anstehen*. Both are single mothers.

In Morgner's *Trobadora Beatriz* and *Amanda*, the paradigmatic mother-and-child couple is Laura Salman and her son Wesselin. No aspect of the reality of women's lives is aired in *Trobadora Beatriz* more than maternity—and the resulting double burden. Morgner calculates her punches in contriving the character and fate of Laura. Married to the committed communist Uwe Parnitzke, Laura, in fictional past time, had a baby as a young professional and exhausted herself doing all the child care and housework besides her job (Uwe was frequently away on business trips). Perhaps because Laura sometimes had to put the baby in child care in spite of a fever, the girl died of pneumonia before her first birthday. Thereafter Laura gave up her academic work, reasoning that "the imposition of back-and-forth trips, repeated daily, between the stooped, down-to-earth activity of housekeeping and those heights where thoughts, after all, dwell, would one day seem too exhausting" (*TB* 174). She went into construction work and divorced Parnitzke. Now, in fictional present time, Laura, unmarried, working as an S-Bahn (suburban train) driver, is expecting a second child. Beatriz and the reader catch their first glimpse of the character who will later be identified as Laura throwing up at Bahnhof Friedrichstrasse. As the reader learns later, she is pregnant. This time Laura gives birth to a son, Wesselin.

In both *Trobadora Beatriz* and its sequel *Amanda* Wesselin's most salient characteristic is that he is constantly sick. In this, the novels imply, he is in no way an unusual child. Wesselin's illnesses run through both works inexorably, like a bass accompaniment to the plot. The conflict between motherhood and work—even when generous child care is available—is summed up in a few sentences: "Laura got a place in a child-care center for infants and toddlers and again drove S-Bahns through the capital city Berlin. Four days after she started work Wesselin came down with bronchitis. Laura took sixteen days of sick child vacation. Eight days of service later the pediatrician diagnosed German measles. At short intervals, angina, diarrhea, and once again bronchitis followed. In three months of work, Laura was absent for more than two, at a time of great shortage of personnel, and she had to listen to the complaint that you didn't have an earthly hope of making up a work schedule with women" (*TB* 146). Lutz, Laura's lover, flees, unable to take a screaming child, while Beatriz and Melusine join Laura in worrying over and caring for the baby.

In *Amanda* Wesselin is older; consequently, the novel treats the reader to the problems posed by a preschooler. Again, these problems are presented as being nothing out of the ordinary. Nothing is wrong with Wesselin: he is an adorable, intelligent, verbal child. We find Laura working night shifts, since only night shifts allow her to deliver Wesselin to preschool in the morning and pick him in the afternoon; working mothers have to accommodate themselves to child-care hours. But Wesselin hates being left alone at night. Consequently, he is often sick, so that his mother has to stay at home with him. He misses his mother at preschool, too, and behaves in ways viewed as eccentric. Operations, epidemics, and accidents vary the sequence of his routine illnesses: in chapter 62 Wesselin is operated on for a double hernia; in chapter 78 he is shut out of preschool for an indefinite period on account of scarlet fever quarantine, just after having been out with bronchitis; in chapter 87 he sprains his thumb sledding. Even with Wesselin in child care, Laura is exhausted. She works all night and then "dragged herself to the second shift. She accomplished the second shift, in which she took care of the chores of the housewife and mother, only by means of the strongest self-discipline. She had no energy left for playing with Wesselin." Laura is not only tired, but plagued by guilt because she does not have enough time and energy to devote to her son.

If Morgner emphasized children's illnesses, Martin in *Nach Freude anstehen*, an extraordinarily naturalistic novel about the difficult, complicated life of a single parent of two children, focuses on the psychological problems that children can develop. Edith Michael lives in Berlin. She has two school-age daughters, a widowed mother who lives in Erkner, and a schoolteacher lover. She works in an industrial center's computer center, and in the course of the narrative she also writes the thesis necessary for her to get an engineering degree. Her work keeps her away from home for about twelve hours a day.

Edith has problems on all fronts, but her main conflict concerns the demands made by the children versus the demands of work and study. To enable Edith to study and also due to complications with her divorce, her older daughter Anne lived with her grandmother in Erkner for several years and went to live with her mother only when she started school. Anne is a problem. She is closer to her grandmother than her mother, does not accept her mother's stricter authority, holds it against her mother that her father (who is now remarried and in the West) left, thinks her mother loves her younger sister more, and is often rude and hurtful to her mother and others. The child also has social problems in school, tending to be targeted as an object of teasing and pranks by her classmates. Her problems are exacerbated when the school finds out that she stole chocolate from a store. The other children torment her as a thief, and she lives in fear.

The incident of Anne's stealing brings on a protracted crisis, during which the family becomes increasingly dysfunctional. Every member suffers psychologically. On top of it Edith, having driven herself too hard, is ill; she is suffering from a gall bladder disorder. What is obvious and what everybody tells Edith is that she needs to spend more time with her children. Yet at the same time, she is under pressure at work. The stopgap solution the novel proposes is to give the single mother a break. A sick leave for a couple of weeks helps Edith begin to find her way out of a situation over which she had all but lost control. It gives her time to consult a psychologist about Anne, have her sent for psychological tests, and take advantage of the professional advice. Whereas Morgner writes with a mix of humor and exaggeration and an unconcealed feminist consciousness-raising agenda, Martin's novel is like a case study, and her only proposal is a pragmatic one: let up on the pressure, give the woman more time.

Many works of fiction portray the specific problems that single mothers face beyond the problem of the double burden. For many women single motherhood meant a life of hard work and loneliness. The protagonist of Doris Paschiller's *Die Würde* (1980) marries because she has a clear picture of what it would be like to raise her child alone and cannot face it: "But the other alternative would mean completely sacrificing herself. Only being a mother, in every opinion that she has. Your battle is mother, first of all mother. To earn bread for your child only as mother. To get to know a man, only as mother. To have only mothers as friends and to bring up future mothers. The whole world is mother. Stick it out, mother. Your child is as lonely as you. His religion is mother, his life is mother."[47] An ostensibly more successful single parent is the heroine of Jutta Schlott's novel *Das liebliche Fest* (The lovely party, 1984). She works as a dramatic producer and has a young son. She has no remarkable problems, either with work or with her child; she herself filed for divorce; but despite her telling herself she must take her life in grip, and her relatively good grip on her life, she experiences her existence as depressing. She is overworked with her full-time job and her child to care for in the evenings. Her emotional life is unsatisfactory, consisting of an off-and-on long-term affair with a married actor. The dreariness of her life comes home to her with a vengeance over an empty Whitsuntide holiday weekend and reaches a shocking conclusion when she slits her wrist.

Various works of fiction make the point that single mothers find it difficult to find male companions. Martin's story "Die Anzeige" (The personal ad, in *Der rote Ballon*, 1977) illustrates this difficulty with a dramatic statistic: when a mother of two responds to a personal ad from a man seeking a woman with children, she receives a letter back from him saying that he got 1,049 responses. Living with children did not make one's social life easier: Zeplin's *Der Maulwurf oder fatales Beispiel weiblicher Gradlinigkeit* (The mole or a fatal example of feminine straightforwardness, 1990) shows that it can be difficult to juggle a lover and a child. The main character Judith's nine-year-old son Timmi, a prominent figure in the story, creates tension with her lover Albrecht. Judith reflects that her love life depends on Timmi's sleep. When Albrecht moves out, Timmi begins to stutter—in relief. Monika D., a character in an interpolated story in Apitz's *Hexenzeit* who is an artist and was a single mother at age nineteen, says in retrospect laconically at age forty: "Because of my son, many relationships didn't work out for me. Once it was jealousy on both sides, once boredom, and once fear that my child and I would bring a financial problem into the house when we moved in. Actually, they all failed. . . . What really counts is my work."[48]

Psychological Interdependence of Women and Children

A number of stories thematize the psychological relations of mothers, especially single mothers, and their children. Some, like

Christa Müller's "Candida" (in *Vertreibung aus dem Paradies* [Expulsion from paradise], 1979), the story of a child whose mother had to put her in a weekly child-care home; Petra Werner's "Der Bronzeelefant" (The bronze elephant, in *Die Lüge hat bunte Flügel* [Lies have bright wings], 1986), about an actress's daughter; and Schlott's "Aussicht" (Prospect, in *Klare Verhältnisse* [Clear conditions], 1989), about a nine-year-old's fearful imaginings when her actress mother leaves her at home alone at night, make the point that the children suffer—or believe they suffer—when their mothers do not have enough time for them. Others focus conversely on the mothers' psychological dependence on their children, which becomes an acute problem when the children reach adolescence. Müller has a number of mountain-climbing stories about a single mother and her son, the most poignant of which is her novel *Die Verwandlung der Liebe* (The transformation of love, 1990), where the son, now an adolescent, first expresses his wish to be independent from his mother as a desire to go mountain climbing without her. Before, he had been her entire life; he needed her, and she gave her life up for him. At age eighteen the son also gets interested in girls and ends up by being entirely callous about his mother's feelings. The mother endures psychological pain comparable to that of being deserted by a lover. Hannelore Lauerwald's "Geliebter Sohn" (Beloved son, in *An einem Donnerstag oder Der Duft des Brotes*, 1975) also concerns a mother whose sole surviving son gives meaning to her life.

Pregnancy, Birth, Abortion, and Contraception

The physical dimension of maternity, that is, pregnancy and childbirth, is a relatively minor topic in GDR women's literature. A few nauseous pregnant women—Morgner's Laura and Zeplin's Lisa—dot the pages of fiction. In "Aus den Akten der Hölle" (From the files of hell, dated 1975 in *Vieräugig oder blind*), Worgitzky gleefully speculates on the notion of male pregnancy. In the same author's *Meine ungeborenen Kinder* the protagonist Martha marvels at "what some women take upon themselves to have a child"[49]— meaning lying in bed for months and being fed with an IV in order to prevent a miscarriage. But beyond this little is made in works written by women of the specific problems of pregnancy. Birth scenes are found in Wolf's *Quest for Christa T.*, where Christa Wolf gives a cursory description of the birth of Christa T.'s first child; in the "Weisses

Ostern" (White Easter) chapter of Morgner's *Hochzeit in Konstantinopel,* which delivers a more detailed account; in Brigitte Reimann's *Franziska Linkerhand,* where we are given a glimpse of a childbearing woman; and in Helga Schütz's *Julia oder Erziehung zum Chorgesang* (Julia, or an education in choral singing, 1980), which summarizes two days of labor in five short sentences. These brief treatments build up to Worgitzky's in *Meine ungeborenen Kinder,* which gives an extensive first-person description of a hospital birth accompanied by a discussion of methods.[50]

Abortion proved to be a much more popular theme than birth. Abortion in the first twelve weeks of pregnancy became legal in the GDR on 9 March 1972. Thereafter, it began to receive a positive profile in GDR literature.[51] Morgner celebrates the new law in *Trobadora Beatriz,* where it constitutes a triumphant high point in the plot (*TB* 328–336). Beatriz jubilates that now the GDR truly is the "promised land" for women (*TB* 335). Morgner even excerpts the speech in which the minister of health justified the bill to the People's Chamber, that is, Parliament, in her novel. As if in support of his rationale, she builds a dangerous illegal abortion into Laura's biography: Laura, refused an abortion as a student and humiliated in her attempt to get one, aborted herself with a knitting needle and dangerously wounded herself (*TB* 109).

A number of stories about or involving abortions focus on the psychological anguish of the woman in deciding whether to abort and her feelings after an abortion. The abortions in Martin's *Der rote Ballon,* Helmecke's "Klopfzeichen" (Tapping code, in *Klopfzeichen*); and Königsdorf's "Unterbrechung" (Interruption, in *Lichtverhältnisse* [Light conditions], 1988) are in this vein. The eighteen-year-old single heroine of Lauerwald's "Wunschzettel" (Wishlist, in *An einem Donnerstag oder Der Duft des Brotes,* assailed by second thoughts in her hospital bed the night before her legal abortion, decides not to abort and abruptly leaves the hospital in the morning. The anguish of a pregnant mother of three in Schlott's "Klare Verhältnisse" (Clear conditions, in *Klare Verhältnisse*), in contrast, quickly cedes to a train of thought that clinches her decision to abort: men want children for egocentric reasons, but pregnancy, childbirth, and child care can eat a woman alive.

The major GDR work on abortion is undeniably Worgitzky's *Meine ungeborenen Kinder* (1982), a 322-page novel devoted to every conceivable aspect of the topic. Worgitzky claims to have done an immense amount of research in order to write the novel. In a lecture she gave in the Humboldt-Universität Ringvorlesung series in 1992, after unification, she described its genesis. She said that she had initially wanted to write a television play about abortion in the late 1960s, but had been told by the dramatic producer—a woman—that it had no chance of being produced. It was only in 1977, after abortion had been legal for five years, that she started work on her novel.[52] Publishing anything on the subject of abortion nevertheless proved far from easy. Gabriele Jähnert notes that "abortion was not a publicly discussed problem in the GDR."[53] Worgitzky's novel, in breaking this taboo, caused considerable debate. The reviews in the GDR were largely negative, but its reception by readers as well as the reviews it received in the BRD (all written by women) were primarily positive.[54]

The novel patently has the didactic intention of bringing the theme of abortion, and beyond that, the conflicts in women's lives, squarely into the public consciousness.[55] What the protagonist, the actress Martha Trubec, says about the play in the novel is also true of the novel itself: "Strangely enough, the dark cloak of taboo is still wrapped around all these complicated events, and I find it is finally time to remove it."[56] The heroine, a successful actress who has a long career behind her, is a glamorous figure, and not at all a victim. The plot is strung along the story of her six abortions and one birth. The choice of an actress as protagonist also allows for a *mise en abyme*: in fictional present time she is acting in a play about abortion, Friedrich Wolf's *Cyankali* (Potassium cyanide). This play, written during the Weimar Republic (it was first performed in 1929), plausibly inspires discussion about abortion "in the old days" among the theater people engaged in the production. It also gives Worgitzky the chance to bring information about the history of abortion in Nazi Germany and in the GDR into the text in the form of program notes authored by Martha.

The idea of plotting the novel around a play production opens a space in which the issue of how an abortion should be shown on stage can be debated. This debate in turn provides the theoretical justification for Worgitzky's merciless, sometimes graphic presentation of abortion in the novel. In fact, according to Worgitzky, the debate over the public staging of abortion originated in discussions over the novel: the author claims that she transposed the discussions she had with her male editors and the debates that arose when she read aloud from her work in progress into her novel, in the guise of Martha's discussions with theater men and in a postperformance public discussion of the play. The argument is always over decorum. Worgitzky's own standpoint is: "One should not be able to dodge these experiences by aestheticizing them."[57] In her view menstruation has to be spoken of openly, abortions not just alluded to but described. In the novel, the actress—a figure for the novelist—demands that the abortion itself be shown on stage. To her mind, "good taste" is irrelevant; the audience must be confronted with the reality of the operation. The dramatic producer Geibel and the director Herrschelmann demur, countering that that the play is chiefly of "historical" interest and without current social significance (pp. 30, 34). The actresses insist that pregnancy and abortions are *still* problems for women. The plot bears the women out when a young actress's pregnancy conflicts with her career and she—typically for Worgitzky fiction—decides to abort so as to take an important stage role. In the end Martha wins out over the doubts of the dramatic producer, and the abortion is staged naturalistically.

Worgitzky's *mise en abyme* also strategically mirrors the reader, bringing him or her into the novel as a figure represented by the play's audience. In the reactions of the spectators that are expressed in a discussion following the play we see possible modes of reception of women's problems: rejecting, uncomprehending, trivializing, and so forth. The producer's censoring of the actress's contribution to the program notes exemplifies men's censoring of women's open self-expression.

The novel has socialist-realist characteristics (*pace* Worgitzky, who averred that such criteria as "typicality" were passé at the time[58]), even though these characteristics do not appear in the classical manner: thus, characters are not typical of their class, but of men and women, young and old. In her conversation with the director of her theater Martha identifies herself as a "representative of [her] sex" and speaks of solidarity among women, thereby implying that women are a class (p. 262). The novel's effectiveness hinges on the reader's accepting her as a "positive heroine." We are meant to concur with Martha's presentation of unwanted pregnancies as an affliction to the female sex that demands easily available abortions, and not quibble at her failure to consider moral issues such as the rights of unborn life or the feelings of her male partners. Nor does the novel invite us to criticize Martha for failing to learn from experience or use contraceptives.

The novel is written in two narrative modes: retrospective first-person narration as a conversation between the protagonist Martha

Trubec and a man, who is presumably her current lover, alternates with third-person narration that follows Martha's perspective. This double form of narration has the advantage of showing women's problems, including abortion, in the past (in Martha's life) versus in the present (in the life of the young actress Emilia Pape, who aborts in favor of her career). The "conversation" fiction of the first-person narrative is strained, given that the male interlocutor is reduced to a mere ear for receiving Martha's immensely long autobiographical confession. Possibly it can be read as a consciously constructed utopian narrative situation that enacts the wish not only that a woman's discourse might be foregrounded, but that a man might listen tirelessly and sympathetically to it. Worgitzky's heroine seizes the male prerogative to take for granted that one can speak with perfect frankness to a member of the opposite sex.

The actress's narrative contrasts the horrors of illegal abortion with the simplicity of abortion once it is legal. Her first five abortions take place in the era of illegal abortion. Her first unwanted pregnancy occurs at age 19. We hear of her desperate attempts to find a doctor who will perform the job, including visits to two money-hungry illegal practitioners in West Berlin. Finally a doctor proposes to wait until the sixth month and then kill the fetus, which will result in a miscarriage. This story is meant to shock with its representation of the grotesqueness of illegal abortion. It ends when the unnerved lovers burn the dead fetus, whom they call "Chlodwig" (playing on "Klo," the familiar German word for "toilet"), in the heating oven in their room. Understandably, this scene shocked many readers.[59] Martha ends her next pregnancy at age 22 by giving birth to her one son. At age 24 or 25, however, she has another abortion, at age 30 another, later two more, and her last at age 37. The abortions are more or less easy depending on whether she has connections, goes abroad, or tries to perform the abortion herself. The pill, which becomes available after her fifth abortion, is rejected as a contraceptive means (as it was typically in the GDR). Martha uses a coil, but it stops working and she finds herself pregnant again. This time, however, abortion is legal.

The novel presents a clear, unambiguous line on abortion: it is a woman's right to abort whenever she wants, for whatever reason, whatever the circumstances. Guilt vis-à-vis the fetus is energetically refused. Martha declares: "By Catholic standards I am a sixfold murderess, by state standards a fivefold lawbreaker. But I, who normally get a guilty conscience pretty quickly—in this case, I refuse to do so"

(p. 315). Her standpoint is validated by the most cogent voice in the public discussion of abortion following the play, that of a 50-year-old woman who condemns the standpoint that women, by aborting, "kill life" (p. 250). It is validated even more conclusively when Martha's younger avatar Emilia decides to abort a child she initially wanted so as to accept a coveted theater role. The book argues for the welfare of the child versus the "rights" of the fetus: according to Martha, a child whose mother does not want it can potentially be so miserable that it would be better off not having been born. Men's "suffering" over abortion is brought in only in the penultimate chapter, as a kind of postscriptum, a peripheral aspect that is interesting but that need not affect what must necessarily be women's unilateral freedom to choose.

But the book's theme is more general than abortion: it wants to show the whole life of a woman and its problems. Like Morgner, Worgitzky talks about the fear with which women grow up, the fact that they always have to think about their bodies. She also airs the problem of combining career and family. The professions of all the women in the book, with the exception of Aunt Erika, who represents the reactionary position, are mentioned. They include a director of documentary radio broadcasts and an ophthalmologist. The novel warns that the problems of women may not appear urgent to the young in today's GDR. Yet it is imperative not to forget the tribulations of a woman in Martha Trubec's generation or indeed of women in previous generations, not to take women's new freedoms for granted or believe that the old problems have been legislated out of existence. Worgitzky ends the novel with the ostensibly positive event of Martha's granddaughter's birth, but takes the opportunity to ask (prophetically, as it happens) whether the future might not bring a step backward instead of a step forward: "Will they again force her to have children?" (p. 322).

Whereas Worgitzky's novel strongly favors legal abortion and sets up a night-and-day contrast between the grim days of illegal abortion and the present, Wiens's *Traumgrenzen*, published a year after *Meine ungeborenen Kinder*, goes so far as to criticize the dismal, unfriendly aspect of *legal* abortions in the GDR. The heroine Nina has to argue with a woman doctor who disapproves of her choice to abort despite the law; conditions in the hospital are portrayed as inhuman; six abortions are mass-produced one after the other.

The enthusiasm for abortion among GDR women accompanied a distrust of the pill. Both Worgitzky and Morgner polemicize extensively against the pill. Worgitzky has her say on the pill in *Meine ungeborenen Kinder*: Martha Trubec insists that she tried the pill when it first came out, but that it made her lose all interest in sex (p. 294). She switched to another brand, which awakened lesbian inclinations but continued to leave her frigid in heterosexual situations. Martha disapproves of feeding women the pill for years or even decades; she believes that no medication can be taken continuously over a long period without negative effects. She asks rhetorically why a medication can't be found for *men*. Morgner, who regarded the pill doubtfully in *Trobadora Beatriz* on account of its unforeseeable medical consequences (*TB* 336), attacks it with vehemence in *Amanda*, now on the grounds of sexual politics. Her opinion in the later novel is that the main effect of the pill is to make women constantly available for sex for the benefit of men: "Even positive exceptions demand that a modern woman today be armed at all times. In other words: immediately ready and in such a manner that the quality of the procedure is not diminished for the man through distraction" (*A* 249). Through the mouths of two characters, Vilma and Laura, she also suggests that the pill has a negative physical effect on women: it takes away their creative drive (*A* 182 and 498).

Interpersonal Relationships

If GDR women writers focus the spotlight on women's double burden, motherhood, single parenthood, and abortion, other "private" issues that might have deserved attention do not receive comparable illumination.[60] In particular, homosexuality is barely treated as a theme in GDR women's literature; it remained taboo until very late, as the publication history of Waldtraut Lewin's story "Dich hat Amor gewiß" (Cupid has you for sure, 1983), which was only authorized for publication nine years after it was written, shows. Madeleine Marti in *Hinterlegte Botschaften: Die Darstellung lesbischer Frauen in der deutschsprachigen Literatur seit 1945* (Messages left: The representation of lesbian women in German-language literature since 1945, 1992) gives a detailed account of the theme of lesbian love in GDR women's literature of the 1970s and 1980s.

Problems with men do not get the lion's share of attention in GDR women's fiction that they get in the West. Aside from the issue of sharing housework and child care and the resulting psychological power struggle, where women ascribe a demeaning attitude to the men who expect them to pick up the pieces at home while they advance their careers, women's problems with men occupy a relatively small chapter. One such, and indeed one of the more prominent, is related to the psychology of the housework-versus-career struggle. It has to do with the fact that career success has traditionally been gendered male, whereas unrecognized, invisible domestic labor has been gendered female. The problem concerns combining a career with a relationship. While many writers wrote abundantly about women's struggles with career and children, Lauerwald, Königsdorf, Morgner, and Renate Feyl also noticed a conflict for women between career success and a relationship. All give the same reason: men find it hard to tolerate a woman's success.

Thus in Lauerwald's "Unterwegs im Regen" (in *An einem Donnerstag oder der Duft des Brotes*) a young man, a scientist, can't bear that his wife, a scientist in the same field, is appointed director of their section. In the story "Pi" Königsdorf's child narrator notes that her mother's boyfriend resents being her subordinate at work: "What he resents the most is that mother is his boss. The guy is an engineer and works in her company."[61] While a man's career success enhances his prospects with the opposite sex, the same thing does not hold true for women. In *Amanda* Morgner has the character Katya S. say that the more successful she was as a poet, the more unhappy she was personally: "Every one of my published books was a professional success and a private defeat" (*A* 31). Through the example of Laura, Morgner shows how the phenomenon of jealousy eludes conscious control. The "ideal man" Benno, Laura's husband, jubilates when Laura becomes known as a writer; over and over again he expresses his happiness. But then he begins to show symptoms: first he becomes jealous of Wesselin, then of other men, and finally of other women, at which point he seeks consolation in alcohol and soon thereafter dies in a car crash caused by drunken driving.

Renate Feyl's ironically entitled historical novel *Idylle mit Professor* (Idyll with professor, 1986) makes career jealousy its central theme. The story is the fictionalized biography of an eighteenth-century woman of letters in Germany, Victoria Gottsched, who was the wife of the famous Johann Christoph Gottsched. Feyl shows how Victoria, who married Gottsched when she was twenty-two and he thirty-five, helped him with his projects, notably translating part of Bayle's dictionary; she also translated the mammoth *Geschichte der königlichen Akademie der schönen Wissenschaften zu Paris* (History of the Royal Academy of Belles Lettres in Paris) from the French, wrote the

Geschichte der lyrischen Dichtkunst der Deutschen (History of German lyric poetry), and wrote comedies. The high point of her career comes when Maria Theresia of Austria calls her "the most learned woman in Germany."[62] According to the novel, it is Gottsched himself, her husband, who consistently opposes and works against her public recognition. Gottsched loves her only when she works for him, when she helps him enhance his public image. When Bayle's dictionary appears, Victoria is disappointed to see that her name is not even mentioned. Gottsched gives as his reason that his wife's name is "automatically" subsumed in his: "When she indicates her disappointment to him, he does not quite know what she wants. Why mention her name separately? Her name is included in his. . . . When two spouses jointly appear before the public with a work, then he represents her! That is very proper!"[63]

Helga Königsdorf in *Respektloser Umgang* (1986), a novel that brings the physicist Lise Meitner back to life, at least in the narrator's imagination, observes that this syndrome may well keep women from seeking fame. Noting that Meitner remained single, the narrator observes that achievements in math and physics do not increase a woman's value as a woman. She speculates that this is one of the main reasons why so few women have gone into science:

> Let's imagine that instead of being a woman, Meitner had been a man. . . . Would this man have had a greater chance of having a family life in addition to his career? Scientific fame would have enhanced his status as a man. But for the woman, fame was more likely to be detrimental. High achievements in physics or mathematics do not increase her value as a woman. Not even today. People should consider this before they cite biological reasons for the low level of interest that girls show in the hard sciences.[64]

Through an interpolated story in *Amanda* involving fictitious interviews with a man and a woman who work in the same building business, Morgner investigates a theme related to that of career jealousy: the differences between a man and a woman's relationship to their work. In her account men have a different psychological investment in their work from women. The man in the story is ambitious and wants power. In his marriage, his wife is "background." She helps him a lot and does all the housework. His woman coworker—who is older than he though lower in the hierarchy—is not so ambitious or power-oriented. She prefers teamwork to being first. She emphasizes that she has to devote a great deal of time to her family.

Whereas he happily tells his life story, hers has to be dragged out of her. When asked whether she would like to become master of works, she unhesitatingly answers "no": "'No', said Inge Petri without hesitation. 'In any case no, but even if I were much better professionally, really big, it would be out of the question. . . . For my husband I'm already too emancipated anyway, he always keeps asking, can't you work shorter hours, six hours or so. . . . If I also wanted to go somewhere in the evenings and over the weekend, my marriage would break up, that's clear. As a woman, you have to play second fiddle, don't you?'" (A 358–359). The woman's testimony makes it clear that she thinks that career success would conflict with her marriage, which, unlike her male colleague, she prioritizes.

Other problems with men—mental cruelty, battering, rape—are occasionally addressed in fiction. Helga Schubert has a number of stories about men's callousness toward women they are close to. Most involve philandering. Thus "Taube Ohren" (Deaf ears, in *Anna kann Deutsch*) is about a man who tries to pick a woman up just after his wife had a baby. "Mondstein" (in *Das verbotene Zimmer* [The forbidden room], 1982) likewise concerns a woman whose husband started an affair with his sister-in-law the day she gave birth to their first child. "Aus dem beruflichen Alltag" (From everyday professional life), in *Anna kann Deutsch* is a depressing story about a woman who has an affair with her boss, who then stays with his wife. The woman commits suicide; her husband soon remarries. A full-length work about a woman's psychological dependence on her abusive, skirt-chasing husband is Christiane Grosz's novel *Die Tochter* (The daughter, 1987). Wife-battering is a topic in Wolf's *Quest for Christa T.*, in Tine Schulze-Gerlach's "Flaschenpfand" (Bottle deposit, 1982), and in Wiens's *Traumgrenzen*; in *Amanda* Morgner mentions a TV report about a shelter for battered women in West Berlin.[65] Rape scenes occur in *Trobadora Beatriz* and in Apitz's *Hexenzeit*. Both of these are blamed on other times and places, however: Beatriz is raped in France, not in the GDR, whereas Apitz's Mathilde is raped in the early years of the GDR, and to boot by the son of a wealthy, property-owning bourgeois family (Mathilde herself is working class). Christine Wolter's "Frühsommer" (in *Wie ich meine Unschuld verlor*, 1976; translated as "Early summer" in Lukens and Rosenberg, *Daughters of Eve*) is a story about sexual assault by a grandfather on a neighboring widow (a friend) that is interesting mainly for the subsequent reactions of the grandfather and his wife. The grandfather resents the woman who resisted his advances and belittles her to his wife. As for the wife, she has tolerated many affairs of her husband's; she feels defenseless, and as if she has to keep her husband from such philandering by making herself slimmer and more attractive. Like wives with womanizing husbands, single women's unsatisfactory affairs with married men are a staple of GDR women's fiction: Königsdorf's "Bolero" (in *Meine ungehörigen Träume*, 1978); Zeplin's "Schattenriß eines Liebhabers" (in *Schattenriß eines Liebhabers*, 1980; translated as "The Shadow of a Lover" in Lukens and Rosenberg, *Daughters of Eve*); and Angela Stachowa's "Resi" (in *Kleine Verführung* [Little seduction], 1983) are among the many examples.

Conclusions

A survey of GDR women's writing of the 1970s and 1980s on the reality of women's everyday lives shows that there is a marked tendency for the feminism in such writing to march with, or rather a step behind, official government policy, that is, to criticize states of affairs that already met with official ideological disapproval (e.g., men not sharing housework), and to laud what had already been made law (abortion). Even the theme of the burdens of motherhood could be seen to have been anticipated in the importance that socialist theory accorded to motherhood, even though in its most radical consequence, the decision not to have children, the critique certainly went well beyond what the GDR, with its concern over the birthrate, considered desirable. There is no open critique of any government policy on women and very little criticism of any condition that the government had the power to change. In all likelihood, self-censorship played a role here.

Yet women's writing is far from being a mere echo of public policy. Especially the foregrounding of the problems of motherhood, but also the attention devoted to relationships with men, go well beyond the repertoire of official themes. In cases where the government took a stand on women's issues, as, for example, the double burden, women authors responded by writing "fiction" that illustrated the problem in great detail and thereby amplified the message that reform was necessary. Sometimes political action presented an author with an opportunity to air a topic she had been unable to publish on previously. Worgitzky's novel on abortion is a case in point.

While women writers plainly thought that the quality of life for women in the GDR left room for improvement, they generally agreed with socialism's solution to the "woman question," as well as with its identification of remaining "contradictions." Even the most assiduous reading between the lines fails to produce any evidence that any of them believed that life for women was better in the West. Morgner especially is adamant that the West is no place for women. In *Trobadora Beatriz* she launches her critique of conditions for women in the GDR only after having painted a lavish picture of the crass sexual exploitation of women by men in the West. The initial premise of *Trobadora Beatriz*, that Beatriz comes back to life in France after a 808-year sleep, is a wonderful opportunity for a spoof on contemporary conditions in the noncommunist countries—which, Beatriz finds, have not changed much since the Middle Ages. Thus, still in France, Beatriz sees a hitchhiker and copies him; she is picked up, but her ride promptly rapes her. After her dress is torn and her money stolen, a Muslim handyman employed in construction work on the site of Beatriz's twelfth-century castle, which was unceremoniously blown up, offers her a dress for sex. The workers tell her she ought to get married and that a pretty woman needn't have emancipatory ideas. In *Amanda* Morgner, having seen the "soft" porn film *Emanuelle*, rages over pornography in the West. (No pornography was sold in the GDR.) Ascribing her views to the character Vilma, she finds it appalling that women are degraded and that powerlessness is made out to be an aphrodisiac for them.[66] In point of family law the BRD looks worse to Morgner: in *Amanda* the "Marriage Con-woman" reflects that equal rights in the GDR means that a woman is a workhorse, but the BRD is worse, since there, after divorce, a woman can be left penniless and lose custody of her children (*A* 259). Another writer who stages an extensive contrast between East and West is Wiens in *Traumgrenzen*. She compares the life of a young woman in the West (Karin) and that of a young woman in the East (Nina). While the West German woman has women's lib and choice of study and political engagement and can drive a taxi to make money, in the East a woman can have a child without it wrecking all her other plans. Even though the GDR is far from perfect (child care and abortions are criticized), the West does not come out looking better, for all the Westerners' automatic assumption that it is.

Into the early 1980s GDR women writers continued to be bemused about "man-hating" Western feminism. In "Das verbotene Zimmer" (The forbidden room, in *Das verbotene Zimmer*, 1982), for example, Schubert writes about a woman's trip to West Berlin. There she visits a women's bookstore, which men are not allowed to enter. The narrator inquires why this is so. Dissatisfied with the answer, she is left merely with the impression that Western feminism is a bizarre and untenable ideology based on the hatred of men.[67]

What Did They Achieve?

If the point of liberating the feminine voice is to improve the actual lives of women by making men as well as women conscious of sexist attitudes and practices that are oppressive to women, did the feminist literature of the GDR in any sense achieve that goal? The literature of the '70s shows men who are blind to the issue of women's oppression. In *Trobadora Beatriz* a soldier draws a blank when Beatriz, newly arrived in the GDR, mentions the exploitation of women: "Beatriz attributed his incomprehension to the ideal conditions of his homeland" (*TB* 100), Morgner concludes ironically. The literature of the '70s at best shows male figures who, like Bem in Worgitzky's "Quäze," sound progressive but behave in ways that show that they have no inclination to renounce their patriarchal prerogatives. These attitudes reflect the documentary evidence. As late as 1988, Annemarie Tröger, stranded at the Peking airport with a group of GDR beer brewers, reports that the men expressed remarkably conservative ideas about women: women in the workplace were the problem with the GDR economy; women's place is in the home.[68]

In contrast, Worgitzky's 1991 novel *Traum vom Möglichen*, which plays in an intellectual, not a working-class, milieu, registers a change. Here, the climate in which men determine what is real, where men feel free to put women into verbal boxes, is portrayed as having ceded to a charged atmosphere where gender-political storms rage from moment to moment. The new ambience portrayed in the novel resembles that in the United States in the 1970s. The main male figure "Bang" is all too aware of "women who call themselves emancipated."[69] He complains: "As a man, one seems downright out of place these days."[70] Relations between the sexes have become tense on account of women's emancipation. Women are sensitized to their discrimination and rebel against it. Men still feel free to make generalizations about "women" publicly—thus: "Women just don't have any sense of irony"[71]—but at their peril: in this novel, women react violently to this kind of remark. On the other hand, women now play men's game: they publicly make disparaging remarks and even jokes about "men." In mixed company women accuse men of being at the top of every hierarchy and of being afraid to show feelings. One women mocks men's driving: "When a woman drives a car, she wants to get somewhere faster; when a man drives, he's playing with dolls."[72] To judge from this novel, the much-missed revolution in consciousness, including the feminist consciousness of women themselves, started to set in about forty years *after* women were emancipated materially, and ironically, just before the demise of the GDR caused a severe setback in their material emancipation. Feminist literature, whose role, as Wolf said in a 1984 interview about literature generally, is to "widen the limits of taboos, to push them always a little bit further," had started to have the desired effect.[73]

Concluding Remarks

Women in the German Democratic Republic found themselves placed in an unusual situation. The government attempted to emancipate them to complete legal, economic, and social equality with men within a few years. Emancipation meant not just de jure equality with men, but an energetic attempt, from above, to overthrow traditional sex roles, particularly those pertaining to women and work. Most notably, it meant integrating the entire female population into every branch of the work force as rapidly as possible. As a result, women enjoyed economic independence from men (though they generally earned less).

The radical nature of the change can best be appreciated when one reflects that the German Democratic Republic, like the Federal Republic of Germany, arose out of the ashes of National Socialism, whose reactionary ideology on women had retarded the emancipation of German women and reinforced traditional sex roles in the 1930s and 1940s. The Nazis restricted women's access to higher education, paid women less and excluded them from senior civil service jobs, opposed the employment of married women, upheld motherhood as women's true vocation, and imposed harsh penalties for abortion. The SED, in contrast, supported women's complete equality with men. It enacted legal equality, enforced factual equality to the extent of its power, and expressed the belief that a change in popular attitudes and customs would follow. While it barely attempted to spread the burden of childraising to the male sex, it did actively try to make motherhood and employment compatible for women. After just twenty-two years of the GDR's forty-year existence, the government deemed that with regard to these centrally important matters, the "woman question" had been "solved."

How did women themselves react to this radical emancipation, which was proclaimed and enacted over and against entrenched patriarchal attitudes and customs? Over the course of forty years, the state socialist policies plainly had a shaping effect on women. In what Gerda Szepansky has called "the quiet emancipation,"[1] women's attitudes and choices regarding work and family changed. GDR women increasingly sought their self-definition in their work. It has consistently been observed that since the fall of the Wall East German women have remained extremely attached to the idea of paid work and have found unemployment hard to tolerate. In the GDR period their financial independence, their guaranteed jobs, made it possible for many of them successfully to establish single-parent families. Their principal complaint had to do with their double day, which the government fully recognized and never ceased to try to palliate. Women felt overburdened with a full-time job plus the after-hours job of child care and housework.

Feminism never became the highly conscious mass movement it was in the West. Yet as the consciousness of an intellectual elite, especially in the 1980s, one can certainly speak of feminism—in the Western sense of the word—in the GDR. Where a political feminism was taboo, but an airing of the "contradictions" in women's lives permitted in literature, writers constituted the vanguard of this GDR feminism, setting its tone. The foregoing chapters have shown that starting in the late 1960s, and particularly in the 1970s, GDR women writers developed a spectrum of feminist positions and arguments. They worked both with and against the Marxist doctrine that constituted their inheritance. Their ideas can be regarded as a product of their socialist context and of socialist ideology inasmuch as the writers generally affirmed and appreciated the government's policies on women. Especially Christa Wolf and Irmtraud Morgner drew on classic Marxist thought, in particular Frederick Engels's theory of the family and August Bebel's ideas on women, to conceptualize women in an extremely positive light, in terms of an ideal communism, a predisposition toward peace, harmony, and ecology, and an image of maternal strength. Some women writers adapted the literary model of socialist realism in their work, using its basic mechanism of identification to construct heroic feminine role models. But Morgner, Wolf, Charlotte Worgitzky, and others took a decisive step against socialist ideology by espousing Western feminism's recognition that women comprise an independent interest group that cuts across class antagonisms. And some writers, for example, Wolf, Gerti Tetzner, and Helga Königsdorf, construed femininity as oppositional to the restrictions, regimentation, and rationalization of state socialism.

While there was some assimilation of Western feminism, above all of the basic idea that women as a group have their own interests and need to defend them, in general East German feminism, in all of its nuances, is different from Western feminism. It responds directly to the specific situation of women in the German Democratic Republic. One form of it, whose strongest representative is Morgner's *Trobadora Beatriz*, sought to perfect the equality envisaged by the socialist state by pushing it to its logical extreme. Trobadora-style feminism applauded the government's efforts to secure legal and economic equality for women, but demanded more: that women be men's social equals, equally active and assertive, equally respected and recognized, equally subjects of desire, equally in control of things. What this position fought against was the bourgeois legacy of conservative gender roles, the traditional mind-set that women are essentially different, that is, desireless, "naturally" maternal, and other-oriented. But another form of GDR feminism, whose earliest and most eloquent exponent was Wolf, held that state socialism was pressuring women to become just like men. Instead, women's *different* voice and ethos should be heard and respected. Wolf and the writers who followed her reacted against the leveling that the socialist solution brought with it, arguing that the masculine model with its one-sided orientation on achievement and rationality was not worth emulating. Instead, so the reasoning went, society as a whole would do well to become more feminine, to cultivate the traditional feminine virtues of loving and nurturing. The *Trobadora* position and the Wolf position were not in contradiction with each other, as Morgner's adoption of the second one in her second novel *Amanda* shows.

GDR feminist writers of the 1970s and to some extent of the 1980s also tackled the crucial job of re-creating a feminine identity by remaking the feminine image in their fiction. Representing woman in her traditional guise would no longer do, but neither would the "socialist model of woman," the workplace heroine who successfully combined work and motherhood in the service of socialism. Instead, GDR feminist writers developed two new feminine types: the strong woman (a feminist permutation of the "positive heroine" of socialist realism, openly intended to refute the traditional image of woman) and the nonconformist rebel (which implicitly criticized the "socialist model woman").

Finally, a broad spectrum of women took to the pen, mainly in the late 1970s and early 1980s, in order to air the insufficiencies of everyday life for women in the GDR. The major themes were the double burden that had been foisted on women—their old role of mother and housewife plus their new role as worker; the problems of motherhood, including single motherhood; and abortion, which had been legalized in 1972, but nevertheless remained a contentious topic.

Notes

Chapter 1. Women, Feminism, and Writing in the German Democratic Republic

1. A relatively tolerant statement from an SED publication: "Disappointed by women's lack of rights in society and in the family in the sphere of influence of capitalism, adherents of feminism want to achieve a change in their situation through a pure women's movement, disengaged from men." Introduction to Bebel, *Die Frau und der Sozialismus*, p. xii, my translation. Except where otherwise indicated, all translations in this book are my own.

2. Böhme, *Die da drüben*, p. 83.

3. Silberman, "Whose Story Is This?" p. 41.

4. Rüß, *Dokumente zur Kunst*, p. 287.

5. Rede Kurt Hagers auf der 6. Tagung des ZK der SED am 6. Juli 1972, in Rüß, *Dokumente zur Kunst*, pp. 510–511.

6. Buckley, *Women and Ideology in the Soviet Union*, pp. 162–163.

7. "Die Frau—der Frieden und der Sozialismus" (Kommunique des Politbüros des ZK der SED, Berlin, den 16. Dezember 1961), reprinted in *Dokumente der revolutionären deutschen Arbeiterbewegung zur Frauenfrage 1848–1974*, p. 260.

8. Erler et al., *Familienpolitik im Umbruch?* pp. 11–12 notes that women tended to take this leave for sick children to its fullest extent. More children became "sick" after the leave was made available than previously. Women apparently took more sick child leave the less happy they were with their jobs. In Sweden, in contrast, mothers may take up to sixty days off annually for sick children, but take on average only ten days off.

9. Statistics are from Schwarz and Zenner, *Wir wollen mehr* and from Erler et al., *Familienpolitik im Umbruch?*

10. Erler et al., *Familienpolitik im Umbruch?* is an example of a West German study; Winkler, *Frauenreport '90* was prepared by the Institut für Soziologie und Sozialpolitik of the GDR in 1990. The East German sociologist Hildegard Nickel, who worked in the Akademie der pädagogischen Wissenschaften of the GDR for ten years, observes that her group did real sociology, but the results never saw the light of day, having been suppressed by the SED (Szepansky, *Die stille Emanzipation*, pp. 93–94).

11. Böhme, *Die da drüben*, pp. 87–88.

12. Dölling, "Culture and Gender," p. 33.

13. Bebel, *Die Frau und der Sozialismus*, p. xxi.

14. Winkler, *Frauenreport '90*, p. 63.

15. Dölling, "Culture and Gender," pp. 32–37.

16. According to Regine Hildebrandt, Minister for Work, Social Issues, Health, and Women in Brandenburg; cited by Szepansky, *Die stille Emanzipation*, pp. 121–122.

17. Ellmenreich, "Operativ-psychologische Einflußnahme," p. 9.

18. Menschik and Leopold, *Gretchens rote Schwestern*, pp. 23, 81.

19. Hogan, "Der Anteil der Arbeit," p. 74.

20. Statistics from Erler et al., *Familienpolitik im Umbruch?* and Schwarz and Zenner, *Wir wollen mehr*.

21. Erler et al., *Familienpolitik im Umbruch*, p. 4; see also pp. 55–57. Salomea G. says in an interview in Fischer and Lux, *Ohne uns ist kein Staat zu machen*, p. 138 that Eastern women are more emancipated, and have more self-confidence; *but* they haven't read the important feminist literature of the West.

22. Erler et al., *Familienpolitik im Umbruch?* p. 57, quoting *Für Dich* editor. Same passage cited by Jaeckel, "Die Frauen," p. 12.

23. Zipser, *DDR-Literatur im Tauwetter*, 3:56, 58.

24. Dodds, "Women in East Germany," pp. 110–111. Some of Dodds and Allen-Thompson's interviewees in *The Wall in My Backyard*, pp. 42, 124, testify to these conservative gender roles.

25. Worgitzky, *Die Unschuldigen*, pp. 208, 213.

26. Merkel, "Keine Zeit," pp. 66–67.

27. Morgner, "Jetzt oder nie!" pp. 37–38, notes that the GDR produced pornography only for export to the West, to get hard currency. Morgner describes her shock and disgust at seeing the movie *Emanuelle* in the 1970s. What particularly horrified her was that her male companions, all Marxists, liked it. Cf. the *Emanuelle* scene in Amsterdam in Morgner, *Amanda*, p. 384.

28. Dölling analyzed photos of men and women in two major GDR magazines, the *Neue Berliner Illustrierte* and the women's magazine *Für Dich* (in "Frauen-und Männerbilder," pp. 35–49). She concludes that photos of men and women at work *do* represent women as competent workers, but they also suggest that men are more competent than women and reinforce the notion that women are subordinate to men in the world of work. Thus photos of men and women together frequently show the man instructing a woman or women. Women, but never men, are often shown doing the same work in long rows, e.g., in factories. High-ranking women are prettified, erasing their status and making them harmless.

29. Schwarz and Zenner, "Ursprünglich," p. 10.

30. Böhme, "Die da drüben," p. 29.

31. Nickel, "Ein perfektes Drehbuch," pp. 77–78.

32. Erler, *Familienpolitik im Umbruch?* p. 18.

33. Böhme (writing in 1983), *Die da drüben*, p. 19; Merkel, "Keine Zeit," pp. 66–72; Merkel, "Leitbilder," p. 373.

34. Commented on by Eva P. in Dodds, *Wall in My Backyard*, pp. 98–100; Liesbeth Mühle in Szepansky, *Die stille Emanzipation*, p. 136; and Merkel, "Leitbilder," p. 374.

35. Kahlau, *Aufbruch!* p. 146; Schenk, "Experiment UFV," p. 124; Schwarz and Zenner, "Ursprünglich," p. 13.

36. Dölling, "Frauenforschung mit Fragezeichen?" p. 47 writes: "The few women in the GDR who successfully demanded independent forms of organization or, as academics, criticized patriarchal structures in spite of these 'achievements,' had received important impulses from the women's movement in Western Europe and the U.S.A." See also Kretzschmar, "Gleichstellung statt Gleichberechtigung," p. 57.

37. Hildegard Nickel in Szepansky, *Die stille Emanzipation*, p. 106.

38. Rosenberg, "Shock Therapy," p. 144, gives a detailed account of this movement, noting: "The speed with which these [feminist] projects blossomed is a direct reflection of the level that feminist consciousness had attained in the GDR before the events of 1989–90."

39. This note is already struck in 1979 by Ahlings and Nordmann, "Arbeiten wie ein Mann," pp. 85–95, an article highly critical of the GDR emancipation of women. More recently Dölling, "Frauenforschung mit Fragezeichen?" p. 40 and Hauser, *Patriarchat als Sozialismus* have worked with the concept.

40. Official communiqués repeatedly stress that public policies must make it possible for women to combine their role as housewife and mother with employment. Thus, for example, it is claimed in "50 Jahre Internationaler Frauentag: Thesen des Zentralkomitees der Sozialistischen Einheitspartei Deutschlands zur Vorbereitung des 8. März, Berlin, Januar 1960," reprinted in *Dokumente der revolutionären deutschen Arbeiterbewegung zur Frauenfrage 1848–1974*, pp. 234–250: "Vacation planning as well as the establishment of service organizations, factory shops, and self-service stores, which help the working woman fulfill her task as employee and as mother, are provided for with equal generosity" (p. 237). The SED program of 1963, adopted by the VI. Parteitag, speaks of harmonizing the "woman's claim to creative work and participation in the life of society" with her "position as housewife and mother" (*Dokumente*, p. 27). It is the state, not the fathers, that will help the mothers in what is perceived to be *their* job of childrearing: "Our mothers no longer alone bear the responsibility for caring for their children. They share it with the government and the entire society." ("Wer die Frauen in ihrer Entwicklung behindert, hemmt den sozialistischen Aufbau," from the Rede des Ministerpräsidenten der DDR, Otto Grotewohl, auf dem VI. Bundeskongreß des Demokratischen Frauenbundes Deutschlands in Weimar, 10. Dezember 1975, in *Dokumente*, 218–221; p. 219.) The program of the IX. Parteitag of the SED, 1976, explicitly endorsed measures such that "women can combine their professional activity even more successfully with their tasks as mother and in the family." (Cited from Bebel, *Die Frau und der Sozialismus*, p. xxi.) The sociologist Hildegard Nickel, who worked at the Akademie der pädagogischen Wissenschaften from 1977 to 1987, notes that research on women there concentrated almost exclusively on the question of how to unify work and motherhood. This unification was viewed as being in the interest of both women and society (Szepansky, *Die stille Emanzipation*, p. 96).

41. Hieblinger, *Frauen in unserem Staat*, pp. 28, 147. Lenin spoke of "mind-deadening, unproductive petty work" in "Rede auf der IV. Konferenz parteiloser Arbeiterinnen der Stadt Moskau," 23. Sept. 1919. Cited from *Marx, Engels, Lenin. Über die Frau und die Familie*, p. 207.

42. Nickel, "Women in the GDR," p. 103; Schwarz and Zenner, "Ausreichend sanft?" p. 148.

43. Dölling, "Frauenforschung mit Fragezeichen?" pp. 44–48.

44. Erler, *Familienpolitik im Umbruch?* pp. 195–197.

45. MacKinnon, *Feminism Unmodified*, p. 38, notes that women have been precluded from combat, from contact jobs in male-only prisons because they might be raped, and from jobs that present health hazards on account of their fertility. Vogel, *Mothers on the Job*, gives a history of protective legislation in the United States and the opposition to its enactment.

46. See MacKinnon, *Feminism Unmodified*, pp. 35–36.

47. Fraser, *Unruly Practices*, p. 144 attributes this term to Diana Pearce, in "Women, Work, and Welfare: The Feminization of Poverty," in *Working Women and Families*, ed. Karen Wolk Feinstein (Beverly Hills, Calif., 1979). That no-fault divorce has impoverished women is the major finding of Weitzman, *Divorce Revolution*. She writes, p. 323, "While most divorced men find that their standard of living improves after divorce, most divorced women and the minor children in their households find that their standard of living plummets. . . . When income is compared to needs, divorced men experience an average 42 percent rise in their standard of living in the first year after divorce, while divorced women (and their children) experience a 73 percent decline."

48. Menschik and Leopold, *Gretchens rote Schwestern*, p. 24, noting that the constitution of 1949 committed the state to creating special institutions and benefits for working women and others, comment: "They had recognized that women started to take advantage of their rights from an unequal, underprivileged position. Therefore, the guarantee of equal rights alone would have been inadequate without these special preferences."

49. "Offener Brief: Geht die Erneuerung an uns Frauen vorbei?" in Kahlau, *Aufbruch!* pp. 25–26.

50. Fraueninitiative *lila offensive*, "Standortbestimmung," in Kahlau, *Aufbruch!* pp. 97–107.

51. Kahlau, *Aufbruch!* p. 34.

52. Dodds's portrait of GDR women in September 1990 after the monetary and just before political unification corroborates this picture. However, she sees a better mood developing by the summer of 1992. (Dodds, "Women in East Germany," pp. 107–114; also Dodds, *Wall in My Backyard*, p. 17.)

53. Beck, "Women and Work," p. 6 notes that in 1997 three-quarters of all American working-age women worked.

54. "BLS Releases New 1998–2000 Employment Projections" (released 30 November 1999). http://stats.bls.gov/emphome.htm.

55. Some comparative statistics: (a) Salary: Rosenberg, *Divided Lives*, p. 247: In the United States women earn 70% of men's salaries. Schwarz and

Zenner, "Ursprünglich," p. 12: in the GDR women earn 60–75% for comparable jobs. (b) Single Parents: Rosenberg, *Divided Lives*, p. 248: 20% of U.S. women are raising their family alone. Gysi, "Frauen in Partnerschaft," p. 104: In 1981, 18% of GDR families were headed by women raising their children alone. (c) Housework: Rosenberg, *Divided Lives*, p. 249: American men perform about 30% of domestic labor. Olsen, "Does Enough Work," p. 600: U.S. women work 20–30 hours a week on housework and child care. Nickel, "Ein perfektes Drehbuch," pp. 77–78: The average GDR family does 40 hours of housework; 75% is done by women.

The enormous difference comes in employment statistics: in 1980 in the United States, only 50% of women were employed, whereas in the GDR, close to 90% of women were employed.

56. Historically, "femininity" and feminine desire have always had to articulate themselves from a position of weakness. Women as material *dependents* have shaped a feminine culture—one which, necessarily, bought into what men, the ruling class, desired, or thought women should be.

57. The German publisher, Rowohlt, brought out a complete translation of the original, in contrast to the English translation published by Knopf in 1983, which was abridged.

58. Beauvoir, *Second Sex*, p. 82.

59. Ibid., p. 112.

60. Ibid, p. 679.

61. Czerkas, Donchenko, and Martin, "Das Verhältnis von Arbeit," p. 146f.

62. Willis, *No More Nice Girls*, p. 121.

63. Schwarzer, *Der "kleine Unterschied,"* pp. 38, 229. She cites the findings of the French sociologist Andrée Michel.

64. Wolf says that since 1968, the West German women's movement influenced East German women intellectuals (Wolf, "From a discussion at Ohio State University. A conversation with Christa and Gerhard Wolf," *FD* 114). She herself mentions extensive reading in Western feminist literature as of about 1980 (Wolf, "Vierte Frankfurter Vorlesung," *DA* 2: 627).

65. MacKinnon, *Feminism Unmodified*, p. 34f. Thus "as applied, the sameness standard has mostly gotten men the benefit of those few things women have historically had" (p. 35). She names custody and alimony. Yet "for women to affirm difference, when difference means dominance, as it does with gender, means to affirm the qualities and characteristics of powerlessness" (p. 39). She mentions women being excluded from combat, which is the normal way to advance in the army, and facing job discrimination on account of their fertility.

66. The only radical "sameness" feminist among GDR women writers is Worgitzky. In *Die Unschuldigen* (1975) she adopted a "sameness" position in order to argue that women should be freed from maternal responsibilities so that they can pursue their careers and vocations, while men are involved with child care. Other writers argue or imply the same conclusion without positing sameness. An outstanding example is Morgner, who capitalizes on women's (culturally predicated) maternal talent as an advantage without therefore concluding that child care should exclusively fall to women. In her vision, men are deficient women.

67. Harris, "Race and Essentialism," p. 612: "Feminist theory at present, especially feminist legal theory, tends to focus on women as passive victims." In the German context, Milz, "Zur deutsch-deutschen Soziologie des Frauenbewußtseins," pp. 340–343, castigates West German sociology for systematically propagating an unquestioned image of women as victims since its beginnings in 1910–1920.

68. Cf. Wendy Brown's critique in *States of Injury*, pp. 128, 133, of MacKinnon's "effort to rectify the masculinism of the law and redress women's equality" through law, which backfires by "interpellating women as unified in their victimization."

69. Morgner, "Aber die großen Veränderungen beginnen leise," p. 19. An English translation of *Trobadora Beatriz*, which was not available when this book went to press, is scheduled to be published by the University of Nebraska Press.

70. Rich, *Of Woman Born*, p. ix.

71. Comparable statements on the trials of motherhood for woman are found in essays Rich wrote dating back to 1971 ("When We Dead Awaken," in *On Lies, Secrets, and Silence*, pp. 33–49). Rich's view is that motherhood is a political institution designed to keep women subservient (*Lies*, pp. 196, 216). Cf. too Rich, *Of Woman Born*.

72. Lützeler, "Von der Arbeiterschaft zur Intelligenz," pp. 241–280.

73. Emmerich, *Kleine Literaturgeschichte der DDR*, pp. 26–27.

74. Hafner, "Nation of Readers," p. 24, notes that a first printing of 500,000 was not unusual for the top writers, while a volume of poetry would typically have a first print run of 2,000 copies. According to Bathrick, *Powers of Speech*, p. 39, the average first edition was 15,000–25,000 copies.

75. Wolf, "A Dialogue with Christa Wolf," p. 10.

76. Schütz in Dodds, *Wall in My Backyard*, p. 108; Maron, *Nach Maßgabe meiner Begreifungskraft*, p. 85.

77. Krauss, "Avant-Garde oder Idyll?" p. 151.

78. Bathrick, *Powers of Speech*, pp. 60, 11. Bathrick discusses the matter in detail on pp. 225–242.

79. Herminghouse, "Schreibende Frauen," p. 353.

80. For a summary of the fuss that critics instigated over Wolf's politics following the publication of *Was bleibt*, see Rey, "'Wo habt ihr bloß alle gelebt,'" or Schoefer, "Attack on Christa Wolf."

81. Wolf, *Auf dem Weg nach Tabou*, pp. 19–20.

82. Ibid., pp. 74, 81–82.

83. Wolf writes in "Berührung. Maxie Wander," in *DA* 1: 205: "These women (in Wander's book) do not see themselves as men's adversaries—unlike certain groups of women in capitalist countries, which are frequently accused of a fanatic hatred toward men." Six years later she remarked similarly: "It seems to me, however unqualified I may be to judge, that part of the inner uncertainty of American women, even those who are highly successful, stems from this lack of economic equality." (Wolf, "From a Discussion at Ohio State University. A Conversation with Christa und Gerhard Wolf" [May 1983], in *FD* 114–115.)

84. See, for example, "Ursprünge des Erzählens. Gespräch mit Jacqueline Grenz," in *DA* 2: 919. At the latest from "Self-experiment" on, Wolf has asserted that women have their own distinct needs and has been highly critical of the way in which socialism has allegedly "emancipated" women by seeking to make them like men. (See, e.g., her interview with Hans Kaufmann, *DA* 2: 799.)

85. Morgner, "Die täglichen Zerstückelungen," in Gerhardt, p. 25.

86. Ibid., p. 24.

87. Morgner, "'Jetzt oder nie!'" Interview by Schwarzer, p. 34.

88. Wolf, *FD* 22.

89. Markgraf, "Die Feministin der DDR," in Gerhardt, *Irmtraud Morgner*, p. 153.

90. Worgitzky, *Die Unschuldigen*; Wolf, "Self-experiment"; and Morgner, *Trobadora Beatriz* are prime examples of works that point out patriarchal laws and customs that communism had not managed to expunge. For example, the state classified a child as a worker, a farmer, or bourgeois by its *father's* profession (Worgitzky, *Die Unschuldigen*, p. 209; Dahn, "Der Stammhalter" [The son and heir] in *Spitzenzeit* [Pique time], pp. 119–120).

Chapter 2. "What Does a Woman Want?" Woman as the Subject of Desire

1. Wolf, "Dialogue with Christa Wolf," p. 12.

2. Morgner has a paragraph on women's dividedness that sounds very much like Beauvoir (Morgner, *Rumba*, pp. 198–199). Moreover, the character Ev argues that women are biologically disadvantaged because childbearing falls to them (p. 32).

3. Beauvoir, *Second Sex*, p. 137. Further page citations will be given in the text.

4. Cited by Jones, *Life and Work of Sigmund Freud*, p. 377.

5. Freud, *Three Essays on the Theory of Sexuality*, pp. 88–94.

6. Girard, *Deceit, Desire, and the Novel*, pp. 53, 56–58. Further page citations will be given in the text.

7. Irigaray, "Blind Spot of an Old Dream of Symmetry" in *Speculum of the Other Woman*, p. 18 passim. Further page citations will be given in the text. Recent psychoanalytic theory associates desire with privilege. In the "rapprochement phase," the toddler is seen to seek recognition as a subject of desire. The toddler's model for his or her desire is—it comes as no surprise—the father. See the discussion in Jessica Benjamin, *Like Subjects, Love Objects*, pp. 120–124.

8. Morgner, *Rumba*, p. 230.

9. Morgner, "'Jetzt oder nie!'" p. 36.

10. Tolstaya, *On the Golden Porch*, p. 57.

11. Thurm, *Verena*, p. 112.

12. Menschik and Leopold, *Gretchens rote Schwestern*, p. 162.

13. Transcribed from the DEFA film *Der Dritte*, by Günther (1972).

14. Tetzner, *Karen W.*, p. 161.

15. Rich, "Husband Right and Father Right," pp. 215–222 in *On Lies*, p. 218.

16. Wolf, *Auf dem Weg nach Tabou*, p. 96.

17. Czapanskiy, "Volunteers and Draftees," pp. 1415–1481; Fineman, "Legal Stories," p. 229.

18. Kirsch, "Merkwürdiges Beispiel," p. 15.

19. Ibid., pp. 15–16.

20. Morgner, "Die täglichen Zerstückelungen," in Gerhardt, *Irmtraud Morgner*, p. 27.

21. Morgner, *Die wundersamen Reisen*, p. 12. Dates of composition according to Eva Kaufmann, "Der Hölle die Zunge rausstrecken," in Gerhardt, *Irmtraud Morgner*, p. 194, n. 15.

22. Morgenstern, *Jenseits der Allee*, pp. 100–101.

23. Lakoff, *Language and Woman's Place*, pp. 30, 7.

24. Ibid., p. 19.

25. Ibid., p. 11.

26. Trömel-Plötz, *Frauensprache*, p. 94.

27. Ibid., p. 138.

28. Putsch, *Das Deutsche als Männersprache*, p. 83. The distinction between speech and action has also been attacked by the legal scholar Catherine A. MacKinnon. In her book on the First Amendment, *Only Words*, p. 30, in which she argues that pornography should not be protected by the First Amendment, she shows that the classic distinction between actions and words frequently does not hold: "Speech acts.... Acts speak." Stanley Fish comments on the speech-action distinction in his essay on the First Amendment, "There's No Such Thing as Free Speech, and It's a Good Thing, Too, p. 105, in *There's No Such Thing*: "Despite the apparent absoluteness of the First Amendment, there are any number of ways of getting around it, ways that are known to every student of the law. In general, the preferred strategy is to manipulate the distinction, essential to First Amendment jurisprudence, between speech and action. If the First Amendment is to make any sense, have any bite, speech must be declared not to be a species of action" (p. 105). For the very purpose of law is to restrict action; if law did not restrict action, there would be no law. Fish shows how First Amendment purists get entangled in contradictions. He observes that "speech always seems to be crossing the line into action"; the arguments for drawing the line, for admitting some kinds of language, like "fighting words," as action while preserving others as "speech," are based on the understanding of the "average person" of these words, and the "average person" is a manipulable concept. His own conclusion is that no speech can definitively be kept on the "speech" side of the line: "There was never anything in the zone [of constitutionally protected speech] to begin with" (p. 106); "insofar as the point of the First Amendment is to identify speech separable from conduct and from the consequences that come in conduct's wake, there is no such speech and therefore nothing for the First Amendment to protect."

29. MacKinnon, *Feminism Unmodified*, pp. 39, 45. She writes more on the subject in other essays in the book, as well as in *Only Words*, pp. 3–10, an attack on First Amendment protection of pornography.

30. Lakoff, *Language and Women's Place*, p. 11.

31. Freud, "Question of Lay Analysis," 20: 212.

32. Freud, *Three Essays on the Theory of Sexuality*, p. 17.

33. E.g. Brownmiller, *Against our Will*, p. 175; Allison and Wrightsman, *Rape*, pp. 172–173, 181–182.

34. Auer, "Trobadora Unterwegs," p. 120.

35. Cf. Romero, "Vertreibung aus dem Paradies," p. 81.

36. De Bruyn, "Geschlechtertausch," pp. 23, 27, 38.

37. Wolf, Interview by Schoeller, FD 87; Interview by Meyer-Gosau, FD 91–92.

38. Wolf, "Speaking of Büchner," AD 180; Wolf, "Ich bin schon für eine gewisse Maßlosigkeit," DA 2: 874.

39. Morgner, 1972 interview by Walther, pp. 53–54.

40. Meier, "Konzerte der Redevielfalt," p. 214, scrutinizes this term and uncovers its ironic potential, noting that Morgner herself says that it is ascribed to a literary figure who uses it to try to sell a manuscript to a press and is thus "equivocal" ("hintersinnig"); Morgner wonders why critics have constantly repeated it. On literary allusions in *Trobadora Beatriz*, see especially Clason, "Mit dieser Handschrift."

41. Nordmann, "Die halbierte Geschichtsfähigkeit der Frau"; Lewis, "Fantasy and Romance"; Bammer, *Partial Visions*; Jahnsen and Meier, "Spiel-Räume der Phantasie"; Emde, "Irmtraud Morgner's Postmodern Feminism"; Lewis, *Subverting Patriarchy*.

42. Meier, "Von schelmischem Spiel zu närrischem Ernst; Jahnsen and Meier, "Spiel-Räume der Phantasie."

43. Emde, "Irmtraud Morgner's Postmodern Feminism."

44. E.g., Damm, "Irmtraud Morgner" who fails to notice the irony in Morgner's presentation of the old Communist "Martha Lehmann" character, p. 138; she finds that Morgner ultimately criticizes Beatriz and validates Laura, pp. 143–144. Auer, "Trobadora unterwegs," pp. 1082–1083, who admires the book greatly, finds it necessary to justify the montage at length, as a technique that registers the conflict between creativity and a woman's life and hence supports the book's main theme. On the limitations of the GDR reception of *Trobadora Beatriz*, see Nordmann, "Die halbierte Geschichtsfähigkeit der Frau," pp. 420–423.

45. Martin, "Socialist Patriarchy and the Limits of Reform," pp. 67–68, criticizes the novel for letting its radical feminist promise evaporate harmo-

niously into a pro-Marxist, pro-GDR message. Emde, "Irmtraud Morgner's Postmodern Feminism," p. 130, stresses the "deconstructive" or destabilizing tendencies of the novel and denies that Laura's pragmatism is validated.

46. Nordmann, "Die halbierte Geschichtsfähigkeit der Frau," pp. 441, 444.

47. Meier, "Von schelmischem Spiel zu närrischem Ernst," p. 249; Jahnsen and Meier, "Spiel-Räume der Phantasie," p. 214. Previously commented on by Bammer, *Partial Visions*, p. 108.

48. Thus Martin, "Socialist Patriarchy and the Limits of Reform," p. 65, notes that Morgner suggests "simultaneity between socialist and feminist struggles" by writing significant historical dates, like 1871 (the date of the Paris Commune) into her fictional history of the Persephonic Organization and Opposition.

49. E.g., Morgner, "'Produktivkraft Sexualität souverän nutzen'" (1975), p. 3; Morgner, "Die täglichen Zerstückelungen" (1976) in Gerhardt, *Irmtraud Morgner*, p. 25, p. 30; Morgner, "Weltspitze sein" (1978), p. 98. By the time of her interview with Schwarzer (1990) she had changed her mind.

50. Morgner, "Apropos Eisenbahn" (1973), in Gerhardt, *Irmtraud Morgner*, p. 19; Morgner, "Die täglichen Zerstückelungen" (1976) in Gerhardt, *Irmtraud Morgner*, p. 30; Morgner, Interview by Rudolph (1977), pp. 167–171; Morgner, "Weltspitze sein" (1978), p. 98; Morgner's remarks in Zipser, *DDR-Literatur im Tauwetter* (1985), p. 23.

51. Morgner, "Apropos Eisenbahn," p. 19.

52. Morgner, "Die täglichen Zerstückelungen" in Gerhardt, *Irmtraud Morgner*, pp. 27–28.

53. Morgner, Interview by Walther (1973), p. 44.

54. Ibid., p. 49; cf. Morgner, "Die täglichen Zerstückelungen" in Gerhardt, *Irmtraud Morgner*, pp. 28–28, and Morgner's remarks in Zipser, *DDR-Literatur im Tauwetter*, p. 43.

55. E.g., Morgner, "Die täglichen Zerstückelungen" in Gerhardt, *Irmtraud Morgner*, pp. 24, 31; Morgner, Interview by Rudolph, pp. 172–174.

56. Kossakowski and Otto, *Psychologische Untersuchungen*, p. 114; Dannhauer, *Geschlecht und Persönlichkeit*, p. 33. The same theme crops up in Hieblinger's 1967 political communiqué on women, *Frauen in unserem Staat*, p. 9: women in the GDR have equal rights, but some de facto inequality still exists, largely due to the persistence of old "ideas" and "habits."

57. Morgner, "Interview mit Irmtraud Morgner," by Kaufmann, p. 1502; she also describes the experience in a chapter of *Amanda*, pp. 99–102.

58. Morgner, "Interview mit Irmtraud Morgner," by Kaufmann, pp. 1498, 1503.

59. Cf. Nordmann, "Die halbierte Geschichtsfähigkeit der Frau," p. 440.

60. *TB*, p. 8; presumably in 1973. The novel takes 5 years; hence Beatriz was 838 in 1968; she slept 808 years and is thus a 30-year-old woman.

61. *Trobadora Beatriz* includes all the pieces Laura wrote for "her" montage novel; the reasons Morgner gives for writing in montage form are the same reasons Laura gives (*TB* 170); and in the sequel to *Beatriz*, *Amanda*, we find out that Laura, like Morgner, has become the author of a famous novel (*A* 121–122).

62. Goethe, *Faust I & II*, p. 30.

63. *A* 18. E.g., Benno tells Beatriz's story as a fairy tale, *TB* 446.

64. Damm, "Irmtraud Morgner," pp. 143–144; Herminghouse, "Die Frau und das Phantastische," p. 251; Martin, "Socialist Patriarchy and the Limits of Reform," pp. 70–72.

65. Lewis, "Fantasy and Romance," p. 253, makes the same point.

66. Morgner, "Interview mit Irmtraud Morgner," by Walther, p. 1010.

67. Damm, "Irmtraud Morgner," p. 144, asserts that Beatriz becomes superfluous and is killed off because the "real social process educates and forms human beings"; Meier, "Von schelmischem Spiel zu närrischem Ernst," p. 249, finds that Beatriz is punished for being too extreme, whether too radical or overly well adjusted.

68. Schmitz-Köster, *Trobadora and Kassandra*, p. 71.

69. Cardinal, "'Be Realistic,'" p. 154.

70. Hanel, *Literarischer Widerstand*, p. 40; Lewis, *Subverting Patriarchy*, p. 150.

71. Goethe, *Faust I & II*, p. 301.

72. Anderson, "Genesis and Adventures," p. 11.

Chapter 3. Praise of the Feminine

1. E.g., Hell's chapter on "Stalinist Motherhood" in *Post-Fascist Fantasies*, pp. 64–102.

2. Hell, *Post-Fascist Fantasies*, pp. 137–250.

3. Morgan, *Ancient Society*, p. 43.

4. Ibid., pp. 532, 539.

5. Ibid., pp. 67–68.

6. Ibid., pp. 247, 552.

7. Ibid., p. 72.

8. Ibid., p. 474.

9. Ibid., p. 345.

10. Ibid., p. 344.

11. Ibid., p. 389.

12. Trautmann, *Lewis Henry Morgan and the Invention of Kinship*, p. 194.

13. Bachofen, *Myth, Religion, and Mother Right*, p. 109.

14. Ibid., p. 107.

15. Morgan, *Ancient Society*, p. 349.

16. Bachofen, *Myth, Religion, and Mother Right*, pp. 94, 142–143.

17. Ibid., pp. 105–106.

18. Ibid., p. 97.

19. Ibid., p. 93.

20. Ibid., p. 105.

21. Ibid., p. 80.

22. Ibid., p. 152.

23. Ibid., pp. 80–81.

24. Ibid., p. 91.

25. Götze, "Zur Entstehungsgeschichte und Verbreitung von Friedrich Engels' Arbeit," p. 44.

26. Engels, *Origin of the Family*, p. 75.

27. Ibid., p. 159.

28. Ibid., pp. 119–120.

29. Ibid., pp. 120–121.

30. Ibid. pp. 220–223.

31. Ibid., pp. 389–390, 475, 480.

32. Ibid., p. 125.

33. Ibid., p. 129.

34. Ibid., p. 128.

35. Ibid., p. 137.

36. Ibid., pp. 137–138.

37. Ibid., p. 221.

38. Morgan, *Ancient Society*, p. 552.

39. Engels, *Origin of the Family*, p. 139.

40. Morgan, *Ancient Society*, p. 342.

41. Engels, *Origin of the Family*, p. 232.

42. Ibid., pp. 187, 112f.

43. Ibid., pp. 170, 233.

44. Ibid., p. 233.

45. Staude, "100 Jahre August Bebels Hauptwerk 'Die Frau und der Sozialismus,'" p. 7.

46. Evans, *Sozialdemokratie und Frauenemanzipation im deutschen Kaiserreich*, p. 40.

47. Partisch, "Bebels Werk," p. 69.

48. Partisch, "Die Verwirklichung des Vermächtnisses von Karl Marx und Friedrich Engels," p. 17; and Partisch, "Bebels Werk," p. 69.

49. Cited by Scholze, "Zur internationalen Konferenz," p. 36.

50. Bebel, *Die Frau und der Sozialismus*, xiii. Further page citations will be given in the text.

51. Bebel, *Die Frau in der Vergangenheit*, p. 6.

52. He writes that one spoke of matrimonium instead of patrimonium and of mater familias instead of pater familias, and that matricide was the most heinous crime—all details taken from Bachofen.

53. Morgan, *Ancient Society*, p. 117: "Theoretically, each tribe was at war with every other tribe with which it had not formed a treaty of peace. Any person was at liberty to organize a war-party and conduct an expedition wherever he pleased. He announced his project by giving a war-dance and inviting volunteers."

54. Thönnessen, *Emancipation of Women*, pp. 47–48.

55. Braun, *Die Frauenfrage*, p. 547.

56. "Aufruf zum ersten Internationalen Frauentag am 19. März 1911," in *Dokumente der revolutionären deutschen Arbeiterbewegung zur Frauenfrage 1848–1974*, p. 62. Yet Zetkin in "Die Arbeiterinnen- und Frauenfrage der Gegenwart" did not make this argument.

57. Bock, "Weibliche Armut," pp. 432–434. Bock notes, p. 441, that these feminists "did not play down sexual difference, but insisted on women's right to be different, and did not see this as an expression of impotence and resignation, but of feminine pride, feminine power and self-assertion."

58. Woolf, *Three Guineas*, p. 110.

59. Bock, "Weibliche Armut," pp. 452–453.

60. Ibid., pp. 442–448.

61. Ibid., pp. 449–450.

62. Frevert, *Women in German History*, p. 233. In 1939 on Mother's Day the state awarded mothers of 4–5 children the bronze cross of honor, of 6–7 children the silver cross, of 8 children or more the gold cross.

63. Buckley, *Women and Ideology in the Soviet Union*, p. 134 writes:

> The Family Law of 1944 . . . tried to promote very large families by the introduction of decorations for motherhood. Women with five children earned a second-class Motherhood Medal and those with six won a first-class Motherhood Medal. First-, second- and third-class awards of Motherhood Glory went to mothers of seven, eight and nine children respectively. Ten children won the jackpot and brought the title of Heroine Mother and a certificate of the Presidium of the Supreme Soviet of the USSR.

64. Firestone, *Dialectic of Sex*, p. 80.

65. The *Berliner Zeitung* of 22 November 1995 reported that a Chicago couple that urgently wanted a child bestially murdered a pregnant woman and cut her fetus out of her body with scissors. (Citing *Washington Post*.)

66. See Czapanskiy, "Volunteers and Draftees," pp. 1415–1481.

67. For an analysis of why mothers traditionally had obligations toward, but no rights to, their children, see Brown, "Mothers, Fathers, and Children," pp. 239–267.

68. Dölling, "Frauen- und Männerbilder," pp. 44, 49.

69. E.g., Othmer-Vetter and Tröger, "Einleitung," p. 3; Schwarz and Zenner, *Wir wollen mehr*, p. 11; cf. Einhorn, *Cinderella*, p. 34.

70. Berghahn and Fritzsche, *Frauenrecht in Ost und West*, pp. 143, 153, 167.

71. Worgitzky, *Meine ungeborenen Kinder*, p. 137.

72. Morgner, Interview by Rudolf, pp. 173, 174.

73. Wolf discusses *Three Guineas* at length in a speech of 1984 (*AD* 82–83).

74. C 200 and 273. Wolf, *Voraussetzungen einer Erzählung*, pp. 156–160, also gives a bibliography.

75. Nicolai, "Christa Wolfs 'Kassandra,'" pp. 139–140; Maisch, *Ein schmaler Streifen Zukunft*, pp. 8, 20–21; West, "Christa Wolf's *Kassandra*," p. 183; Preußer, "Projektionen und Mißverständnisse," p. 78.

76. Davis, *First Sex*, p. 78.

77. Daly, *Beyond God the Father*, pp. 94, 34.

78. Wolf, "Warum schreiben Sie?" *DA* 1: 75.

79. Mohr, "Productive Longing," p. 225, already discerned the utopian qualities in *The Quest for Christa T.* in a 1971 article. Huyssen, "Traces of Ernst Bloch," demonstrates parallels between *The Quest for Christa T.* and the philosophy of Bloch as set forth in *Das Prinzip Hoffnung*, but more recent critics—Maisch, *Ein schmaler Streifen Zukunft*, p. 82; Kuhn, *Christa Wolf's Utopian Vision*, p. 227; and Hörnigk, *Christa Wolf*, p. 126—say that Wolf denies having known Bloch at the time.

80. For the history of this opposition, which started in 1966, see Stephan, "Die wissenschaftlich-technische Revolution," pp. 25–31.

81. Critics have come round to the idea that Wolf's interest in self-realization is gender specific (Adams, "Christa Wolf," p. 126; Vanhelleputte, "Christa Wolf und der Bankrott des patriarchalischen Prinzips," p. 16) and have recognized that her female figures carry utopia (Berghahn, "Die real existierende Utopie," p. 293; Kaufmann, ". . . schreiben, als ob," p. 25).

82. Lennox makes the same conjecture in "'Der Versuch, man selbst zu sein,'" p. 221.

83. Kossakowski and Otto, *Psychologische Untersuchungen*, p. 112; Dannhauer, *Geschlecht und Persönlichkeit*, p. 13.

84. Wolf, "Origins of Narration," *FD* 125.

85. Wilke, "Between Female Dialogics and Traces of Essentialism," pp. 252, 259, makes the opposite argument: that from "Self-experiment" on

Christa Wolf continues to adhere to an essentialistic model of femininity, asserting an "authentic female identity," unlike, say, Ingeborg Bachmann or Elfriede Jelinek.

86. Klotz, *Das Verhältnis von allgemeiner sozialer Frage und Frauenfrage*, 1: 16–19.

87. Hell, *Post-Fascist Fantasies*, p. 165.

88. Translation from Wolf, "Tomcat's New Philosophy of Life," in *Thinking It Over*, p. 175.

89. Wolf, "Documentation," p. 107. Wolf uses "love" with Musilian force: for Musil, author of *The Man Without Qualities*, the universe of love is the "other condition," the mystic, utopian dimension of acceptance and unity, which opposes "violence" (rationality, hierarchy) as its antithesis.

90. E.g., *DA* 2: 845, 847, and 876; also "value scale"—*Wertskala, DA* 2: 845 and "value system"—*Wertsystem, DA* 2: 875.

91. Krauss, "Avant-Garde oder Idyll?" dates her acquaintance with Woolf's work to 1976 (p. 155).

92. E.g., Lennox, "'Nun ja!'" p. 231; Greiner, "'Mit der Erzählung geh ich in den Tod,'" p. 108; Gutjahr, "'Erinnerte Zukunft,'" p. 72.

93. She nevertheless qualifies in her 1983 Ohio State interview that nineteenth-century positivism, rationalism, and scientific spirit all led to the huge danger of war that we are in today (*FD* 111).

94. Wolf, "Origins of Narration," *FD* 124; cf. *C* 282.

95. Wolf, "Illness and Love Deprivation," *AD* 74.

96. Wolf, *Voraussetzungen einer Erzählung*, p. 122.

97. Girnus, "Wer baute das siebentorige Theben," p. 444.

98. Jankowsky, "New Sense or Nonsense?" p. 404.

99. Pickle, "'Scratching Away the Male Tradition,'" p. 36; Harbers, "'Widersprüche hervortreiben,'" pp. 271–278.

100. On the irony of Cassandra's imprisonment in a "hero's grave"—where the hero is symbolic of aggressive masculinity—see Guthrie, "Reconstructed Subject," p. 183. Nicolai, *Christa Wolf, Kassandra*, p. 52, notes that this grave is formed of chiffres of femininity (hollow, willow).

101. *C* 155; "Berliner Begegnung," *DA* 1: 441; *C* 233.

102. Kuhn, *Christa Wolf's Utopian Vision*, p. 188, notes that Wolf implicitly criticizes the antinomic categories in Aristotle's *Poetics*.

103. West, "Christa Wolf's *Kassandra*," p. 170, asserts that "the concept of a primaeval Great Goddess, with an exclusively female priesthood to match, is dubious."

104. E.g., Stephens, "'Die Verführung der Worte,'" p. 142; Schmidt, "Über gesellschaftliche Ohnmacht," p. 120.

105. On the willow as a symbol for motherliness and fertility as well as for sterility and chastity, see Maisch, *Ein schmaler Streifen Zukunft*, pp. 10–11.

106. Roebling, "'Hier spricht keiner meine Sprache,'" p. 225.

107. Nicolai, "Christa Wolfs 'Kassandra,'" p. 414; and Maisch, *Ein schmaler Streifen Zukunft*, pp. 23–35 discuss Wolf's/Cassandra's psychologizing.

108. Already in C 264, Wolf hints that she is planning a *roman à clef*. In *Parting from Phantoms*, p. 214, she says the message of the novel was that Troy, that is, the GDR, must fall. The most extensive reading of the novella as a *roman à clef* is Jenkinson, "Loyalty and Its Limits."

109. Wolf, *Parting from Phantoms*, p. 57.

110. Wolf, *Medea*, trans. John Cullen, p. 171.

111. Morgner, Interview by Walther in *Meinetwegen Schmetterlinge*, p. 47.

112. E.g., Morgner, "Die täglichen Zerstückelungen," in Gerhardt, pp. 25, 30.

113. Lewis, *Subverting Patriarchy*, pp. 250–268, writes on this topic extensively.

114. See Löffler, "Vergnügliche und gescheite Hexerei," p. 7; Berger, "*Amanda* von Irmtraud Morgner," p. 5; Engler, "Die wahre Lüge der Kunst," p. 137.

115. In this novel Morgner correctly identifies mother right with Minoan culture, p. 227.

116. Morgner, "Interview mit Irmtraud Morgner," by Kaufmann, p. 1498.

117. Even the otherwise wholly positive figure Arke is made to seem somewhat paranoid on one occasion. Arke believes that anti-DDR, antipeace forces have caged Beatriz, when if fact it turns out to have been gardeners.

118. Marcuse, *Eros and Civilization*, p. 161.

119. *Amanda*, p. 67; the parallel between Faust and Prometheus is drawn explicitly on p. 244.

120. Morgner, "Interview mit Irmtraud Morgner," by Kaufmann, p. 1503. Morgner also mentions in the text of the novel, through the voice of Arke, that Goethe calls attention to the destructive consequences of the Faust figure in *Faust II* (p. 243).

121. Streller, "Sirenen und Hexen," p. 431, who discusses allusions to *Faust* and other works from the German canon, notes that Amanda is born on Goethe's birthday in Morgner's birth year.

122. These include above all Streller, "Göttinnen, Seherinnen, Hexen," pp. 263–271; Pietsch, "Goethe as a Model for Feminist Writing?" pp. 212–219; Reid, "From Adolf Hennecke to Star Wars," pp. 154–156; Streller, "Sirenen und Hexen," pp. 427–441; and Druxes, *Feminization of Dr. Faustus*.

123. Bovenschen, "Contemporary Witch," pp. 83–84.

124. Meier, "Konzerte der Redevielfalt," pp. 217, 220, finds a Stalinist detail in Morgner's Walpurgisnacht—as well as a Nazi slogan in the first commentary.

125. Herminghouse, "Wunschbild, Vorbild oder Porträt," p. 285, notes that there had been on average 10 percent of women in the Central Committee and none in the Politbüro. The situation did not improve by the time of the *Wende*: Schubert in Süssmuth and Schubert, *Gehen die Frauen in die Knie?* p. 94, writes: "In the Politburo there were only men and in the Central Committee only a few women."

126. Meier, "Konzerte der Redevielfalt," p. 226.

127. In a question-and-answer session following a public reading of her work in Solothurn in 1984, in *Die Hexe im Landhaus*, p. 72, Morgner fends off the argument that women in power (the example in point is Thatcher) are no better than men in power. She insists that women cannot be expected to bring a new style into politics unless they have parity. "The 'Iron Lady' is no argument at all. A woman alone amongst many men has to imitate their style." In present-day politics, women have to fight: "If something is very important, you have to fight for it."

128. Königsdorf, *Respektloser Umgang*, pp. 111–113, 46–48.

129. Apitz, *Hexenzeit*, pp. 207–212.

Chapter 4. Writing Women's Images

1. Marx and Engels, *German Ideology*, p. 64.

2. "Communist Manifesto," in McLellan, ed., *Marxism: Essential Writings*, p. 34.

3. Thompson, *Making of the English Working Class*, p. 12.

4. Brecht, *Bad Time for Poetry*, p. 1.

5. Benjamin, "Theses on the Philosophy of History," p. 256.

6. *VII. Schriftstellerkongreß*, p. 79.

7. Ibid., pp. 89, 90.

8. Beard, *Woman as Force in History*, pp. 54–76.

9. Braun, *Die Frauenfrage*, p. 1.

10. Ibid.

11. Morgner, "Interview mit Irmtraud Morgner," by Walther, p. 1012.

12. *VII. Schriftstellerkongreß*, p. 112.

13. Morgner, *Die wundersamen Reisen*, p. 17; *TB*, pp. 66 and 194.

14. See Hell's discussion of the pervasiveness of such "father discourse" in SED ideology and early GDR fiction, in *Post-Fascist Fantasies*, pp. 25–63.

15. *VII. Schriftstellerkongreß*, p. 112.

16. Ibid., p. 113.

17. Morgner, "Die Perlen des Phantastischen," p. 35.

18. Morgner, *Die wundersamen Reisen*, p. 16.

19. Ibid., p. 13.

20. Ibid., p. 156.

21. Morgner, "Die Perlen des Phantastischen," p. 35.

22. Morgner, "Die täglichen Zerstückelungen," in Gerhardt, p. 26.

23. Robin, *Socialist Realism*, p. xxvi.

24. Buehler, *Death of Socialist Realism in the Novels of Christa Wolf*, p. 35.

25. These types are discussed by Trommler, "Von Stalin zu Hölderlin"; Herminghouse, "Wunschbild, Vorbild oder Porträt"; and Herminghouse, "Schreibende Frauen."

26. Dannhauer, *Geschlecht und Persönlichkeit*, p. 33.

27. Ibid., p. 183.

28. Herminghouse, "Wunschbild, Vorbild oder Porträt," p. 286; see also Rosenberg, "Emancipation," p. 351.

29. Böck, "'Ich schreibe,'" p. 67. Herminghouse, "Schreibende Frauen," discusses historical novels written about women in the 1950s.

30. This feature of GDR literature has been frequently remarked, e.g., by Herminghouse, "Wunschbild, Vorbild oder Porträt," p. 286; and by Rosenberg, "Emancipation," p. 358. For a commentary on the history of the female victim, the heroine, and the heroine-victim figure in literature written by both men and women generally (though not in the GDR), see Weigel, "Die geopferte Heldin und das Opfer als Heldin."

31. E.g., as early as 1963 Reimann spoke of the "antiquated positive hero" in her diary (*Die geliebte, die verfluchte Hoffnung*, p. 152). Worgitzky, "Meine ungeborenen Kinder," in *Ohne Frauen ist kein Leben*, p. 111, said that criteria like "typicality" were "stupid, long since out-of-date stuff" when she wrote *Meine ungeborenen Kinder*.

32. Selbmann, *Der deutsche Bildungsroman*, p. 18.

33. Trommler, "Die Kulturpolitik der DDR," pp. 16–21, 61.

34. Mayer, *Der deutsche Bildungsroman*, p. 342, traces the terminological development.

35. Trommler, "Von Stalin zu Hölderlin," p. 155.

36. Herminghouse, "Schreibende Frauen," pp. 343–344, 347.

37. *Flight of Ashes* was published after the fall of the Wall by the Union-Verlag in 1990.

38. E.g., Lennox, "'Nun ja!'" pp. 225, 236–239; Schmitz-Köster, *Trobadora und Kassandra*, pp. 28–79.

39. Biddy Martin, "Socialist Patriarchy and the Limits of Reform," p. 67, criticizes Morgner's *Trobadora Beatriz* for "constraining" its own subversive, feminist impulses by "the conceptual coherence of an orthodox Marxist analysis and loyalty to the GDR status quo." Lennox, "'Nun ja!'" pp. 238–239, follows suit in assessing *Trobadora Beatriz* as containing *less* radical feminist criticism than Wolf's "Self-experiment."

40. Hilzinger, "Als ganzer Mensch zu leben . . . ," p. 46. Scholz, "Zum Bild der Frau in der DDR-Literatur," p. 136, underscores the importance of *Christa T.* for the beginning of GDR discussion of "women's literature" and "feminine writing."

41. Labovitz, *Myth*, writes, p. 221: "Rarely has this genre encountered such a departure from the traditional image." She asked Wolf if she had intended her novel as a *Bildungsroman*; Wolf said she had not, and assented to the designation only after Labovitz said she had in mind "a specific 'female' *Bildungsroman*, departing from traditional conceptions," p. 242, n. 33.

42. Herminghouse, "Schreibende Frauen," p. 348, states the historical significance of the novel succinctly.

43. E.g., Mohr, "Productive Longing," p. 197; Berghahn, "Die real existierende Utopie," p. 282; Dröscher, *Subjektive Authentizität*, p. 80.

44. After Reich-Ranicki wrote in his review that Christa T. is suffering from "the GDR" ("Christa Wolfs unruhige Elegie," in *Die Zeit*, 23 May 1969; reprinted in *Entgegnung*, p. 245), many critics followed suit, phrasing the criticism in various different ways. Thus Mohr, "Productive Longing," p. 212: "The disease of the blood also stands for the—curable—disease of the society in which the attempt to say 'I' cannot yet be undertaken." Berghahn, "Die real existierence Utopie," pp. 284–285; and Hammerstein, "Warum nicht Christian T.?" p. 25, argue similarly. Labovitz, *Myth*, p. 229: "Christa T. is seen to suffer and die as a result of the extraordinary conflict between her artistic existence and her socialist Utopian vision, and the static and fixed state machinery." Dröscher, *Subjektive Authentizität*, p. 103, points out that since Christa T. dies in 1963 Wolf's criticism must be directed at the preceding period, the 1950s, not at the period during which she wrote the novel.

45. Herminghouse, "Wunschbild, Vorbild oder Porträt?" p. 317.

46. For the early publication history and reception in the GDR see Mohr, "Productive Longing," pp. 217–219.

47. Thus Mauser, "Subjektivität—Chance oder Verirrung?" p. 173, believes that the narrator selectively foregrounds aspects of Christa T.'s character that demand consideration if the GDR is to become a humane socialist society.

48. Love, "Christa Wolf and Feminism," p. 37.

49. Ibid.; Clausen, "Difficulty of Saying 'I'"; and Labovitz, *Myth* give the book an enthusiastic reading. Lennox, e.g., in "Christa Wolf and the Women Romantics," p. 40, and Adams, "Christa Wolf," pp. 129–130, deplore the novel's ending, where Christa T. finds happiness as a veterinarian's wife. Voris, "The Hysteric and the Mimic," p. 250, impervious to the narrator's idealization of the Christa T. figure and reading the book against the grain, finds that the narrator in fact succeeds, in her reconstruction of Christa T., in essentializing and glorifying woman as mother, "whose substance is love."

50. Stephan, "Christa Wolf," p. 153.

51. Hammerstein, "Warum nicht Christian T.?" pp. 18–19.

52. Werner, "'Unter den Linden' von Christa Wolf," pp. 274–275, 277, traces both of these ideas, which continue to loom large in the rest of Wolf's oeuvre, as well as the Undine motif, to Ingeborg Bachmann.

53. Tetzner, *Karen W.*, p. 39.

54. Schmitz-Köster, *Trobadora and Kassandra*, p. 52.

55. Tetzner, *Karen W.*, p. 113.

56. Nagelschmidt wrote of *Karen W.* in 1991: "What a lot of courage it took, after all, to let her heroine break loose." Cited by Hauser, *Patriarchat als Sozialismus*, p. 212.

57. Rosenberg, "Another Perspective," p. 195; Herminghouse, "Schreibende Frauen," p. 350.

58. Wolf, *Q* 123: "the advantage of being a woman."

59. The government did, however, make it difficult for people to abandon certain careers for which they had been selected and trained at the government's expense, notably that of teacher. See Dodds, *Wall in My Backyard*, p. 67.

60. Kosing, *Wörterbuch der marxistisch-leninistischen Philosophie*, pp. 45–46.

61. Königsdorf, *Meine ungehörigen Träume*, pp. 128–129.

62. Maron, *Flight of Ashes*, p. 56.

63. Maron, *Defector*, p. 160.

64. Cf. Anderson, "Creativity and Nonconformity in Maron's *Überläuferin*," p. 145.

65. Linklater, "Erotic Provocations," p. 155.

66. Ibid., p. 161.

67. Krause, *Gefesselte Rebellin*, p. 239.

68. Reimann, *Franziska Linkerhand*, p. 486.

69. Ibid., p. 569.

70. Ibid., pp. 334, 332.

71. Ibid., p. 527.

72. Ibid., p. 582.

73. Ibid., pp. 35–36.

74. Ibid., p. 38.

75. Ibid., p. 40.

76. Ibid., p. 284.

77. Ibid., p. 178.

78. Ibid., p. 178.

79. Ibid., p. 284.

80. Ibid., p. 189.

81. Schowalter, "Towards a Feminist Poetics," p. 32, observes about the American context: "Hating one's mother was the feminist enlightenment of the fifties and sixties; but it is only a metaphor for hating oneself."

82. Thurm, *Verlangen*, pp. 72–73.

83. Ibid., p. 69.

84. Ibid., p. 66.

85. Pirskawetz, *Der Stille Grund*, p. 33.

86. Ibid., p. 50.

87. Ibid., pp. 164–165.

88. Ibid., pp. 424–425.

89. Ibid., p. 421.

90. Ibid., p. 8.

91. Wolter, *Die Alleinseglerin*, p. 111.

92. Worgitzky, *Die Unschuldigen*, p. 5; p. 215 in the diary.

93. Worgitzky documents favorable and unfavorable responses to her heroine in "Meine ungeborenen Kinder," in *Ohne Frauen ist kein Leben*, pp. 121–125.

94. Worgitzky, *Meine ungeborenen Kinder*, p. 68.

95. Ibid., p. 69.

96. Ibid., p. 70.

97. Ibid., p. 134.

98. Ibid., p. 136.

99. Ibid., pp. 251–252.

100. Ibid., p. 252.

101. Pulkenat, "Geschichte der Töchter," pp. 1189–1190, citing Annegret Schmidjell, *Quartier auf Probe: Tendenzen feministischer Literaturpraxis aus der neuen Frauenbewegung* (Stuttgart: Hans-Dieter Heinz Akademischer Verlag, 1986), p. 83, on FRG women's literature.

102. Schmidt, "Concept of Identity," pp. 429–447.

Chapter 5. The Reality of Women's Lives

1. Zeplin, *Schattenriß*, 167.

2. Worgitzky, "Meine ungeborenen Kinder," p. 112.

3. Ibid., p. 130.

4. Ibid, p. 135.

5. Schwarzer, *Der "kleine Unterschied,"* e.g., pp. 121, 130.

6. That much GDR women's literature since the later 1970s has been concerned with making problems visible and changing consciousness has been noted by Romero, "Vertreibung aus dem Paradies," p. 73; Rosenberg, "Emancipation of Women," p. 359; and Rosenberg, "Redefining the Public and the Private," p. 144.

7. Rossi, "Equality Between the Sexes," pp. 105–119. Her main point is that child-care facilities are necessary.

8. Menschik and Leopold, *Gretchens rote Schwestern*, p. 147; p. 145, citing Annelies Albrecht, "15 Milliarden Stunden für Hausarbeit in der DDR," *Markforschung*, H 1 (1971), p. 7ff. The remaining hours were done by children, grandparents, and so forth.

9. Hieblinger, *Frauen in unserem Staat*, pp. 28–29; Menschik and Leopold, *Gretchens rote Schwestern*, pp. 102, 105, 148.

10. Menschik and Leopold, *Gretchens rote Schwestern*, pp. 67, 102. Menschik and Leopold trace the rapid exodus of women from full-time to part-time work starting in 1967 to the shortening of the workweek in that year: whereas it had been 45 hours spread over 6 days, it became 43 3/4 hours spread over 5 days. The working day became 45 minutes longer, which to women with children apparently seemed too long.

11. Morgner, *Rumba*, p. 198. Morgner, *Hochzeit in Konstantinopel*, p. 52.

12. Rossi, "Equality between the Sexes," p. 132: "In the family . . . women seem to have an important superordinate position. However high . . . father's occupational status outside the home, when he returns at night, he is likely to remove his white shirt and become a bluecollar Mr. Fixit or mother's helper."

13. Menschik and Leopold, *Gretchens rote Schwestern*, p. 198.

14. E.g. Hieblinger, *Frauen in unserem Staat*, p. 143.

15. In Heidtmann, *Im Kreislauf der Windeln*, p. 234.

16. Ibid, pp. 235–236.

17. Lauerwald, *An einem Donnerstag oder Der Duft des Brotes*, p. 37.

18. Königsdorf, *Der Lauf der Dinge*, p. 81.

19. Apitz, *Hexenzeit*, p. 179.

20. According to Hildebrandt, *Zwölf schreibende Frauen*, pp. 53, 58, who interviewed Martin, Bem is closely modeled on Martin herself.

21. Martin, *Der rote Ballon*, p. 91.

22. Ibid., p. 20.

23. Martin, *Nach Freude anstehen*, p. 55.

24. Ibid., p. 56.

25. Ibid.

26. Ibid., p. 57.

27. Morgner, *Hochzeit in Konstantinopel*, p. 52.

28. In Schubert, *Schöne Reise*, p. 33.

29. Apitz, *Hexenzeit*, pp. 134–167.

30. Morgner, "Notturno," p. 31.

31. Morgner, *Rumba*, p. 32.

32. Ibid., p. 159.

33. Königsdorf, *Meine ungehörigen Träume*, p. 114.

34. Morgner, "Interview mit Irmtraud Morgner," by Kaufmann, p. 1495.

35. Wolf, *Parting from Phantoms*, p. 68.

36. This story of a mother's shrinking ambitions modifies one told as Karla's in "Notturno" (1964), p. 14, and retold in *Rumba* (1965), p. 166.

37. Worgitzky, *Die Unschuldigen*, pp. 100–101.

38. Wiens, *Traumgrenzen*, p. 95.

39. Ibid., p. 146.

40. Ibid., p. 185.

41. Menschik and Leopold, *Gretchens rote Schwestern*, pp. 25, 37; Drauschke and Stolzenburg, *Alleinerziehen*, p. 58; Dodds, "Women in East Germany," p. 109.

42. Drauschke and Stolzenburg, *Alleinerziehen*, pp. 92–93.

43. Ibid., p. 14.

44. Menschik and Leopold, *Gretchens rote Schwestern*, p. 113.

45. Szepansky, *Die stille Emanzipation*, p. 11. See also Szepansky, pp. 49, 168, 258.

46. Menschik and Leopold, *Gretchens rote Schwestern*, p. 104; Winkler, *Frauenreport '90*, pp. 143–144.

47. Paschiller, *Die Würde*, p. 13.

48. Apitz, *Hexenzeit*, pp. 76–77.

49. Worgitzky, *Meine ungeborenen Kinder*, p. 293.

50. Wolf, *Q*, 134; Reimann, *Franziska Linkerhand*, p. 233; Schütz, *Julia*, p. 137; Worgitzky, *Meine ungeborenen Kinder*, pp. 146f.

51. Herminghouse, "Wunschbild, Vorbild oder Porträt," p. 296, observes that before the 1972 abortion law was passed, authors depicted only the horrors of self-abortion and illegal abortions and the woman's resulting self-accusation. A novel of 1973, Jurek Becker's *Irreführung der Behörden*, already presents an illegal abortion undertaken in 1960 as the best solution.

52. Worgitzky, "Meine ungeborenen Kinder," in *Ohne Frauen ist kein Leben*, p. 108.

53. Jähnert, "Einleitung," in *Ohne Frauen ist kein Leben*, p. 7.

54. Worgitzky, "Meine ungeborenen Kinder," pp. 117–125.

55. Testified to by ibid., p. 112. Today, Worgitzky, ibid., p. 119, believes that she was successful in breaking down a taboo: "Everywhere I go people tell me that people who read the book (mainly women, but also men) suddenly talk to each other about things that fear and shame used to make them keep silent about."

56. Worgitzky, *Meine ungeborenen Kinder*, p. 54. Further page citations will be given in the text.

57. Worgitzky, "Meine ungeborenen Kinder," p. 112.

58. Ibid., p. 111.

59. Ibid., p. 117.

60. Another one that did receive attention was women's aging and old age. Jokiniemi, "Beyond Hags and Old Bags?" pp. 145–162; and Schmitz-

Köster, *Trobadora und Kassandra*, p. 116 note that a considerable amount of fiction on these topics started to be published in the 1980s.

61. Königsdorf, *Der Lauf der Dinge*, p. 81.

62. Feyl, *Idylle*, p. 138.

63. Ibid., p. 110.

64. Königsdorf, *Respektloser Umgang*, pp. 82–83.

65. Wolf, *Q* 132; Schulze-Gerlach, "Flaschenpfand," in Heidtmann, ed., *Im Kreislauf der Windeln*, pp. 30–39; Wiens, *Traumgrenzen*, p. 199; Morgner, *A* 213. Kersten, "Role of Women in GDR Films Since the Early 1970s," pp. 55, 57, 60, mentions some GDR films that depict battering: Hermann Zschoche's *Bürgschaft für ein Jahr* (1981), based on a novel by the same title by Tine Schulze-Gerlach; Heiner Carow's *Bis daß der Tod euch scheidet* (1979) and Carow's *So viele Träume* (1986).

66. *A* 383f. In her interview with Schwarzer, p. 38, Morgner says that she saw *Emanuelle*—her first pornographic film—in the mid-1970s and hated it for showing how a woman was psychologically butchered.

67. Schubert, *Das verbotene Zimmer*, pp. 91–92.

68. Tröger, "Brief an eine französische Freundin," p. 115.

69. Worgitzky, *Traum vom Möglichen*, p. 83.

70. Ibid., p. 131.

71. Ibid., p. 244.

72. Ibid., p. 127.

73. Wolf, "Dialogue with Christa Wolf," p. 9.

Concluding Remarks

1. The title of Szepansky's book of interviews with GDR women is *Die stille Emanzipation* (The quiet emancipation).

Bibliography

Adams, Marion. "Christa Wolf: Marxismus und Patriarchat." In *Frauenliteratur: Autorinnen—Perspektiven—Konzepte*, 123–137. Bern: Lang, 1983.

Ahlings, Gabi and Ingeborg Nordmann. "Arbeiten wie ein Mann und wie eine Frau dazu. Frauen in der DDR." *Weibliche Utopien—männliche Verluste. Frauen und Linke. Ästhetik und Kommunikation* 37 (1979): 85–95.

Allison, Julie A. and Lawrence S. Wrightsman. *Rape: The Misunderstood Crime*. Newbury Park, CA: Sage, 1993.

Altbach, Edith Hoshino et al., eds. *German Feminism: Readings in Politics and Literature*. Albany: State University of New York Press, 1984.

Anderson, Edith. "Genesis and Adventures of the Anthology *Blitz aus heiterm Himmel*." *Studies in GDR Culture and Society* 4 (1984): 1–14

———, ed. *Blitz aus heiterem Himmel*. Rostock: Hinstorff Verlag, 1975.

Anderson, Susan C. "Creativity and Nonconformity in Maron's *Überläuferin*." *Women in German Yearbook* 10 (1995): 143–160.

Apitz, Renate. *Evastöchter. Ein Dutzend Dutzendgeschichten*. Rostock: Hinstorff, 1981.

———. *Hexenzeit. Roman*. Rostock: Hinstorff, 1984.

Auer, Annemarie. "Trobadora unterwegs oder Schulung in Realismus." *Sinn und Form*, 1976, no. 5: 1067–1106. Shorter version in *Irmtraud Morgner. Texte, Daten, Bilder*, edited by Marlis Gerhardt, 117–149. Frankfurt a.M.: Luchterhand, 1990.

Bachofen, J. J. *Das Mutterrecht. Eine Auswahl.* Edited by Hans Jürgen Heinrichs. Frankfurt a.M.: Suhrkamp, 1975.

——. *Myth, Religion, and Mother Right. Selected Writings.* Translated by Ralph Mannheim. Princeton: Princeton University Press, 1973.

Bammer, Angelika. *Partial Visions. Feminism and Utopianism in the 1970s.* New York: Routledge, 1991.

Baranskaya, Natalya. *A Week Like Any Other.* Seattle: Seal Press, 1990.

Barckhausen, Christine. *Schwestern: Tonbandprotokolle aus sechs Ländern.* Berlin: Verlag der Nation, 1985.

Bathrick, David. *The Powers of Speech: The Politics of Culture in the GDR.* Lincoln: University of Nebraska Press, 1995.

Baume, Brita. "Heldinnen nach Plan: Zur literarischen Sozialisation und zum Umgang mit der Frauenfrage in der DDR." In *Der weibliche multikulturelle Blick*, edited by Brita Baume and Hannelore Scholz, 113–124. Berlin: Trafo, 1995.

Beard, Mary. *Woman as Force in History.* New York: MacMillan, 1946.

Beauvoir, Simone de. *The Second Sex.* Translated and edited by H. M. Parshley. New York: Random House, 1989.

Bebel, August. *Die Frau in der Vergangenheit, Gegenwart und Zukunft.* Zürich: Verlags-Magazin (J. Schabelitz), 1883. Second edition of *Die Frau und der Sozialismus.*

——. *Die Frau und der Sozialismus.* Berlin: Dietz Verlag, 1979.

——. *Woman and Socialism.* Translated by Meta L. Stern. New York: Socialist Literature Co., 1910.

Beck, Barbara. "Women and Work." Survey in *The Economist*, 18–24 July 1998, pp. 1–16, special supplement following p. 56.

Benjamin, Jessica. *Like Subjects, Love Objects.* New Haven: Yale University Press, 1995.

Benjamin, Walter. "Theses on the Philosophy of History." In *Illuminations*, edited by Hannah Arendt, translated by Harry Zohn, pp. 253–264. New York: Schocken, 1969.

Berger, Christel. "*Amanda* von Irmtraud Morgner." Review of *Amanda*, by Irmtraud Morgner. *Sonntag*, 29 May 1983, p. 5.

Berghahn, Klaus L. "Die real existierende Utopie im Sozialismus. Zu Christa Wolfs Romanen." In *Literarische Utopien von Morus bis zur Gegenwart*, edited by Klaus L. Berghahn and Hans Ulrich Seeber, 275–297. Königstein: Athenäum, 1983.

Berghahn, Sabine and Andrea Fritzsche. *Frauenrecht in Ost und Westdeutschland: Bilanz—Ausblick.* Berlin: Basisdruck, 1991.

Boa, Elisabeth and Janet Wharton, eds. *Women and the* Wende: *Social Effects and Cultural Reflections of the German Unification Process.* Amsterdam: Rodopi, 1994.

Böck, Dorothea. "'Ich schreibe, um herauszufinden, warum ich schreiben muß.' Frauenliteratur in der DDR zwischen Selbsterfarung und ästhetischem Experiment." *Feministische Studien*, 1990, no. 1: 61–74.

Bock, Gisela. "Weibliche Armut, Mutterschaft und Rechte von Müttern in der Entstehung des Wohlfahrtsstaats 1890–1950." In *Geschichte der Frauen*, edited by Georges Duby and Michelle Perrot, vol. 5 (*20. Jahrhundert*), edited by Françoise Thébaud, 427–461. Frankfurt a.M. and New York: Campus Verlag, 1995.

Böhme, Irene. *Die da drüben—Sieben Kapitel DDR.* W. Berlin: Rotbuch, 1984.

Bovenschen, Silvia. "The Contemporary Witch, the Historical Witch and the Witch Myth: The Witch, Subject of the Appropriation of Nature and Object of the Domination of Nature." Translated by Jeannine Blackwell, Johanna Moore, and Beth Weckmueller. *New German Critique* 15 (1978): 83–119.

Braun, Lily. *Die Frauenfrage.* Leipzig: Hirzel, 1901.

Brecht, Bertolt. *Bad Time for Poetry. Was it? Is it? 152 Poems and Songs.* Edited and introduced by John Willett. London: Methuen: 1995.

Brown, Carol. "Mothers, Fathers, and Children: From Private to Public Patriarchy." In *Women and Revolution*, edited by Lydia Sargent, 239–267. Boston: South End Press, 1981.

Brown, Wendy. *States of Injury.* Princeton: Princeton University Press, 1995.

Brownmiller, Susan. *Against Our Will: Men, Women, and Rape.* New York: Simon & Schuster, 1975.

Brüning, Elfriede. *Partnerinnen.* Frankfurt a.M.: Fischer, 1982. First published in the GDR in 1978.

Buckley, Mary. *Women and Ideology in the Soviet Union.* Ann Arbor: University of Michigan Press, 1989.

Buehler, George. *The Death of Socialist Realism in the Novels of Christa Wolf.* Frankfurt a.M.: Lang, 1984.

Cardinal, Agnès. "'Be Realistic: Demand the Impossible'. On Irmtraud Morgner's Salman Trilogy." In *Socialism and the Literary Imagination*, edited by Martin Kane, 147–161. New York: Berg, 1991.

Clason, Synnöve. "'Mit dieser Handschrift wünschte sie in die Historie einzutreten': Aspekte der Erbrezeption in Irmtraud Morgners Roman 'Leben und Abenteuer der Trobadora Beatriz . . .'" *Weimarer Beiträge* 36 (1990): 1128–1145.

Clausen, Jeanette. "The Difficulty of Saying 'I' as Theme and Narrative Technique in the Works of Christa Wolf." In *Gestaltet und Gestaltend: Frauen in der deutschen Literatur*, edited by Marianne Burkhard. Amsterdamer Beiträge zur neueren Germanistik 10 (1980): 319–333.

Czapanskiy, Karen. "Volunteers and Draftees: The Struggle for Parental Equality." *UCLA Law Review* 38 (1991): 1415–1481.

Czerkas, Andreas, Nadia Donchenko, and Biddy Martin. "Das Verhältnis von Arbeit und gesellschaflicher Veränderung in feministischer Theorie und Literatur der BRD." In *Arbeit als Thema in der deutschen Literatur vom Mittelalter bis zur Gegenwart*, edited by Reinhold Grimm and Jost Hermand, 146–170. Königstein: Athenäum, 1979.

Dahn, Daniela. *Spitzenzeit*. Halle: Mitteldeutscher Verlag, 1980.

Daly, Mary. *Beyond God the Father: Toward a Philosophy of Women's Liberation*. Boston: Beacon, 1973.

Damm, Sigrid. *Cornelia Goethe*. Frankfurt a.M.: Insel, 1988. First published by Aufbau-Verlag, Berlin and Weimar, 1987.

———. "Irmtraud Morgner: Leben und Abenteuer der Trobadora Beatriz nach Zeugnissen ihrer Spielfrau Laura." *Weimarer Beiträge* 9 (1975): 138–148.

Dannhauer, Heinz. *Geschlecht und Persönlichkeit. Eine Untersuchung zur psychischen Geschlechtsdifferenzierung in der Ontogenese*. Berlin: Deutscher Verlag der Wissenschaften, 1977.

Davis, Elizabeth Gould. *The First Sex*. New York: Putnam, 1971.

De Bruyn, Günter. "Geschlechtertausch." In *Blitz aus heiterem Himmel*, edited by Edith Anderson, 7–45. Rostock: Hinstorff Verlag, 1975.

Diemer, Susanne. "'Die Mauer zwischen uns wird immer großer'— Anmerkungen zur DDR-Frauenbewegung im Umbruch." In *Lebensweise und gesellschaftlicher Umbruch in Ostdeutschland*, edited by G. Meyer, G. Riege, and D. Strützel, 343–363. Erlangen: Palm & Enke, 1992.

Dodds, Dinah. "Women in East Germany: Emancipation or Exploitation?" In *Women and the* Wende: *Social Effects and Cultural Reflections of the German Unification Process*, edited by Elizabeth Boa and Janet Wharton, 107–114. Amsterdam: Rodopi, 1994.

―――― and Pam Allen-Thompson, eds. *The Wall in My Backyard. East German Women in Transition.* Amherst: University of Massachusetts Press, 1994.

Dölling, Irene. "Culture and Gender." In *The Quality of Life in the German Democratic Republic,* edited by Marilyn Rueschemeyer and Christiane Lemke, 27–47. London: M. E. Sharpe, 1989.

――――. "Frauen- und Männerbilder: Eine Analyse von Fotos in DDR-Zeitschriften." *Feministische Studien,* 1990, no. 1: 35–49.

――――. "Frauenforschung mit Fragezeichen? Perspektiven feministischer Wissenschaft." In *Wir wollen mehr als ein "Vaterland": DDR-Frauen im Aufbruch,* edited by Gislinde Schwarz and Christine Zenner, 35–55. Reinbek bei Hamburg: Rowohlt, 1990.

Dokumente der revolutionären deutschen Arbeiterbewegung zur Frauenfrage 1848–1974. Leipzig: Verlag für die Frau, 1975.

Drauschke, Petra and Margit Stolzenburg. *Alleinerziehen, eine Lust? Chancen und Risiken für Ostberliner Frauen nach der Wende.* Paffenweiler: Centaurus-Verlagsgesellschaft, 1995.

Dröscher, Barbara. *Subjektive Authentizität: Zur Poetik Christa Wolfs zwischen 1964 und 1975.* Würzburg: Königshausen & Neumann, 1993.

Druxes, Helga. *The Feminization of Dr. Faustus: Female Identity Quests from Stendhal to Morgner.* University Park: Pennsylvania State University Press, 1993.

Eckart, Gabriele. *So sehe ick die Sache; Protokolle aus der DDR; Leben im Havelländischen Obstanbaugebiet.* Köln: Kiepenheuer und Witsch, 1984.

Ehrenreich, Barbara and D. English. *Witches, Midwives, Nurses.* Old Westbury, NY: Feminist Press, 1973.

Einhorn, Barbara. *Cinderella Goes to Market: Citizenship, Gender and Women's Movements in East Central Europe.* London: Verso, 1993.

Ellmenreich, Renate. "Operativ-psychologische Einflußnahme." In *Frauen im Visier der Stasi.* Dokumentation zur Tagung "Frauen im Visier der Stasi" vom 12.11.94 im Haus am Köllnischen Park, Berlin, edited by Annette Maennel, 8–17. Berlin: Redaktion "Weibblick," 1994.

Emde, Silke von der. "Irmtraud Morgner's Postmodern Feminism: A Question of Politics." *Women in German Yearbook* 10 (1995): 117–142.

Emmerich, Wolfgang. *Kleine Literaturgeschichte der DDR.* Darmstadt: Luchterhand, 1989.

Engels, Frederick. *The Origin of the Family, Private Property, and the State*. New York: International Publishers, 1990.

Engler, Jürgen. "Die wahre Lüge der Kunst." Review of *Amanda*, by Irmtraud Morgner. *neue deutsche literatur* 31 (1983), no. 7: 135–144.

Erler, Gisela, Monika Jaeckel, Uta Meier, Rudolf Pettinger, Jürgen Sass, *Familienpolitik im Umbruch? Ergebnisse einer explorativen Studie zu familienpolitischen Maßnahmen in der DDR, Polen, Sowjetunion und Ungarn*. München: Deutsches Jugendinstitut e.V, June 1990.

Evans, Richard J. *Sozialdemokratie und Frauenemanzipation im deutschen Kaiserreich*. Translated by W. G. Sebald in consultation with the author. Berlin: Dietz, 1979.

Feyl, Renate. *Idylle mit Professor*. Berlin: Neues Leben, 1986.

——— . *Der lautlose Aufbruch: Frauen in der Wissenschaft*. Darmstadt: Luchterhand, 1981.

Fineman, Martha Albertson. "Legal Stories, Change, and Incentives—Reinforcing the Law of the Father." *New York Law School Law Review* 37 (1992): 227–249.

Firestone, Shulamith. *The Dialectic of Sex. The Case for Feminist Revolution*. New York: Morrow, 1970.

Fischer, Erica and Petra Lux. *Ohne uns ist kein Staat zu machen: DDR-Frauen nach der Wende*. Köln: Kiepenheuer & Witsch, 1990.

Fish, Stanley. *There's No Such Thing as Free Speech and It's a Good Thing, Too*. New York: Oxford University Press, 1994.

Fraser, Nancy. *Unruly Practices: Power, Discourse, and Gender in Contemporary Social Theory*. Minneapolis: University of Minnesota Press, 1994. First published in 1989.

Freud, Sigmund. "The Question of Lay Analysis." In *The Standard Edition of the Complete Psychological Works of Sigmund Freud*, vol. 20, pp. 177–250. Translated by James Strachey. London: Hogarth Press, 1981.

——— . *Three Essays on the Theory of Sexuality*. Translated by James Strachey. N.P.: Basic Books, n.d.

Frevert, Ute. *Women in German History*. Oxford: Berg, 1988.

Fries, Marilyn Sibley, ed. *Responses to Christa Wolf: Critical Essays*. Detroit: Wayne State University Press, 1990.

Gerber, Margy. "Impertinence, Productive Fear and Hope: The Writings of Helga Königsdorf." In *Socialism and the Literary Imagination. Essays on East German Writers*, edited by Martin Kane, 179–194. New York: Berg, 1991.

Gerhard, Ute. "Die staatlich institutionalisierte 'Lösung' der Frauenfrage. Zur Geschichte der Geschlechterverhältnisse in der DDR." In *Sozialgeschichte der DDR*, edited by Hartmut Kaelble, Jürgen Kocka, and Hartmut Zwahr, 383–403. Stuttgart: Klett-Cotta, 1994.

Gerhardt, Marlis. *Irmtraud Morgner*. Frankfurt a.M.: Luchterhand, 1990.

Girard, René. *Deceit, Desire, and the Novel*. Translated by Yvonne Frecerro. Baltimore: Johns Hopkins, 1965.

Girnus. Wilhelm. "Wer baute das siebentorige Theben." *Sinn und Form* 35 (1983): 439–447.

Goethe, Johann Wolfgang von. *Faust I & II*. Edited and translated by Stuart Atkins. Boston: Suhrkamp/Insel, 1985.

Götze, Ruth. "Zur Entstehungsgeschichte und Verbreitung von Friedrich Engels' Arbeit 'Der Ursprung der Familie, des Privateigentums und des Staats.'" *Mitteilungsblatt der Forschungsgemeinschaft "Geschichte des Kampfes der Arbeiterklasse um die Befreiung der Frau,"* 1984, no. 3: 44–50.

Gray, Francine du Plessix. *Soviet Women: Walking the Tightrope*. New York: Doubleday, 1989.

Greiner, Bernhard. "'Mit der Erzählung geh ich in den Tod': Kontinuität und Wandel des Erzählens im Schaffen von Christa Wolf." In *Erinnerte Zukunft*, edited by Wolfram Mauser, 107–140. Würzburg: Königshausen und Neumann, 1985.

Grosz, Christiane. *Die Tochter*. Berlin und Weimar: Aufbau, 1991. First published in 1987.

Guthrie, John. "The Reconstructed Subject: Christa Wolf, *Kassandra*." In *The German Novel in the Twentieth Century. Beyond Realism*, edited by David Midgley, 179–193. Edinburgh: Edinburgh University Press, 1993.

Gutjahr, Ortrud. "'Erinnerte Zukunft': Gedächtnisrekonstruktion und Subjektkonstitution im Werk Christa Wolfs." In *Erinnerte Zukunft*, edited by Wolfram Mauser, 53–80. Würzburg, Königshausen und Neumann, 1985.

Gysi, Jutta. "Frauen in Partnerschaft und Familie: Sozialistisches Leitbild oder patriarchialisches Relikt." In *Wir wollen mehr als ein "Vaterland": DDR-Frauen im Aufbruch*, edited by Gislinde Schwarz and Christine Zenner, 90–119. Reinbek bei Hamburg: Rowohlt, 1990.

Haase, Horst et al., eds. *Geschichte der Literatur der deutschen demokratischen Republik*. Berlin/GDR: Verlag Volk und Wissen, 1976.

Hafner, Katie. "A Nation of Readers Dumps Its Writers." *New York Times Magazine*, 10 January 1993: 23–26, 46–48.

Hammerstein, Katharina von. "Warum nicht Christian T.? Christa Wolf zur Frauenfrage, untersucht an einem frühen Beispiel: *Nachdenken über Christa T.*" *New German Review* 3 (1987): 17–29.

Hanel, Stephanie. *Literarischer Widerstand zwischen Phantastischem und Alltäglichem. Das Romanwerk Irmtraud Morgners*. Pfaffenweiler: Centaurus, 1995.

Harbers, Henk. "'Widersprüche hervortreiben': Eros, Rationalität und Selbsterkenntnis in Christa Wolfs Erzählung 'Kassandra'." *Neophilologus* 71 (1987): 266–284.

Harris, Angela P. "Race and Essentialism in Feminist Legal Theory." *Stanford Law Review* 42 (1990): 581–607.

Hauser, Kornelia. *Patriarchat als Sozialismus. Soziologische Studien zu Literatur aus der DDR*. Hamburg: Argument-Verlag, 1994.

Heidtmann, Horst, ed. *Im Kreislauf der Windeln. Frauenprosa aus der DDR*. Weinheim und Basel, Beltz Verlag, 1982.

Heitlinger, Alena. *Women and State Socialism*. Montreal: McGill-Queens University Press, 1979.

Hell, Julia. *Post-Fascist Fantasies: Psychoanalysis, History, and the Literature of East Germany*. Durham, NC: Duke University Press, 1997.

Helmecke, Monika. *Klopfzeichen*. Berlin: Verlag Neues Leben, 1979.

Helwig, Gisela. *Frau und Familie in beiden deutschen Staaten*. Köln: Verlag Wissenschaft und Politik Berend von Nottbeck, 1982.

Herminghouse, Patricia A. "Die Frau und das Phantastische in der neueren DDR-Literatur: Der Fall Irmtraud Morgner." In *Die Frau als Heldin und Autorin*, edited by Wolfgang Paulsen, 248–266. Bern: Francke, 1979.

———. "Legal Equality and Women's Reality in the German Democratic Republic." In *German Feminism: Readings in Politics and Literature*, edited by Edith Hoshino Altbach et al., 41–46. Albany: State University of New York Press, 1984.

———. "The Rediscovery of Romanticism: Revisions and Reevaluations." *Studies in GDR Culture and Society* 2 (1982): 1–17.

———. "Schreibende Frauen in der Deutschen Demokratischen Republik." In *Frauen Literatur Geschichte: Schreibende Frauen vom Mittelalter bis zur Gegenwart*, edited by Hiltrud Gnüg and Renate Möhrmann, 338–353. Stuttgart: Metzler, 1985.

———. "Wunschbild, Vorbild oder Porträt? Zur Darstellung der Frau im Roman der DDR." In *Literatur und Literaturtheorie in der DDR*, edited by Peter Uwe Hohendahl and Patricia Herminghouse, 281–334. Frankfurt a.M.: Suhrkamp, 1976.

Herrmann, Ursula. "Die Verarbeitung von Ideen aus Friedrich Engels' Schrift 'Der Ursprung der Familie, des Privateigentums und des Staats' durch August Bebel in seinem Buch 'Die Frau und der Sozialismus.'" *Informationen des Wissenschaftlichen Rates "Die Frau in der sozialistischen Gesellschaft"* (1985), no. 6.

Hieblinger, Inge. *Frauen in unserem Staat. Einige Probleme der Förderung der Frau unter den Bedingungen der wissenschaftlich-technischen Revolution in der DDR*. Berlin: Staatsverlag der Deutschen Demokratischen Republik, 1967.

Hildebrandt, Christel. *Zwölf schreibende Frauen in der DDR: Zu den Schreibbedingungen von Schriftstellerinnen in der DDR in den 70er Jahren*. Hamburg: Frauenbuchvertrieb, 1984.

Hilzinger, Sonja. *"Als ganzer Mensch zu leben..." Emanzipatorische Tendenzen in der neueren Frauen-Literatur der DDR*. Frankfurt a.M.: Lang, 1985.

Hogan, Heidrun. "Der Anteil der Arbeit an der 'Menschwerdung der Frauen': Frauenerwerbsarbeit in der DDR." In *Irmtraud Morgners hexische Weltfahrt*, edited by Kristine von Soden, 73–84. Berlin: Elefanten Press, 1991.

Hohendahl, Peter Uwe und Patricia Herminghouse, eds. *Literatur und Literaturtheorie in der DDR*. Frankfurt a.M.: Suhrkamp, 1976.

Hölder, Egon, ed. *Im Trabi durch die Zeit—40 Jahre Leben in der DDR*. Stuttgart: Metzler-Poeschel, 1992.

Hörnigk, Therese. *Christa Wolf*. Göttingen: Steidl, 1989.

Huyssen, Andreas. "Traces of Ernst Bloch: Reflections on Christa T." In *Responses to Christa Wolf. Critical Essays*, edited by Marilyn Sibley Fries, 233–247. Detroit: Wayne State University Press, 1989. First published in German in 1975.

Irigaray, Luce. *Speculum of the Other Woman*. Translated by Gillian C. Gill. Ithaca: Cornell University Press, 1992. First published in 1974.

Jaeckel, Monika. "Die Frauen im vereinten Deutschland." In Rita Süssmuth and Helga Schubert, *Gehen die Frauen in die Knie?*, edited by Michael Haller, 9–42. Zürich: pendo-verlag, 1990.

Jahnsen, Doris and Monika Meier. "Spiel-Räume der Phantasie: Irmtraud Morgner: 'Leben und Abenteuer der Trobadora Beatriz nach Zeugnissen ihrer Spielfrau Laura.'" In *Verrat an der Kunst? Rückblicke auf die DDR-Literatur*, edited by Karl Deiritz and Hannes Krauss, 209–214. Berlin: Aufbau, 1993.

Jankowsky, Karen H. "New Sense or Nonsense? Christa Wolf's *Kassandra* and 'weibliches Schreiben' in the GDR." *Amsterdamer Beiträge zur Neueren Germanistik* 29 (1989): 397–414.

Jenkinson, David. "Loyalty and its Limits: Christa Wolf's *Kassandra* as a 'Schlüsselerzählung.'" In *Literature on the Threshold: The German Novel in the 1980s*, edited by Arthur William Stuart Parkes and Roland Smith, 235–252. New York: Berg, 1990.

Jokiniemi, Miriam. "Beyond Hags and Old Bags? Portrayals of Women's Old Age in Recent GDR Prose Fiction." *Studies in GDR Culture and Society* 9 (1989): 145–162.

Jones, Ernest. *Life and Work of Sigmund Freud*. Edited and abridged in one volume by Lionel Trilling and Steven Marcus. N.p.: Basic Books, 1961.

Kahlau, Cordula, ed. *Aufbruch! Frauenbewegung in der DDR. Dokumentation*. München: Verlag Frauenoffensive, 1990.

Kaufmann, Eva. "DDR-Schriftstellerinnen, die Widersprüche und die Utopie." *Women in German Yearbook* 7 (1991): 107–120.

———. "Der Hölle die Zunge rausstrecken: Der Weg der Erzählerin Irmtraud Morgner." In *Irmtraud Morgner. Texte, Daten, Bilder*, edited by Marlis Gerhardt, 172–195. Frankfurt a.M.: Luchterhand, 1990. First published in 1984.

———. "'. . . schreiben, als ob meine Arbeit noch und immer wieder gebraucht würde'. Überlegungen zur Utopie bei Christa Wolf." In *Christa Wolf in feministischer Sicht*, edited by Michel Vanhelleputte, 23–32. Frankfurt a.M.: Lang, 1992.

Kersten, Heinz. "The Role of Women in GDR Films Since the Early 1970s." *Studies in GDR Culture and Society* 8 (1988): 47–64.

Kirsch, Sarah. "Merkwürdiges Beispiel weiblicher Entschlossenheit." In *Die ungeheuren bergehohen Wellen auf See*, 7–24. Berlin: Eulenspiegel Verlag, 1973.

———. *Die Pantherfrau*. Berlin and Weimar: Aufbau, 1973.

Klotz, Sibyll-Anka. "Das Verhältnis von allgemeiner sozialer Frage und Frauenfrage in August Bebels Hauptwerk "Die Frau und der Sozialismus" und dessen Rezeption in der BRD-Literatur der siebziger und achtziger Jahre." Ph.D. diss., Humboldt-Universität 1989. 2 vols.

Königsdorf, Helga. *Der Lauf der Dinge*. Berlin and Weimar: Aufbau Verlag, 1988. First published in 1982.

———. *Lichtverhältnisse: Geschichten.* Berlin: Aufbau Verlag, 1988.

———. *Meine ungehörigen Träume.* Berlin and Weimar: Aufbau Verlag, 1981. First published in 1978.

———. *Respektloser Umgang.* Berlin and Weimar, Aufbau Verlag, 1989. First published in 1986.

Kosing, Alfred. *Wörterbuch der marxistisch-leninistischen Philosophie.* Berlin: Dietz, 1986.

Kossakowski, Adolf and Karlheinz Otto, eds. *Psychologische Untersuchungen zur Entwicklung sozialistischer Persönlichkeiten.* Berlin: Volk und Wissen, 1971.

Krause, Barbara. *Gefesselte Rebellin: Brigitte Reimann.* Biographischer Roman. Berlin: Verlag Neues Leben, 1994.

Krauss, Angela. *Das Vergnügen.* Berlin: Aufbau Verlag, 1984.

Krauss, Hannes. "Avant-Garde oder Idyll? Christa Wolf's Discovery of Modernity." Translated by Andrew Barker. In *In the Party Spirit: Socialist Realism and Literary Practice in the Soviet Union, East Germany and China*, edited by Hilary Chung et al., 150–157. Amsterdam: Rodopi, 1996.

Kretzschmar, Ute. "Gleichstellung statt Gleichberechtigung: Frauenpolitik nach der 'Wende.'" In *Wir wollen mehr als ein "Vaterland": DDR-Frauen im Aufbruch*, edited by Gislinde Schwarz and Christine Zenner, 56–69. Reinbek bei Hamburg: Rowohlt, 1990.

Krüger, Ingrid, ed. *Die Heiratsschwindlerin: Erzählungen der DDR.* Darmstadt: Luchterhand, 1983.

Kuhn, Anna. *Christa Wolf's Utopian Vision: From Marxism to Feminism.* Cambridge: Cambridge University Press, 1988.

Labovitz, Esther Kleinbord. *The Myth of the Heroine: The Female "Bildungsroman" in the Twentieth Century. Dorothy Richardson, Simone de Beauvoir, Doris Lessing, Christa Wolf.* New York: Lang, 1986.

Lakoff, Robin. *Language and Woman's Place.* New York: Harper and Row, 1989. First published in 1975.

Lambrecht, Christine. *Männerbekanntschaften: freimütige Protokolle.* Halle: Mitteldeutscher Verlag, 1986.

Lange, Sigrid. "Two Generations of Women's Literature in the GDR: A Study of Power and Feminism." In *In the Party Spirit: Socialist Realism and Literary Practice in the Soviet Union, East Germany and China*, edited by Hilary Chung et al., 166–174. Amsterdam: Rodopi, 1996.

Lauerwald, Hannelore. *An einem Donnerstag oder Der Duft des Brotes. Erzählungen.* Berlin: Verlag Tribüne, 1975.

Lemke, Christiane. "Beyond the Ideological Stalemate: Women and Politics in the FRG and the GDR in Comparison." *German Studies Review* 13 (DAAD Special Issue), 1990: 87–94.

Lennox, Sara. "Christa Wolf and the Women Romantics." *Studies in GDR Culture and Society* 2 (1982): 31–44.

———. "'Nun ja! Das nächste Leben geht aber heute an': Prosa von Frauen und Frauenbefreiung in der DDR." In *Literatur der DDR in den siebziger Jahren*, edited by P. U. Hohendahl and P. Herminghouse, 224–258. Suhrkamp: Frankfurt, 1983.

———. "'Der Versuch, man selbst zu sein': Christa Wolf und der Feminismus." In *Die Frau als Heldin und Autorin*, edited by Wolfgang Paulsen, 217–222. Bern: Franke, 1979.

Lewin, Waldtraut. "Dich hat Amor gewiß." In *Kuckucksrufe und Ohrfeigen: Erzählungen.* Berlin: Verlag Neues Leben, 1983.

Lewis, Alison. "Fantasy and Romance: A Feminist Poetics of Subversion and the Case of Irmtraud Morgner." *Southern Review* 22 (1989): 244–255.

———. *Subverting Patriarchy: Feminism and Fantasy in the Works of Irmtraud Morgner.* Oxford: Berg, 1995.

Liebmann, Irina. *Berliner Mietshaus. Begegnungen und Gespräche.* Halle-Leipzig: Mitteldeutscher Verlag, 1982.

Linklater, Beth. "Erotic Provocations: Gabriele Stötzer-Kachold's Reclaiming of the Female Body?" *Women in German Yearbook* 13 (1997): 151–170.

Löffler, Anneliese. "Vergnügliche und gescheite Hexerei." Review of *Amanda*, by Irmtraud Morgner. *Berliner Zeitung*, 14 June 1983, p. 7.

Love, Myra. "Christa Wolf and Feminism: Breaking the Patriarchal Connection." *New German Critique* 16 (1979): 31–53.

Lukens, Nancy and Dorothy Rosenberg, trans. and ed. *Daughters of Eve. Women's Writing from the German Democratic Republic.* Lincoln: University of Nebraska Press, 1993.

Lützeler, Paul Michael. "Von der Arbeiterschaft zur Intelligenz: Zur Darstellung sozialer Mobilität im Roman der DDR." In *Literatur und Literaturtheorie in der DDR*, edited by Peter Uwe Hohendahl and Patricia Herminghouse, 241–280. Frankfurt a.M.: Suhrkamp, 1976.

MacKinnon, Catherine A. *Feminism Unmodified. Discourses on Life and Law.* Cambridge: Harvard University Press, 1987.

———. *Only Words.* Cambridge: Harvard University Press, 1993.

Maisch, Christine. *Ein schmaler Streifen Zukunft: Christa Wolfs Erzählung "Kassandra."* Würzburg: Königshausen and Neumann, 1986.

Marcuse, Herbert. *Eros and Civilization.* Boston: Beacon, 1955.

Markgraf, Nikolaus. "Die Feministin der DDR." *Frankfurter Rundschau,* 24 May 1975. Reprinted in Gerhardt, *Irmtraud Morgner: Texte, Daten, Bilder,* 150–155. Frankfurt a.M.: Luchterhand, 1990.

Maron, Monika. *The Defector.* Translated by David Newton Marinelli. London: Readers International, 1988.

———. *Flight of Ashes.* Translated by David Newton Marinelli. London: Readers International, 1986.

———. *Flugasche.* Berlin: Union Verlag, 1990. First published in the Federal Republic of Germany in 1981.

———. *Nach Maßgabe meiner Begreifungskraft.* Frankfurt a.M.: Fischer, 1993.

———. *Die Überläuferin.* Frankfurt a.M.: Fischer, 1986.

Marti, Madeleine. *Hinterlegte Botschaften. Die Darstellung lesbischer Frauen in der deutschsprachigen Literatur seit 1945.* Stuttgart: Metzler, 1992.

Martin, Biddy. "Socialist Patriarchy and the Limits of Reform: A Reading of Irmtraud Morgner's *Life and Adventures of Troubadora Beatriz as Chronicled by Her Minstrel Laura.*" *Studies in Twentieth Century Literature* 5 (1980): 59–74.

Martin, Brigitte. *Nach Freude anstehen.* Berlin: Buchverlag der Morgen, 1983. First published in 1981.

———. *Der rote Ballon. Geschichten um Brigge Bem.* Berlin: Der Morgen, 1977.

Marx, Engels, Lenin. *Über die Frau und die Familie.* Leipzig: Verlag für die Frau, 1976.

Marx, Karl and Frederick Engels. *The German Ideology.* Edited by C. J. Arthur. New York: International Publishers, 1993.

Mauser, Wolfram. "Subjektivität—Chance oder Verirrung? Zu Christa Wolfs 'Nachdenken über Christa T.'" *Sprachkunst* 12, no. 1 (1981): 171–185.

Mayer, Gerhart. *Der deutsche Bildungsroman: Von der Aufklärung bis zur Gegenwart*. Stuttgart: Metzler, 1992.

McLellan, David, ed. *Marxism: Essential Writings*. Oxford: Oxford University Press, 1989.

Meier, Monika. "Konzerte der Redevielfalt: Die Walpurgisnacht-Darstellungen in der 'Amanda' Irmtraud Morgners." *Literatur für Leser* 4 (1990): 213–227.

——. "Von schelmischem Spiel zu närrischem Ernst: Die Dialogisierung geschlechtsspezifischer Denkformen und Redeweisen in den Romanen 'Leben und Abenteuer der Trobadora Beatriz' und 'Amanda' von Irmtraud Morgner." *Weimarer Beiträge* 38 (1992): 245–258.

Menschik, Jutta and Evelyn Leopold. *Gretchens rote Schwestern: Frauen in der DDR*. Frankfurt a.M.: Fischer, 1974.

Merkel, Ina. "Keine Zeit. Niemals." In *Irmtraud Morgners hexische Weltfahrt*, edited by Kristine von Soden, 66–72. Berlin: Elefanten Press, 1991.

——. "Leitbilder und Lebensweisen von Frauen in der DDR." In *Sozialgeschichte der DDR*, edited by Hartmut Kaelble, Jürgen Kocka, and Hartmut Zwahr, 359–382. Stuttgart: Klett-Cotta, 1994.

—— et al. *Ohne Frauen ist kein Staat zu machen*. Hamburg: Argument-Verlag, 1990.

Milz, Helga A. "Zur deutsch-deutschen Soziologie des Frauenbewußtseins: Paradigmenwechsel der Frauenforschung in Ost und West." *Berliner Journal für Soziologie*, 1996, no. 3: 339–362.

Mohr, Heinrich. "Productive Longing: Structure, Theme, and Political Relevance in Christa Wolf's *The Quest for Christa T.*" In *Responses to Christa Wolf. Critical Essays*, edited by Marilyn Sibley Fries, 196–232. Detroit: Wayne State University Press, 1989. First published in German in 1971.

Morgan, Lewis Henry. *Ancient Society*. Tuscon: University of Arizona Press, 1985. First published in 1877.

——. *League of the Iroquois*. New York: Carol Publishing Group, 1993. First published in 1851.

Morgenstern, Beate. *Jenseits der Allee*. Berlin and Weimar: Aufbau, 1979.

Morgner, Irmtraud. "Aber die großen Veränderungen beginnen leise." Interview by Erika Nowak. *Für Dich* 21 (1978): 17–20.

——. *Amanda*. Darmstadt: Luchterhand, 1983.

———. "Am Ende bleibt das eigene Leben." Interview by Synnöve Clason. *Die Zeit*, 6 November 1992, p. 6 Literatur.

———. "Apropos Eisenbahn." In *Irmtraud Morgner. Texte, Daten, Bilder*, edited by Marlis Gerhardt, 17–23. Frankfurt a.M.: Luchterhand, 1990. First published in 1974.

———. "Des Kaisers alte neue Kleider." Interview by Gisela Lindemann. *Die Zeit*, Number 30, 22 July 1988, p. 34 Literatur.

———. "Frauenstaat." Interview by Harrie Lemmens. *Konkret* 10 (1984): 54–61.

———. "Gespräch mit Irmtraud Morgner." Interview by Doris Berger. *GDR Monitor* 12 (1984–1985): 29–37.

———. *Die Hexe im Landhaus. Gespräch in Solothurn*. Zürich: Rauhreif Verlag, 1984.

———. *Hochzeit in Konstantinopel*. Berlin and Weimar: Aufbau, 1968.

———. Interview by Ekkehart Rudolph. In *Aussage zur Person. Zwölf deutsche Schriftsteller im Gespräch mit Ekkehart Rudolph*, 157–177. Tübingen: Horst Erdmann Verlag, 1977.

———. Interview by Joachim Walther. In Joachim Walther, *Meinetwegen Schmetterlinge: Gespräche mit Schriftstellern*, 42–54. Berlin: Der Morgen, 1973.

———. "Interview mit Irmtraud Morgner." By Eva Kaufmann. *Weimarer Beiträge* 9 (1984): 1494–1514.

———. "Interview mit Irmtraud Morgner." By Joachim Walther. *Weltbühne* 32 (1972): 1010–1013.

———. "'Jetzt oder nie! Die Frauen sind die Hälfte des Volkes!'" Interview by Alice Schwarzer. *Emma*, January 1990: 32–39.

———. *Leben und Abenteuer der Trobadora Beatriz nach Zeugnissen ihrer Spielfrau Laura*. Berlin: Aufbau, 1974.

———. "Life and Adventures of Trobadora Beatriz as Chronicled by Her Minstrel Laura—Twelfth Book." Translated by Karen R. Achberger and Friedrich Achberger. *New German Critique* 15 (1978): 121–146.

———. "Notturno." In *Neue Texte. Almanach für deutsche Literatur*, 7–36. Berlin and Weimar: Aufbau Verlag: 1964.

———. "Die Perlen des Phantastischen." Interview by Klara Obermüller. *Die Weltwoche*, no. 13, 30 March 1977, p. 35.

――. "'Produktivkraft Sexualität souverän nutzen.' Ein Gespräch mit der DDR-Schriftstellerin Irmtraud Morgner." Interview by Karin Huffzky. *Frankfurter Rundschau*, no. 188, 16 August 1975, Feuilleton page iii.

――. *Rumba auf einen Herbst*. München: DTV, 1995.

――. "Die täglichen Zerstückelungen. Gespräch mit Ursula Krechel." *Journal der Frauenoffensive* 5 (1976). Reprinted in *Irmtraud Morgner. Texte, Daten, Bilder*, edited by Marlis Gerhardt, 24–33. Frankfurt a.M.: Luchterhand, 1990.

――. "Weltspitze sein und sich wundern, was noch nicht ist." Interview by Oskar Neumann. *Kürbiskern* 1 (1978): 95–99.

――. *Die wundersamen Reisen Gustavs des Weltfahrers*. Berlin and Weimar, Aufbau, 1972.

Mudry, Anna, ed. *Gute Nacht, du Schöne. Autorinnen blicken zurück*. Frankfurt a.M.: Luchterhand, 1991.

Müller, Christa. "Candida." In *Vertreibung aus dem Paradies*. Berlin and Weimar: Aufbau, 1979.

――. *Die Verwandlung der Liebe*. Berlin and Weimar: Aufbau, 1990.

Müller, Christine. *Männer-Protokolle*. Berlin: Buchverlag Der Morgen, 1985.

Nagelschmidt, Ilse. "Sozialistische Frauenliteratur: Überlegungen zu einem Phänomen der DDR-Literatur in den siebziger und achtziger Jahren." *Weimarer Beiträge* 35 (1989): 450–471.

――. "40 Jahre Gleichberechtigung im Sozialismus." *Frauen in der Geschichte*, 1992, no. 3: 5–18.

Nickel, Hildegard. "Ein perfektes Drehbuch: Geschlechtertrennung durch Arbeit und Sozialisation." In *Wir wollen mehr als ein "Vaterland": DDR-Frauen im Aufbruch*, edited by Gislinde Schwarz and Christine Zenner, 73–89. Reinbek bei Hamburg: Rowohlt, 1990.

――. "Women in the GDR: Will Renewal Pass them By?" *Women in German Yearbook* 6 (1991): 99–107.

――. "Zur Lage der Frauen in der früheren DDR." In Rita Süssmuth and Helga Schubert, *Gehen die Frauen in die Knie?*, edited by Michael Haller, 149–158. Zürich: pendo-verlag, 1990. Reprinted in excerpt from *Aus Politik und Zeitgeschichte* 16–17 (1990).

Nicolai, Rose. *Christa Wolf, Kassandra: Interpretation*. With Doris Thimm. München: Oldenbourg, 1989.

Nicolai, Rosemarie. "Christa Wolfs 'Kassandra'. Quellenstudien und Interpretationsansätze." In *Literatur für Leser*, 1985, no. 3: 137–155.

Nordmann, Ingeborg. "Die halbierte Geschichtsfähigkeit der Frau. Zu Irmtraud Morgners Roman *Leben und Abenteuer der Trobadora Beatriz nach Zeugnissen ihrer Spielfrau Laura*." *Amsterdamer Beiträge zur neueren Germanistik* 11/12 (1981): 419–462.

Norton, Roger C., ed. and trans. *Voices East and West: German Short Stories Since 1945*. New York: Ungar, 1984.

Ohne Frauen ist kein Leben. Edited by Zentrum Interdisziplinäre Frauenforschung. Berlin: Verlag Christine Hoffmann, 1994.

Olsen, Frances. "Does Enough Work Make Women Free? Part-Time and Full-Time Work Strategies for Women." *The Indian Journal of Social Work* 53 (1992): 599–610.

Othmer-Vetter, Regine and Annemarie Tröger. "Einleitung." *Zwischenzeiten—Frauenforschung aus der DDR*. *Feministische Studien* 8:1 (1990): 3–9.

Panitz, Eberhard. *Unter den Bäumen regnet es zweimal*. Halle (Saale): Mitteldeutscher Verlag, 1969.

Partisch, Gudrun. "Bebels Werk "Die Frau und der Sozialismus"—Orientierungshilfe für die Frauenpolitik in der DDR?" *Frauen in der Geschichte*, 1991, no. 2: 68–74.

Paschiller, Doris. *Die Würde*. Berlin: Verlag der Morgen, 1980.

Pickle, Linda Schelbitzki. "'Scratching Away the Male Tradition': Christa Wolfs *Kassandra*." *Contemporary Literature* 27 (1986): 32–47.

Pietsch, Hildegard. "Goethe as a Model for Feminist Writing? The Adaptation of a Classical Author in Irmtraud Morgner's *Amanda. Ein Hexenroman*." In *The Age of Goethe Today*, edited by Gertrud Bauer Pickar and Sabine Cramer, 212–219. München: Fink, 1990.

Pirskawetz, Lia. *Der Stille Grund*. Berlin: Verlag Neues Leben, 1985.

Preußer, Heinz-Peter. "Projektionen und Mißverständnisse. Über den Nobilitierungsdiskurs der westlichen Rezeption und einige Unvermeidbarkeiten im Umgang mit Christa Wolf, ihrer Erzählung 'Kassandra' und den sie begleitenden 'Voraussetzungen.'" In *Christa Wolf*, Text & kritik, vol. 46 (Neufassung), 68–87. München: Verlag edition text & kritik, 1994.

Pulkenat, Maria. "Geschichte der Töchter: Autobiographische Erzählprosa von DDR-Autorinnen der achtziger Jahre." *Weimarer Beiträge* 36 (1990): 1185–1190.

Pusch, Luise. *Das Deutsche als Männersprache*. Frankfurt a.M.: Suhrkamp, 1984.

Quataert, Jean H. *Reluctant Feminists in German Social Democracy, 1885–1917.* Princeton: Princeton University Press, 1979.

Reich-Ranicki, Marcel. "Christa Wolfs unruhige Elegie." In *Entgegnung. Zur deutschen Literatur der siebziger Jahre,* 240–248. Stuttgart: Deutsche Verlags-Anstalt, 1981. First published in *Die Zeit,* 23 May 1969, pp. 21–22.

Reid, J. H. "From Adolf Hennecke to Star Wars—the Fortunes of 'Faust' in the GDR." In *Neue Ansichten. The Reception of Romanticism in the Literature of the GDR,* edited by Howard Gaskill, Karin McPherson, and Andrew Barker, 142–159. Amsterdam: Rodopi, 1990.

Reimann, Brigitte. *Franziska Linkerhand.* München: DTV, 1990. Originally published: Berlin: Verlag Neues Leben, 1974.

———. *Die geliebte, die verfluchte Hoffnung.* Darmstadt: Luchterhand, 1983.

Rey, William H. "'Wo habt ihr bloß alle gelebt': Christa Wolfs Dilemma in ihrem Verhältnis zur DDR." *Germanic Review* 66 (1991): 89–95.

Rich, Adrienne. *Of Woman Born: Motherhood as Experience and Institution.* New York: Norton, 1995.

———. *On Lies, Secrets, and Silence.* New York: Norton, 1979.

Robin, Régine. *Socialist Realism. An Impossible Aesthetic.* Translated by Catherine Porter. Stanford: Stanford University Press, 1992.

Roebling, Irmgard. "'Hier spricht keiner meine Sprache, der nicht mit mir stirbt.' Zum Ort der Sprachreflexion in Christa Wolfs *Kassandra.*" In *Erinnerte Zukunft,* edited by Wolfram Mauser, 207–232. Würzburg: Königshausen & Neumann, 1985.

Romero, Christine Zehl. "Vertreibung aus dem Paradies: Zur neuen Frauenliteratur in der DDR, " *Studies in GDR Culture and Society* 3 (1983): 71–85.

Rosenberg, Dorothy. "Another Perspective: Young Women Writers in the GDR." *Studies in GDR Culture and Society* 4 (1984): 187–197.

———. "The Emancipation of Women in Fact and Fiction: Changing Roles in GDR Society and Literature." In *Women, State, and Party in Eastern Europe,* edited by Sharon L. Wolchik and Alfred G. Meyer, 344–361. Durham, NC: Duke Unversity Press, 1985.

———. "GDR Women Writers: The Post-War Generation. An Updated Bibliography of Narrative Prose, June 1987." *Women in German Yearbook* 4: 233–241.

———. "On Beyond Superwomen: The Conflict Between Work and Family Roles in GDR Literature." *Studies in GDR Culture and Society* 3 (1983): 87–100.

———. "Redefining the Public and the Private: Women Writers in the GDR." In *Frauen-Fragen in der deutschsprachigen Literatur seit 1945*, edited by Mona Knapp and Gerd Labroisse, 131–157. Amsterdam: Amsterdamer Beiträge zur neueren Germanistik 29 (1989).

———. "Shock Therapy: GDR Women in Transition from a Socialist Welfare State to a Social Market Economy." *Signs* 17 (1991): 129–151.

Rosenberg, Rosalind. *Divided Lives: American Women in the Twentieth Century*. London: Penguin, 1993.

Rossi, Alice S. "Equality Between the Sexes: An Immodest Proposal." In *The Woman in America*, edited by Robert Jay Lifton, 98–143. Boston: Houghton Mifflin, 1968.

Röth, Uta. "Die klassenlose Gretchenfrage: Über die Vereinbarkeit von Beruf und Familie." In *Wir wollen mehr als ein "Vaterland": DDR-Frauen im Aufbruch*, edited by Gislinde Schwarz and Christine Zenner, 132–144. Reinbek bei Hamburg: Rowohlt, 1990.

Rüdenauer, Erika, ed. *Dünne Haut. Tagebücher von Frauen aus der DDR*. Köln: Weltkreis, 1988. Lizenzausgabe des Mitteldeutscher Verlags Halle.

Rueschemeyer, Marilyn and Hanna Schissler. "Women in the Two Germanies." *German Studies Review* (DAAD Special Issue 1990): 72–85.

Rüß, Gisela, ed. *Dokumente zur Kunst-, Literatur- und Kulturpolitik der SED 1971–1974*. Stuttgart: Seewald Verlag, 1976.

Sargent, Lydia, ed. *Women and Revolution: A Discussion of the Unhappy Marriage of Marxism and Feminism*. Boston: South End Press, 1981.

Schaffer, Harry G. *Women in the Two Germanies: A Comparative Study of a Socialist and a Non-Socialist Society*. New York: Pergamon Press, 1981.

Schenk, Christina. "Experiment UFV." In *Irmtraud Morgners hexische Weltfahrt*, edited by Kristine von Soden, 124–135. Berlin: Elefanten Press, 1991.

Scherer, Gabriele. *Zwischen 'Bitterfeld' und 'Orplid': Zum literarischen Werk Irmtraud Morgners*. Bern: Lang, 1992.

Schlott, Jutta. *Klare Verhältnisse. Erzählungen*. Berlin: Verlag Neues Leben, 1989.

———. *Das liebliche Fest*. Berlin: Verlag Neues Leben, 1984.

Schmidt, R. "Über gesellschaftliche Ohnmacht und Utopie in Christa Wolfs *Kassandra*." *Oxford German Studies* 16 (1985): 109–121.

Schmidt, Ricarda. "The Concept of Identity in Recent East and West German Women's Writing." In *German Literature at a Time of Change: 1989–1990: German Unity and German Identity in Literary Perspective*, edited by Arthur Williams, Stuart Parkes, and Roland Smith, 429–447. Bern: Lang, 1991.

———. "Truth, Language and Reality in Christa Wolf." In *Socialism and the Literary Imagination: Essays on East German Writers*, edited by Martin Kane, 107–123. New York: Berg, 1991.

Schmitz, Dorothee. *Weibliche Selbstentwürfe und männliche Bilder. Zur Darstellung der Frau in DDR-Romanen der siebziger Jahre*. Frankfurt a.M.: Lang, 1983.

Schmitz-Köster, Dorothee. *Trobadora und Kassandra und . . . Weibliches Schreiben in der DDR*. Köln: Pahl-Rugenstein, 1989.

Schoefer, Christine. "The Attack on Christa Wolf." *The Nation*, 22 October 1990, 446–449.

Schoeps, Karl-Heinz and Richard A. Zipser. "Kurzer Überblick über die Geschichte der DDR-Literatur." In *DDR-Literatur im Tauwetter*, 3 vols. New York: Peter Lang, 1985, 1: 17–36.

Scholz, Hannelore. "Zum Bild der Frau in der DDR-Literatur." In *Unterm neuen Kleid der Freiheit das Korsett der Einheit: Auswirkungen der deutschen Vereinigung für Frauen in Ost und West*, edited by Christel Faber and Traute Meyer, 131–152. Berlin: Edition Sigma Rainer Bohn Verlag, 1992.

Scholze, Siegfried. "Zur internationalen Konferenz anläßlich des 100. Jahrestages des Erscheinens von Bebels Buch 'Die Frau und der Sozialismus' im Februar 1979—ein kritischer und selbstkritischer Nachtrag," *Frauen in der Geschichte*, 1992, no. 2: 35–40.

Schowalter, Elaine. "Towards a Feminist Poetics." In *Women Writing and Writing about Women*, edited by Mary Jacobus, 22–41. London: Croom Helm, 1979.

Schubert, Helga. *Anna kann Deutsch*. Berlin: Aufbau-Verlag, 1975.

———. *Blickwinkel. Geschichten*. Berlin: Aufbau-Verlag, 1984.

———. *Lauter Leben. Geschichten*. Berlin: Aufbau-Verlag, 1977. First published in 1975.

———. *Schöne Reise. Geschichten*. Berlin: Aufbau-Verlag, 1988.

———. *Das verbotene Zimmer*. Darmstadt and Neuwied: Luchterhand, 1982.

Schütz, Helga. *In Annas Namen*. Berlin: Aufbau-Verlag, 1986.

———. *Julia oder Erziehung zum Chorgesang*. Berlin: Aufbau, 1975.

Schwarz, Gislinde and Christine Zenner. "Nachbetrachtung: Ausreichend sanft? Ausreichend zornig? Frauen zwischen Mut und Verzweiflung." In *Wir wollen mehr als ein "Vaterland": DDR-Frauen im Aufbruch*, edited by Gislinde Schwarz and Christine Zenner, 145–155. Reinbek bei Hamburg: Rowohlt, 1990.

———. "Ursprünglich war da mal eine Frau: Die Geschichte eines Briefes." In *Wir wollen mehr als ein "Vaterland": DDR-Frauen im Aufbruch*, edited by Gislinde Schwarz and Christine Zenner, 7–14. Reinbek bei Hamburg: Rowohlt, 1990.

———, eds. *Wir wollen mehr als ein "Vaterland": DDR-Frauen im Aufbruch*. Reinbek bei Hamburg: Rowohlt, 1990.

Schwarzer, Alice. *Der "kleine Unterschied" und seine großen Folgen*. Frankfurt a.M.: Fischer, 1994. First published in 1975.

Scott, Hilda. *Does Socialism Liberate Women? Experiences from Eastern Europe*. Boston: Beacon, 1974.

Seidemann, Maria. "Der hilfreiche Rabe," in *Das Kostüm*, pp. 62–65. Berlin and Weimar: Aufbau, 1982. First published in *Der Tag an dem Sir Henry starb*. Berlin: Eulenspiegel-Verlag, 1980.

Selbmann, Rolf. *Der deutsche Bildungsroman*. Stuttgart: Metzler, 1984.

VII. Schriftstellerkongreß der Deutschen Demokratischen Republik. Protokoll (Arbeitsgruppen). Berlin and Weimar: Aufbau, n.d.

Silberman, Marc. "Whose Story Is This?" In *Contentious Memories: Looking Back at the GDR*, edited by Jost Hermand and Marc Silberman, 25–57. New York: Peter Lang, 1998.

Soden, Kristine von, ed. *Irmtraud Morgners hexische Weltfahrt*. Berlin: Elefanten Press, 1991.

Stachowa, Angela. *Kleine Verführung*. Halle: Mitteldeutscher Verlag, 1983.

Staritz, Dieter. *Geschichte der DDR*. Frankfurt a.M.: Suhrkamp, 1989.

Staude, Fritz. "August Bebels Hauptwerk 'Die Frau und der Sozialismus' in seiner aktuellen Bedeutung." *Mitteilungsblatt der Forschungsgemeinschaft "Geschichte des Kampfes der Arbeiterklasse um die Befreiung der Frau,"* 1980, no. 3: 5–15.

———. "100 Jahre August Bebels Hauptwerk 'Die Frau und der Sozialismus.'" *Mitteilungsblatt der Forschungsgemeinschaft "Geschichte des Kampfes der Arbeiterklasse um die Befreiung der Frau,"* 1979, no. 1: 5–20.

Stephan, Alexander. "Christa Wolf." In *Neue Literatur der Frauen: Deutschsprachige Autorinnen der Gegenwart*, edited by Heinz Puknus, 149–158. München: Beck, 1980.

———. "Die wissenschaftlich-technische Revolution in der Literatur der DDR." *Der Deutschunterricht* 30, no. 2 (1978): 18–34.

Stephens, Anthony. "'Die Verführung der Worte'—von *Kindheitsmuster* zu *Kassandra*." In *Wolf: Darstellung—Deutung—Diskussion*, edited by Manfred Jurgensen, 127–147. Bern: Francke, 1984.

Streller, Siegfried. "Göttinnen, Seherinnen, Hexen: Zur Goethe-Rezeption in Christa Wolfs 'Kassandra' und Irmtraud Morgners Hexenroman 'Amanda.'" In Streller, *Wortweltbilder. Studien zur Deutschen Literatur*, 255–271. Berlin: Aufbau Verlag, 1986.

———. "Sirenen und Hexen zwischen Blocksberg und Parnaß. Zur Traditionswahl des Phantastischen in Irmtraud Morgner's Hexenroman 'Amanda.'" In *Kulturelles Erbe zwischen Tradition und Avantgarde*, edited by Thomas Metscher and Christian Marzahn, 427–441. Köln: Böhlau Verlag, 1991.

Struzyk, Brigitte. *Caroline unterm Freiheitsbaum. Ansichtssachen*. Darmstadt: Luchterhand, 1988.

Süssmuth, Rita and Helga Schubert. *Gehen die Frauen in die Knie?* Edited by Michael Haller. Zürich: pendo-verlag, 1990.

Szepansky, Gerda. *Die stille Emanzipation. Frauen in der DDR*. Frankfurt a.M.: Fischer, 1995.

Tetzner, Gerti. *Karen W*. Halle: Mitteldeutscher Verlag, 1974.

Thompson, E. P. *The Making of the English Working Class*. London: Victor Gollancz, 1963.

Thönnessen, Werner. *The Emancipation of Women: The Rise and Decline of the Women's Movement in German Social Democracy 1863–1933*. Translated by Joris de Bres. London: Pluto Press, 1973.

Thurm, Brigitte. *Verena*. Rostock: VEB Hinstorff Verlag, 1972.

———. *Verlangen*. Rostock: Hinstorff Verlag, 1985. First published in 1981.

Tolstaya, Tatyana. *On the Golden Porch*. Translated by Antonina W. Bouis. New York: Random House, 1990.

Trautmann, Thomas R. *Lewis Henry Morgan and the Invention of Kinship.* Berkeley: University of California Press, 1987.

Tröger, Annemarie. "Brief an eine französische Freundin. Die Intelligenz in der Wende—Gedanken zu den Veränderungen in der DDR." *Feministische Studien*, 1990, no. 1: 113–122.

Trömel-Plötz, Senta. *Frauensprache: Sprache der Veränderung.* Frankfurt a.M: Fischer, 1991. First published in 1982.

Trommler, Frank. "Die Kulturpolitik der DDR und die kulturelle Tradition des deutschen Sozialismus." In *Literatur und Literaturtheorie in der DDR*, edited by Peter Uwe Hohendahl and Patricia Herminghouse, 13–72. Frankfurt a.M.: Suhrkamp, 1976.

——. "Von Stalin zu Hölderlin: Über den Entwicklungsroman in der DDR." In *Basis. Jahrbuch für Deutsche Gegenwartsliteratur*, 2 (1971): 141–190.

Vanhelleputte, Michel. "Christa Wolf und der Bankrott des patriarchalischen Prinzips oder die Voraussetzungen ihres Entwurfs eines weltverändernden Feminismus." In *Christa Wolf in feministischer Sicht*, edited by Michel Vanhelleputte, 13–22. Frankfurt a.M.: Lang, 1992.

Vogel, Lise. *Mothers on the Job: Maternity Policy in the U.S. Workplace.* New Brunswick, NJ: Rutgers University Press, 1993.

Voris, Renate. "The Hysteric and the Mimic: Reading Christa Wolf's *The Quest for Christa T.*" In *Writing the Woman Artist: Essays on Poetics, Politics, and Portraiture*, edited by Suzanne W. Jones, 232–258. Philadelphia: University of Pennsylvania Press, 1991.

Wander, Maxie. *Guten Morgen, du Schöne.* Darmstadt: Luchterhand, 1979.

——. *Leben wär eine prima Alternative.* Edited by Fred Wander. Darmstadt: Luchterhand, 1980.

Waschescio, Petra. *Vernunftkritik und Patriarchatskritik: Mythische Modelle in der deutschen Gegenwartsliteratur. Heiner Müller, Irmtraud Morgner, Botho Strauß, Gisela von Wysocki.* Bielefeld: Aisthesis Verlag, 1994.

Weigel, Sigrid. "Die geopferte Heldin und das Opfer als Heldin. Zum Entwurf weiblicher Helden in der Literatur von Männern und Frauen." In *Die verborgene Frau: Sechs Beiträge zu einer feministischen Literaturwissenschaft*, with contributions by Inge Stephan and Sigrid Weigel, 138–152. Berlin: Argument Verlag, 1983.

Weinbaum, Batya. *The Curious Courtship of Women's Liberation and Socialism.* Boston: South End Press, 1978.

Weitzman, Lenore J. *The Divorce Revolution*. New York: Free Press, 1985.

Werner, Hans-Georg. "'Unter den Linden' von Christa Wolf." In *Erworbene Tradition: Studien zu Werken der sozialistischen deutchen Literatur*, edited by Günter Hartung et al., 256–298. Berlin: Aufbau, 1977.

Werner, Petra. *Die Lüge hat bunte Flügel*. Berlin: Neues Leben, 1986.

West, Stephanie. "Christa Wolf's *Kassandra*: A Classical Perspective." *Oxford German Studies* 20–21 (1991–1992): 164–185.

Wiens, Maya. *Traumgrenzen*. Berlin: Verlag Neues Leben, 1983.

Wilke, Sabine. "Between Female Dialogics and Traces of Essentialism: Gender and Warfare in Christa Wolf's Major Writings." *Studies in Twentieth-Century Literature* 17 (1993): 243–262.

Willis, Ellen. *No More Nice Girls. Countercultural Essays*. Hanover, NH: Wesleyan University Press, 1992.

Winkler, Gunnar, ed. *Frauenreport '90*. Berlin: Verlag Die Wirtschaft, 1990.

———, ed. *Sozialreport '90: Daten und Fakten zur sozialen Lage in der DDR*. Berlin: Verlag Die Wirtschaft, 1990.

Wolf, Christa. "A Dialogue with Christa Wolf." With Grace Paley. *Newsletter*, American Center of Pen International, no. 53 (1984): 8–13.

———. "A Tomcat's New Philosophy of Life." In *Thinking It Over. 30 Stories from the German Democratic Republic*, edited by Hubert Witt, 171–197. Berlin: Seven Seas, 1977.

———. *Auf dem Weg nach Tabou. Texte 1990–1994*. Köln: Kiepenheuer & Witsch, 1994.

———. *The Author's Dimension. Selected Essays*. Introduction by Grace Paley. Edited by Alexander Stephan. Translated by Jan van Heurck. New York: Farrar, Straus and Giroux, 1993.

———. *Cassandra. A Novel and Four Essays*. Translated by Jan van Heurck. New York: Farrar Straus Giroux, 1984.

———. *Die Dimension des Autors. Essays und Aufsätze, Reden und Gespräche 1959–1985*, 2 vols. Frankfurt a.M.: Luchterhand, 1987.

———. *Divided Heaven*. Translated by Joan Becker. Introduction and Bibliography by Jack Zipes. N.p.: Adler's Foreign Books, 1983. First published in 1965 by Seven Seas Books, Berlin, G.D.R.

———. "Documentation: Christa Wolf." *German Quarterly* 57 (1984): 91–115.

———. *The Fourth Dimension. Interviews with Christa Wolf.* Translated by Hilary Pilkington. Introduction by Karin McPherson. London: Verso, 1988.

———. *Gesammelte Erzählungen.* Frankfurt a.M.: Luchterhand, 1988.

———. *Der geteilte Himmel.* Halle/Saale: Mitteldeutscher Verlag, 1963.

———. *Kassandra.* Darmstadt: Luchterhand, 1983.

———. *Kein Ort. Nirgends.* Berlin: Aufbau, 1979.

———. *Medea. A Modern Retelling.* Translated by John Cullen. London: Virago, 1998.

———. *Medea. Stimmen.* N.p.: Luchterhand, 1996.

———. *Nachdenken über Christa T.* Neuwied and Berlin: Luchterhand, 1970.

———. *No Place on Earth.* Translated by Jan van Heurck. New York: Farrar, Straus, Giroux, 1982.

———. *Parting from Phantoms. Selected Writings, 1990–1994.* Translated and annotated by Jan van Heurck. Chicago: University of Chicago Press, 1997.

———. *The Quest for Christa T.* Translated by Christopher Middleton. New York: Farrar, Straus and Giroux, 1970.

———. "Self-Experiment: Appendix to A Report." *New German Critique* 13 (1978): 109–131.

———. *Voraussetzungen einer Erzählung: Kassandra.* Darmstadt: Luchterhand, 1983.

———. *Was bleibt. Erzählung.* München: DTV, 1994. First published in 1990.

———. *What Remains and Other Stories.* Translated by Heike Schwarzbauer and Rick Takvorian. New York: Farrar, Straus and Giroux: 1993.

Wolter, Christine. *Die Alleinseglerin.* Zürich: Benziger, 1982.

———. *Wie ich meine Unschuld verlor: Erzählungen.* Berlin and Weimar: Aufbau-Verlag, 1976.

Woolf, Virginia. *Three Guineas.* San Diego: Harcourt Brace, n.d. First published in 1938.

Worgitzky, Charlotte. *Meine ungeborenen Kinder.* Berlin: Buchverlag Der Morgen, 1982.

———. "Meine ungeborenen Kinder." In *Ohne Frauen ist kein Leben*, edited by Zentrum für interdisziplinäre Frauenforschung, 107–125. Berlin: Verlag Christine Hoffmann, 1994.

———. *Traum vom Möglichen*. Berlin: Morgenbuch Verlag, 1991.

———. *Die Unschuldigen*. Berlin: Der Morgen, 1975.

———. *Vieräugig oder blind*. Berlin: Der Morgen, 1985. First published in 1978.

Zeplin, Rosemarie. *Der Maulwurf oder fatales Beispiel weiblicher Gradlinigkeit*. Berlin and Weimar: Aufbau, 1990.

———. *Schattenriß eines Liebhabers*. Frankfurt a.M.: Ullstein, 1984. First published in 1980.

Zetkin, Clara. "Die Arbeiterinnen- und Frauenfrage der Gegenwart." Berliner Arbeiterbibliothek. Edited by Max Schippel. No. 3. Berlin: Verlag der "Berliner Volks-Tribüne," Berlin, 1889.

Zipser, Richard A. *DDR-Literatur im Tauwetter*, vol. 3 (*Stellungnahmen*). "With Karl-Heinz Schoeps." New York: Lang, 1985.

Index

abortion, 13, 25, 205; declared illegal, 17; legalization of, 7, 8; literary treatment of, 29, 33, 191–95, 200, 208, 236 n.51; in Morgner, *Trobadora Beatriz*, 62, 65, 66, 191; in Wiens, *Traumgrenzen*, 33, 162, 183, 195; in Worgitzky, *Meine ungeborenen Kinder*, 33, 161–62, 191–95; in Worgitzky, *Unschuldigen, Die*, 162
Aeschylus, 100–101
Andersen, Hans Christian, 168
Anderson, Edith, *Blitz aus heiterem Himmel* (Lightning out of a blue sky), 68, 88, 94
Apitz, Renate, 28; *Hexenzeit* (Time of witches), 47, 124, 175, 177, 189, 199; "Jahr der Wibke Winter, Das" (The year of Wibke Winter), 155
Arnim, Bettina von, 97
Auclert, Hubertine, 84
Auer, Annemarie, 54, 88

baby year, 6, 10, 11
Bachmann, Ingeborg, 100, 231 n.52
Bachofen, J.J., 75, 88, 102, 106; and Bebel, 83; and Engels, 79; *Mutterrecht, Das*, 77–79; and Wolf, 56, 100
Bakhtin, Mikhail, 58
Baranskaya, Natalya, *A Week Like Any Other*, 180
Barckhausen, Christiane, *Schwestern* (Sisters), 170
Bathrick, David, 24
Beard, Charles, 126
Beard, Mary, 128
Beauvoir, Simone de, 40, 44, 179; *The Second Sex*, 19, 20, 36–39, 61
Bebel, August, 2, 18, 31, 75, 84, 86; and Morgner, 88–89, 109, 112, 206; and Western feminism, 19; and Wolf, 28, 37, 56, 88–89, 100, 101, 106, 206; *Woman and Socialism*, 4–5, 75–76, 81–84
Benjamin, Jessica, 217 n.7
Benjamin, Walter, 126–27, 129
Bernstein, Eduard, 84
Biermann, Wolf, 24

Bildungsroman, 32, 137, 230 n.41. See also novel of education
birthrate, 2, 7, 8, 12, 82, 85–86
Bitterfeld Way, 67, 151
Blitz aus heiterem Himmel. See Anderson, Edith
Bock, Gisela, 84
Böhme, Irene, 7
Bonaparte, Marie, 41
Braun, Lily, 84, 128
Braun, Volker, 127
Brecht, Bertolt, 124, 126–27, 128, 129, 130–31
Brown, Wendy, 215 n.68
Brüning, Elfriede, *Partnerinnen* (Women partners), 183

censorship, 23–24, 29, 62, 103, 114, 117
child care, 10, 15, 17, 82; Bebel's view on, 5, 82; literary treatment of, *see under* double burden, literary treatment of; single mother, in fiction. See also child-care facilities
child-care facilities, 2, 6, 184–86
Critical Theory, 90, 97
Croce, Benedetto, 126

Daly, Mary, 88
Damm, Sigrid, *Cornelia Goethe*, 136
Dannhauer, Heinz, 59, 134
Davis, Elizabeth Gould, 88
De Bruyn, Günter, "Geschlechtertausch" (Sex change), 55
Dilthey, Wilhelm, 137
Diner, Helen, 88
Dodds, Dinah, 9, 213 n.52
Dölling, Irene, 10, 11, 13, 86, 211 n.28, 211 n.36
double burden, 10, 12, 17, 29, 171, 206; literary treatment of, 29, 33, 170–78, 186–88, 196–97, 201, 208

double day. *See* double burden
Dritte, Der (Her Third), 46

Eckart, Gabriele, *So sehe ick die Sache* (The way I see things), 170
Eckstein-Diener, Berta, 88
Ehrenreich, Barbara, 117
employment statistics, 7–8, 16, 17–18, 171, 214 n.55, 234 n. 10
Engels, Frederick, 2, 28, 31; and Bebel, 82–83; *Communist Manifesto*, 80; *German Ideology*, 125–26; and Morgner, 88–89, 111, 112, 206; and mother right, 75, 100; *Origin of the Family, Private Property, and the State*, 5, 75, 79–81, 82, 101; and Western feminism, 19, 38; and Wolf, 28, 37, 88–89, 100, 101, 106, 206
English, D., 117
Entwicklungsroman, 134, 137. See also novel of education
Erler, Gisela Anna, 13
Erziehungsroman, 137. See also novel of education

Familiengesetzbuch der Deutschen Demokratischen Republik (Family statutes of the German Democratic Republic), 172
family benefits, 2, 6–7, 15, 17, 184; criticism of, 12–13; generational conflict and, 11. See also baby year; child-care facilities
Feuchtenberger, Anke, 118
Feyl, Renate, 28; *Idylle mit Professor* (Idyll with professor), 136, 197–98; *lautlose Aufbruch, Der: Frauen in der Wissenschaft* (The soundless startoff: women in science), 136
Firestone, Shulamith, 85
Fish, Stanley, 218 n.28

Frau—der Frieden und der Sozialismus, Die (Woman—peace, and socialism), 5–6, 134–35
Fret, Rosemarie, 28
Freud, Sigmund, 3, 41, 42, 43, 47, 53–54
Frisch, Max, 140

Gilligan, Carol, 20, 53, 55
Girard, René, 42–43
Girnus, Wilhelm, 102
Gloger, Gotthold, 88
Goethe, Johann Wolfgang von, 26, 136; *Faust*, 59–60, 62, 66, 115–16, 117; *Pandoras Wiederkunft: Ein Festspiel* (Pandora's return: a festival play), 115; *Wilhelm Meisters Lehrjahre* (Wilhelm Meister's apprenticeship years), 137
Graves, Robert, 88
Grosz, Christiane, *Die Tochter* (The daughter), 199
Günderrode, Karoline von, 55–56, 97, 132
Günther, Egon, 46

Hager, Kurt, 3
Hammerstein, Katharina von, 143
Harris, Angela P., 215 n.67
Heine, Heinrich, 173
Hell, Julia, 75, 92
Helmecke, Monika, 28, 33; "Erich," 47; "Klopfzeichen" (Tapping code), 191; "Lauf weg—kehr um" (Run away—turn around), 178; "September 30," 180
Herminghouse, Patricia, 24, 134, 137, 228 n.125, 236 n.51
Heussi, Karl, 126
Heym, Stefan, 23
Hieblinger, Inge, 220 n.56
Hill, Anita, 54

Hilzinger, Sonja, 139
Hitler, Adolf, 85
Hoffmann, E.T.A., 93
Homer, 105
Honecker, Erich, 3, 169
housework, 10, 12, 29, 171–72, 200, 214 n.55; literary treatment of, *see under* double burden, literary treatment of; monthly day off for, 7, 12; socialist ideas on, 5, 12, 81, 82

Iliad, 105
Irigaray, Luce, 43

Jähnert, Gabriele, 192
Jakobs, Karl-Heinz, 88
Jankowsky, Karen, 102
Jones, Tamara, 17

Kachold, Gabriele. *See* Stötzer-Kachold, Gabriele
Kafka, Franz, 182
Kaufmann, Hans, 95
Kirsch, Sarah, 24, 27, 36; "Merkwürdiges Beispiel weiblicher Entschlossenheit" (Strange example of female determination), 47–50, 54; *Panther Woman, The* (*Die Pantherfrau*), 169
Kleist, Heinrich von, 97
Klotz, Sibyll-Anka, 91
Koetter-Johnschker, Renate, 28; "Im Kreislauf der Windeln" (In the diaper cycle), 172–73
Königsdorf, Helga, 28, 33, 144, 207; "Bolero," 55, 200; "Heimkehr einer Prinzessin" (Homecoming of a princess), 180; "Hochzeitstag in Pizunda" (Wedding day in Pizunda), 147; "Pi," 175, 197; *Respektloser Umgang* (Disrespectful company), 124, 198; "Unterbrechung"

Königsdorf, Helga *(continued)* (Interruption), 191; "Unverhoffter Besuch" (The unexpected visit), 147
Kossakowski, Adolf, 59
Krauss, Angela, 28
Küchenmeister, Claus, 127

Lacan, Jacques, 42
Lakoff, Robin, 52, 53
Lambrecht, Christine, *Männerbekanntschaften* (Male acquaintances), 170
Lange, Inge, 82
Lauerwald, Hannelore, 28, 172, 190; "Eines Tages . . ." (One day . . .), 150; "Geliebter Sohn" (Beloved son), 190; "Unterwegs im Regen" (On the road in the rain), 174, 197; "uralte Geschichte, Die" (The age-old story), 150; "Wunschzettel" (Wishlist), 191
Lenin, Vladimir Ilyich, 2, 212 n.41
Leopold, Evelyn, 185, 213 n.48, 234 n.10
Lewin, Waltraud, "Dich hat Amor gewiß" (Cupid has you for sure), 196
Liebmann, Irina, *Berliner Mietshaus* (Berlin apartment house), 170
lila offensive, 15, 16
Love, Myra, 141
Lukács, Georg, 137
Lutheran Church, 11

MacKinnon, Catherine A., *Feminism Unmodified*, 2, 52–53, 54, 55, 213 n.45, 214 n.65; *Only Words*, 218 n.28
Maisch, Christine, 88
Marcuse, Herbert, 115
Maron, Monika, 28, 138; *Defector, The* (*Die Überläuferin*), 148, 165; *Flight of Ashes* (*Flugasche*), 148

Marti, Madeleine, 196
Martin, Brigitte, 28; "Anzeige, Die" (The personal ad), 189; *Nach Freude anstehen* (Standing in line for happiness), 176–77, 186, 187–88; *rote Ballon, Der. Geschichten um Brigge Bem* (The red balloon. Stories about Brigge Bem), 176, 191
Marx, Karl, 28, 37, 79; *Communist Manifesto*, 80; *German Ideology*, 125–26
maternity leave, 6, 15. See also baby year
matriarchy. See mother right
Meier, Monika, 58, 121
Menschik, Jutta, 185, 213 n.48, 234 n.10
Merkel, Ina, 9, 16
Millett, Kate, 20
Milz, Helga A., 215 n.67
Morgan, Lewis Henry, 75–81, 83, 100; *Ancient Society*, 76–77, 78, 81; *League of the Iroquois*, 76
Morgenstern, Beate, 28; "Mädchen Mirka, Das" (The girl Mirka), 183; "Im Spreekahn" (In the Spree boat), 51
Morgner, Irmtraud, 11, 23, 28–29, 172; and Beauvoir, 19, 36–37, 57, 61, 119; and Bebel, 88–89, 109, 112, 206; on child care, 215 n.66; on children and career, 180; commitment to socialism, 24–27, 87; communism and the feminine in, 74–75, 89, 206; and Engels, 88–89, 111, 112, 206; feminism in, 25–27, 123–24, 139, 228 n.127; on motherhood, 108; on patriarchy and war, 88; on pornography, 201, 211 n.27, 237 n.66; praise of the feminine in, 74, 90; and Western feminism, 19, 21, 26–27, 206–207; on women's condition, 36; on

women's desire, 43, 44, 50; on women's genius, 29, 37; on women's history, 32, 128–30; on women's imagination, 40, 50; on women's speech, 30

Works:

   Amanda, 111–23; battering in, 199; birth-control pill in, 196; on censorship, 62, 114, 117; communism and the feminine in, 30, 74, 112; *Entrückung* in, 116; and *Faust*, 115–17; matriarchy in, 111–12; men in, 71, 175, 197, 198–99; motherhood in, 108, 110, 181, 185, 186–87; nurturing in, 31, 111, 113–14; pacifism in, 70, 111–13; praise of the feminine in, 74, 112, 207; shopping in, 175; West in, 201; women's desire in, 44, 77, 116; women's history in, 32, 130, 131; women's role models in, 154; women's voice in, 54–55, 113

   Hochzeit in Konstantinopel (Wedding in Constantinople), 27; birth scene in, 191; double day in, 171, 177; heroine type in, 40, 59; parthenogenesis in, 108; scientist in, 110–11

   Leben und Abenteuer der Trobadora Beatriz nach Zeugnissen ihrer Spielfrau Laura (Life and adventures of Trobadora Beatriz as chronicled by her minstrel Laura), 36, 50, 57–71; abortion in, 191; birth-control pill in, 196; *Entrückung* in, 116; and *Faust*, 58, 59–61, 62, 66–67; feminism in, 207; heroine type in, 59, 135, 138; matriarchy in, 109–10; megalomania in, 58, 59, 63–66, 68–70, 179; motherhood in, 31, 108, 110, 180–81, 186–87; nurturing in, 31; pacifism in, 111; pregnancy in, 186, 190; rape in, 199, 201; science in, 110–11; socialist feminism in, 26, 58, 109, 138; West in, 201; Western reception of, 21, 28; women's desire in, 44, 67–68, 70–71, 131; women's genius in, 59, 63, 68, 70; women's history in, 32, 128–29, 130–31; women's oppression in, 171, 202

   "Gospel of Valeska" ("Die gute Botschaft der Valeska"), 51, 68–70, 110, 174

   "Seil, Das" (The tightrope), 178

   "Notturno," 21, 179

   Rumba auf einen Herbst (Rumba to an autumn), 44, 171; motherhood in, 179; in *Trobadora Beatriz*, 57; women's dividedness in, 37, 217 n.2

   wundersamen Reisen Gustavs des Weltfahrers, Die (The amazing travels of Gustav the globetrotter), 50; matriarchy in, 70, 108–109; women's history in, 128–29, 130

motherhood: Adrienne Rich on, 21, 215 n.71; Beauvoir on, 37–38; Bebel on, 5, 82, 82–84; combin-

motherhood: Adrienne Rich on *(continued)*
  ability of work and, 2, 8, 12, 15, 17–18, 82, 87, 171, 212 n.40; as defining the image of women, 11, 75, 76, 86–87, 134, 205; GDR policies on, 6–7, 11, 87; GDR statistics on, 8; image of in GDR, 22; as literary theme, 21, 37, 108–10, 123–24, 143, 154, 161–65, 178–91, 200, 207–208; rewards for, 84–86, 224 n.62, 224 n.63; work and, 10, 171. *See also* maternity leave; mother right; *Mutterschutzgesetz*; single mother
mother right, 106; and Bachofen, 77–78, 100, 102; and Bebel, 83; and Engels, 5, 80
Müller, Christa, 28; "Candida," 186, 190; *Verwandlung der Liebe, Die* (The transformation of love), 190
Müller, Christine, *Männer-protokolle* (Male statements), 170
Mutterschutzgesetz (law protecting prenatal and postnatal mothers), 14–15

neopositive heroine, 149–65
Nickel, Hildegard, 210 n.10, 212 n.40
Nicolai, Rose, 88
Noll, Dieter, 137
Nordmann, Ingeborg, 58
novel of education, 32, 137, 138–39, 149–61. *See also* Bildungsroman

Otto, Karlheinz, 59

Paley, Grace, 22, 36, 181
Panitz, Eberhard, 9, 46
parental leave, 6. *See also* baby year; maternity leave; sick child leave

Paschiller, Doris, 28; *Die Würde* (Dignity), 150, 188–89
Pirskawetz, Lia, 28; *Der Stille Grund*, 155, 157–60, 165
Plath, Sylvia, 154
Plenzdorf, Ulrich, 139
positive hero(ine), 21, 136, 138, 165, 207–208; Reimann on, 230 n.31; and Wolf, 93, 142; and Worgitzky, 193. *See also* neopositive heroine
primitive communism, 31; and Bebel, 83; and Engels, 5; and Morgan, 81; and Morgner, 112; and Wolf, 106
Pusch, Luise, 52

quotas, 15–16

Ranke-Graves, Robert von, 88
Reimann, Brigitte, 27, 32; *Franziska Linkerhand*, 32, 138, 150–54, 191
Rich, Adrienne, 21, 48, 215 n.71
Roebling, Irmgard, 107
Rosenberg, Dorothy, 211 n.38
Roussel, Nelly, 84
Rouzade, Léonie, 84
Rücker, Günther, 46
Rüdenauer, Erika, *Dünne Haut. Tagebücher von Frauen aus der DDR* (Thin skin: Diaries of women from the GDR), 170

Sander, Helke, 165
Schiller, Friedrich von, 97
Schlott, Jutta, 28; "Aussicht" (Prospect), 190; *liebliche Fest, Das* (The lovely party), 189; "Klare Verhältnisse" (Clear conditions), 191
Schmidt, Ricarda, 165
Schmitz-Köster, Dorothee, 145
Schneider, Rolf, 9
Schopenhauer, Arthur, 42

Schubert, Helga, 28, 228 n.125; "Aus dem beruflichen Alltag" (From everyday professional life), 199; "Ausnahme, Die" (The exception), 179–80; "Mondstein" (Moonstone), 177, 199; "Taube Ohren" (Deaf ears), 199; "verbotene Zimmer, Das" (The forbidden room), 201–202
Schulz, Max Werner, 137
Schulze-Gerlach, Tine, "Flaschenpfand" (Bottle deposit), 199
Schütz, Helga, 28; *Julia oder Erziehung zum Chorgesang* (Julia, or an education in choral singing), 191
Schwarzer, Alice, 19, 20–21, 169; interview with Morgner, 27, 44
Seidemann, Maria, 28; "Der hilfreiche Rabe" (The helpful raven), 178
sick child leave, 6–7, 10, 11, 12, 184, 209 n.8; in Morgner, 187
Silberman, Marc, 3
single mother, 10, 25, 184–85; in fiction, 66, 110, 178, 184–90, 208; GDR benefits for, 6–7, 15, 184; statistics, 8, 214 n.55
socialist realism, 21, 133, 136–38, 206–208; and Wolf, 28, 92–93, 140; and Worgitzky, 193
Stachowa, Angela, 28; "Resi," 200
Stalin, Joseph Vissarionovich, 85, 133
Stötzer-Kachold, Gabriele, 24, 138, 149, 165
Strittmatter, Eva, 25
Struzyk, Brigitte, *Caroline unterm Freiheitsbaum* (Caroline under the freedom tree), 136
Szepansky, Gerda, 185, 206

Tetzner, Gerti, 23, 27, 32, 207; *Karen W.*, 47, 138, 144–46, 157

Thomas, Clarence, 54
Thompson, E.P., 126
Thomson, George, 88
Thönnessen, Werner, 84
Thurm, Brigitte, 28, 32, 165; *Verena*, 45; *Verlangen* (Desire), 155–57
Tolstaya, Tatyana, 45
Treder, Uta, 165
Tröger, Annemarie, 202
Trömel-Plötz, Senta, 52

Ulbricht, Walter, 3
Unabhängiger Frauenverband (Independent Women's Association), 16–17, 117, 118

Wander, Maxie, 11; *Guten Morgen, Du Schöne* (Good morning, you beautiful creature), 25, 87, 170
Weitzman, Lenore J., 213 n.47
Werner, Petra, 28; "Der Bronzeelefant" (The bronze elephant), 190
Wiens, Maya, 28, 33, 150, 165; *Traumgrenzen* (Dream limits), 163–65, 183–84, 185, 195, 200, 201
Willis, Ellen, 19
Wolf, Christa, 11, 23, 27, 28; on abortion, 48; and Beauvoir, 36–37; and Bebel, 28, 37, 56, 88–89, 100, 101, 106, 206; commitment to socialism, 24–25; communism and the feminine in, 31, 74–75, 89, 206; and Engels, 28, 37, 88–89, 100, 101, 106, 206; feminism in, 24–25, 96, 123–24, 207, 216 n.84; on literature's function, 22, 203; masculine vs. feminine in, 31, 51, 74, 94–99, 102, 107; on patriarchy and war, 88, 91, 99–100, 101–102; praise of the feminine in, 74, 90; and

Wolf, Christa *(continued)*
  Romanticism, 91, 97, 135; and SED, 24; social critique in, 89–90; and Western feminism, 25, 206–207, 214 n.64, 216 n.83; on women's history, 96–99, 131–32; on women's speech, 30; women's values in, 96–97
  Works:
    "Berührung" (Touching), 143
    Cassandra (*Kassandra*), 99–108; communism and the feminine in, 56, 74, 106; masculine vs. feminine in, 31, 74, 102, 107; matriarchy in, 56, 91, 102, 105–107; and pacifism, 91; political allegory in, 103, 107; praise of the feminine in, 74; Wolf's reading for, 88; woman as victim in, 105, 123; women's voice in, 56–57, 102–105
    Divided Heaven (*Der geteilte Himmel*), 28, 31, 92–93, 152, 171
    "Lectures on Poetics" (*Voraussetzungen einer Erzählung: Kassandra*), 56, 88, 91, 100–102, 107, 132; censorship of, 23, 102
    Medea, 91, 107–108, 132
    "New Life and Opinions of a Tomcat" ("Neue Lebensansichten eines Katers"), 31, 93–94
    No Place on Earth (*Kein Ort. Nirgends*), 97
    Parting from Phantoms (*Auf dem Weg nach Tabou*), 24, 181
    Quest for Christa T., The (*Nachdenken über Christa T.*), 65, 139–43; birth scene in, 190; criticism of GDR in, 28, 140–41; historical significance of, 27, 135, 139–40; nonconformist heroine in, 40, 137–38, 141–42; as novel of education, 32, 139, 230 n.41; quest for identity in, 39, 141–42; wife battering in, 140, 199
    Schatten eines Traumes, Der (The shadow of a dream), 97
    "Self-experiment" ("Selbstexperiment"), 94–96; career vs. children in, 183–84; gender difference in, 90, 96; masculine vs. feminine in, 31, 51, 94–95; men's life-style in, 146; quest for identity in, 39, 143; women's voice in, 55, 56, 101, 103
    "Shadow of a Dream, The" ("Der Schatten eines Traumes"), 55, 132, 169
    Sommerstück (Summer piece), 165
    "Speaking of Büchner" ("Von Büchner sprechen"), 56, 98, 102, 132
    "Truth You Can Expect, The" ("Die zumutbare Wahrheit"), 100
    "Unter den Linden," 39, 143–44, 146
    What remains (*Was bleibt*), 24
    "Your Next Life Begins Today" ("Nun ja! Das nächste Leben geht aber heute an"), 97
Wolf, Friedrich, 192
Wolter, Christine, 28, 172; *Alleinseglerin, Die* (The solo yachtswoman), 155, 160–61,

165; "Early summer" ("Frühsommer"), 199; "Ich habe wieder geheiratet" (I have married again), 101, 174–75
Woolf, Virginia, 85, 88, 97, 103
Worgitzky, Charlotte, 27, 150, 161, 165, 169, 172; career vs. children in, 181–82; "sameness feminism" in, 161, 215 n. 66; and Western feminism, 206–207; on women's speech, 30
Works:
"Aus den Akten der Hölle" (From the files of hell), 190
"Eva," 179
"Hänsel und Gretel. Kein Märchen" (Hansel and Gretel. Not a fairy-tale), 186
"Karriere abgesagt" (Career cancelled), 177–78
"Leben wie im Paradies" (Life as in paradise), 161

Meine ungeborenen Kinder (My unborn children), 33, 162–63, 164, 190–96, 200; birth control pill in, 195–96
"Quäze," 161, 173–74, 182, 202–203
Traum vom Möglichen (Dream of possibilities), 163, 202–203
Unschuldigen, Die (The innocents), 9, 161–62, 164, 182, 215 n.66

Zeplin, Rosemarie, 28, 54; "kleine Seejungfrau, Die" (The little mermaid), 168–69, 190; *Maulwurf oder fatales Beispiel weiblicher Gradlinigkeit, Der* (The mole or a fatal example of feminine straightforwardness), 189; "The Shadow of a Lover" ("Schattenriß eines Liebhabers"), 200
Zetkin, Clara, 2, 84, 86, 109